David T. Johnston

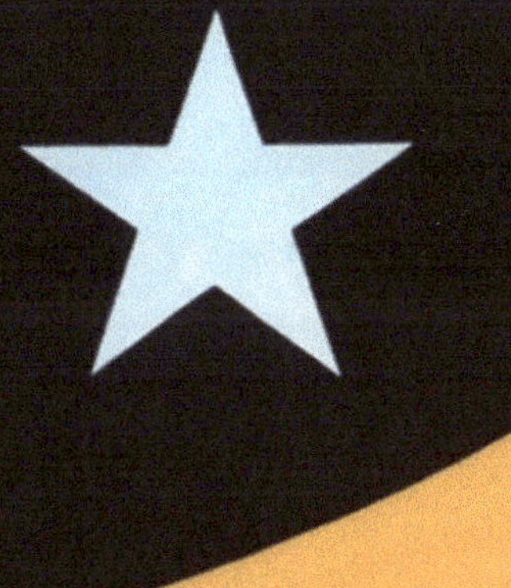

I AM THE WAY

David T. Johnston

I Am the Way

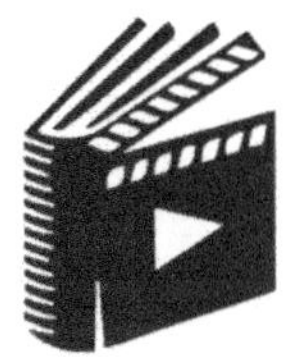

I AM THE WAY

Copyright © 2021 **David T. Johnston**

All rights reserved. No part of this book may be used or reproduced by any means, graphic, electronic, or mechanical, including photocopying, recording, taping or by information storage and retrieval system without the written permission of the author except in the case of brief quotations embodied in critical articles and reviews.

Book Films Media
2780 South Jones Blvd Suite
200- 4007 Las Vegas, NV
89146 United States
+1 725-238-6534
support@bookfilmsmedia.com

Because of the dynamic nature of the Internet, any web addresses or links contained in this book may have changed since publication and may no longer be valid. The views expressed in the work are solely those of the author and do not necessarily reflect the views of the publisher, and the publisher hereby disclaims any responsibility for them.

ISBN (Paperback): 979-8-9896059-1-0

ISBN (Ebook): 979-8-9896059-2-7

Printed in the United States of America

The cover design is based on an image of a painting by the author.

The Descent of Light

The principal image on the cover is based on a painting called *The Descent of Light*. The image consists of three parts: a six-pointed star, a five-pointed star, and a swoosh of descending light. The symbolic meaning of the six-pointed star is the union of fire and water. The upward-pointing triangle represents the fire of aspiration, and the downward-pointing triangle represents the descent of healing water, known in alchemy as *aqua permanens*, the water of life. Variations of this symbol are well-known as the Star of David and the Seal of Solomon, which point to its significance. The five-pointed star is symbolic of the individual center of being, the quintessence and centered four. Spiritual traditions speak of the descending light of consciousness, in Christianity known as the Holy Spirit. This image, then, symbolizes the Descent of Consciousness that comes along with both the six-pointed star and the individual star.

Contents

Preface

I put *I Am the Way* together as a document illustrating the individuation process as articulated by C. G. Jung. Jung put considerable emphasis on the image that come by way of dreams and true fantasy, through which the individual can learn to embrace a transformation of personality and widened consciousness. Jung encouraged not only an active engagement with dreams, but also a process he calls active imagination, which is a dynamic meditation involving a dialogue between the ego and the unconscious, eventually, the archetypes of the collective unconscious. The archetype in-itself is the principle by which we apprehend the world and move into action, which requires ethical considerations. The archetypal image is the form given to the archetype that varies according to individual, culture, and time in history.

Jung's challenge to the individual, then, is to form a relationship between the ego and the archetype through the image, while bringing in the ethical dimension. This process can be done through any art form, including, art, poetry, music, and dance or, simply, with inner dialogue. I have sought meaning/meaninglessness in the images both by taking account of synchronicities and by amplifying the images not only with personal associations but, more importantly, with archetypally relevant material, which tie the images to universal truths. For this reason, I amplify the images in this book with historically relevant archetypal material, but not personal associations, which are only relevant to me. Along with giving form to the image through painting and clay, this process has helped me become more conscious over time.

My chosen way has been through art, and I have followed Jung and the Jungian tradition in Jung's belief that the psyche is constituted by images. In fact, I have painted, worked in clay, and used art as a meditative process for some forty-five years now. The images that appear in this book are from relatively early in the process. I have never painted for commercial reasons or to exhibit my work, although, over the years, I have exhibited paintings to selected audiences, who, typically, have had an interest in Jungian psychology.

Beyond Jung, I am following a tradition that dates back some 40,000–60,000 years ago, the testimony for which can be found in an ancient rock and cave paintings found throughout the world. There is a difference,though, in that the approach promoted by Jung concerns individuals and their relationship to the image, even though the images are archetypal with universal value. In contrast, the images found on rock and cave paintings are, typically, part of a collective ritual or rituals that may have taken place repeatedly or as special notations to mark a sacred site.

The images in this book are, for the most part, not predetermined, but they are based on spontaneous outpourings from the unconscious that present themselves in dreams either fully painted or drawn or otherwise given form, or partially completed but inviting completion with the aid of my imagination. As I allude to above, the purpose of an active meditative process is both for the sake of increasing consciousness, living a "meaningful" life and for the realization of the Self. This requires self-reflection and the integration of the material emerging from the unconscious into consciousness. It means reconciling the opposites in the psyche,including meaning and meaninglessness.

PART I
Essays

It is as if we did not know or else continuously forget, that everything of which we are conscious is an image and image *is* psyche.

—C. G. Jung[1]

It is as if something somewhere were 'known' in the form of images—but not by us.

—Marie-Louise von Franz[2]

CHAPTER 1

Art and the Individuation Process

Introduction

The psychology of C. G. Jung emphasizes the central importance of the image to becoming conscious. The high importance of the image for the growth of consciousness is related to the fact that images are intrinsic to life. In fact, according to Jung, becoming conscious involves the transformation of a drive stimulus into consciousness via the image, which he regards as "the cultural instinct *par excellence.*"[3] Thus, dreams, visions,and true fantasy (fantasiavera) constitute primary sources of images that can potentially enlarge consciousness and the experience of life.

Jung encourages a form of meditation he calls active imagination, which can take many forms, including writing, dancing, painting, and working in other art media. Whereas dreams provide access to the unconscious, even the deeper or collective unconscious in a relatively passive process, active imagination is the royal road to the unconscious. The advantage active imagination has over dreams is that, whereas dreaming is a passive process that happens to the dreamer, active imagination essentially involves a dialogue between the conscious ego and the archetypes of the collective unconscious. It is a dynamic process that engages the psyche according to its actual concerns and involvements at the moment, at least according to what is actually constellated in the unconscious psyche at the time.

The ability and importance given to registering images from the unconscious into consciousness dates back thousands of years, in some places as early as some 40–60,000 years ago, in ancient rock paintings found throughout the world at a time, which Theodor Abt characterizes as the dawn of the human spirit.[4] Art as active imagination is an important way for the contemporary individual to activate the deeper sources within in order to augment individual consciousness and further the process of individuation. When art is based on true fantasy, it can also bring to conscious awareness new aspects and qualities of consciousness for the culture at large.

The meaning of images that emerge into consciousness through dreams, art, or active imagination has its roots in what was formerly essentially unknown and, typically, inaccessible to consciousness. For art in general, cultural distance, reflection, and the study of changing historical art expressions can bring to conscious awareness the meaning of major cultural and political movements and the evolution of consciousness. Similarly, with a self-reflective religious (spiritual) attitude, the meaning of a painting or series of paintings done as a form of active imagination can become more conscious overtime by taking into account synchronicity or meaningful coincidences between the painting, dreams, visions, and life experiences. This process can be aided by amplifying the images with both personal associations and archetypally relevant material. The more functions of consciousness brought to bear in examining the image, the wider the potential understanding.

Amplifications on Individual Paintings

These images are not precalculated but are spontaneous products from the unconscious that appear in dreams either fully painted or drawn, or as unfinished but inviting completion with the aid of the artist's imagination. The purpose of this meditation process is to gain consciousness for both the sake of a meaningful life and for the sake of the realization of the Self. What follows are amplifications on archetypal images depicted in individual paintings. Since the images have archetypal references, they depict fundamental ways of apprehending life and blueprints for action. This is the reason for their psychological importance and reality. There is no attempt to bring in personal references in this presentation, but that is essential for the process to be meaningfully integrated by the artist. At least, there is a need to witness and reflect on the archetypal patterns depicted in the paintings as they are being subjectively experienced synchronistically.

CHAPTER 2

The Way of Art

The Aesthetic View of Life and Individuation

Abstract

In this paper, I discuss the nature of art or the aesthetic view of life by examining the thoughts on this subject of several respected authorities in different branches of the humanities. First, I survey those who recommend an aesthetic attitude to life as a guide to conduct. These writers all tend to subsume the ethical attitude to the aesthetic. By and large, they argue that it leads not only toward the experience of beauty but also to wholeness. I then take up Jung's argument, which I support with that of Sri Aurobindo's, that the aesthetic way is not enough, but that a strong moral effort is required to give sustaining power to life. I conclude by arguing that individuation requires a broad perspective, the psychological, in order to integrate all the different noble instincts of the psyche. The way of art, still valid, then becomes subordinated to the art of life.

Introduction

Joseph Campbell extols the way of art, drawing a parallel between it and the path of the mystic or yoga. Indeed, a case can be made that Campbell's ultimate message is directly related to this path.[5] Following one's bliss, seeking the experience of life rather than the meaning of life, the search for beauty, the aesthetic life, and the way of art are a single path. The aesthetic attitude to life is essentially one that is nonjudgmentally open to experience.[6] The artist, and an artistic life, simply exemplifies a path that is open to "ordinary" people as the way of art.

In this paper, I examine the way of art or the aesthetic path and its strengths and shortcomings for the process of individuation. As Miller observes, there is a distinct difference between Campbell's message and that of Jung's.[7] Whereas Jung's path is concerned with the question of meaning and meaninglessness, Campbell stresses openness to the "rapture…associated with being alive."[8] Moreover, whereas Jung's path has to do with individuation—that is, becoming the unique individual one essentially is, which not only includes the incarnation of the Self but also increased differentiation of one's nature—Campbell sees individuation in terms of distinguishing individual differences as an illusion.[9] He supports his line of thinking with a quote from Schopenhauer that "individuation is but an appearance in a field of space and time."[10]

First, I argue the case for the aesthetic life and the path of art and beauty. I enlist some heavy artillery; in addition to Campbell himself, I refer to the arguments of two eminent contemporary psychologists Rollo May and James Hillman, art educator Frances Wilson, and Romantic dramatist and poet Friedrich Schiller. To give further support to the aesthetic attitude, I also refer to a poem by Canadian poet Irving Layton. I then argue Jung's case: that the aesthetic path alone is not up to the difficult task of individuation. In the process, I enlist the support of Sri Aurobindo, a supreme poet and master yogi. I conclude by showing how the way of art can be integrated to serve the process of individuation as Jung defines it.

On the Defense of the Aesthetic Attitude

Joseph Campbell writes compellingly about the way of art, arguing that the artist and the mystic are exposed to the same reality, which artists reflect in their master works.[11] For Sri Aurobindo, the primary intention of art is the unveiling of beauty.[12] Campbell argues that art normally aspires to beauty and "to the sensuous glorification of life," although, he writes, it can move "beyond perception [to] the purely conceptual, apprehensible by the intellect [alone]."[13]

Although art aspires toward beauty, there is, Campbell is quick to add, a need to distinguish proper art from improper art. He does so based on a classification borrowed from James Joyce. True to the meaning of the word *aesthetic*, from the Greek *aisthetikos*, "perceptive," and aisthanesthai, "to perceive, to feel," proper art, Campbell argues, requires disinterested perception, apprehension, and feeling.[14] Indeed, the adjective *aesthetic* refers to appreciating the beautiful accordingly while the noun refers to the philosophy of art and of the beautiful. Improper art, on the other hand, is not disinterested and serves commercial, ethical, sociological, political, or other forces. It can be either didactic, at the service of propaganda, or pornographic, exciting feelings of desire, loathing, or fear. Whereas improper art is kinetic and encourages action for the benefit of the ego, proper art is static, derived from the Greek *statikos*, "causing to stand," inducing the experience of what Campbell refers to as "aesthetic arrest."[15]

Through "aesthetic arrest," proper art raises the mind above the duality of desire, fear, and loathing, beyond the opposites. At that point, one contemplates beauty, which comes with wholeness, harmony, and radiance, the experience of the "whatness of a thing."[16] This, observes Campbell, is the source of the healing power of art, by means of which "beauty… illuminate(s) the senses, still(s) the mind, and enchant(s) the heart."[17] It also shows the relationship between the way of art and the mystic's path as both, in their own way, seek to go beyond the dualities of the conditioned world.

Campbell supports his argument by showing how Buddhist discipline is essentially the same as that of the artist. Proper art requires detachment from the ingredients of improper art—that is, from instilling desire, loathing, or fear and the desire to use art for didactic or pornographic purposes. Likewise, Buddhist discipline requires detachment from *kama* or desire, *mara* or fear of death, and *dharma* or social duties and commitments. Indeed, art in India has traditionally been considered to be one path to the Divine requiring, according to Ananda Coomaraswamy, "discipline [yoga]" and "attention [dharana]" to be "consummated in self-identification [samadhi] with the object or theme of contemplation."[18]

Although Campbell doesn't say so explicitly, the way of art, as he understands it, is one instance of what can be generalized as an aesthetic path or a path in search of beauty that is open to someone other than the artist. Moreover, as I suggested in the introduction, that is indeed the path that Campbell espouses. As Wendy Doniger observes, for Campbell, beauty is the ruling archetype, and as Richard Underwood notes, "It is the way of art and the artist that Campbell opens up for us."[19] Moreover, Campbell's enjoining us to seek the experience of being alive and open to experience, rather than seeking meaning *per se*, is an aesthetic path. It is based on the root meaning of the word *aesthetic*, which is "to perceive," "to apprehend," "to feel," and implying not to judge. In this context, what is meant by feelings are such emotions as "being astonished by," "being surprised at," "being in wonder at," "being struck by," "being in awe of," etc., something beautiful, along with the attending sensation.

It means being open to the senses, the imagination, and the evaluative heart of beauty. [20] In this way, Campbell's path is based on a "Buddhist-like vision," a kind of Zen that has considerable appeal for some people.[21]

In *My Quest for Beauty*, Rollo May takes a position on art, beauty, and the aesthetic attitude that is somewhat similar to that of Campbell.[22] Influenced by Friederich Schiller, who sees beauty as being able to "tame down the savageness of life," May contends that art is an antidote to violence.[23] Moreover, he argues that the person of tomorrow will have the artist's attitude, which, for him, comes with a sense of wholeness.

When considering the value of art for psychological well-being, unlike Campbell, May stays within Western tradition, although he arrives at a similar truth. He suggests that classic Greek beauty takes one beyond the duality of emotions to the "center of being."[24] In addition, he quotes Schiller to the effect that beauty is a place of pure contemplation, which unites the world of the senses to that of the idea. Therefore, argues May, not only does art keep us in touch with the sensuous reality of life, along with beauty, it is "an inseparable…part of our capacity to be conscious and to think."[25] I would rather say that inasmuch as art puts us in touch with the idea, it does so through Eros and feeling rather than thinking. Nonetheless,through art, one can be exposed to a wide range of ideas that can be taken up by the intellect.

May refers to Hellenic thought, effectively observing that experience of beauty is that of the *To Kalon*, the beautiful, splendidly imminent in the many. He also refers to Aristotle's idea that beauty is the condition of harmony. Finally, he picks up on the Greek sense of ethics, which is primarily based on beauty and harmony. For Plato, goodness, along with truth, is subordinated to beauty, and goodness—the goal of the ethical life— consists in acting harmoniously with one's fellow human being.[26] "For all true Greeks," writes May, "the noble life was first of all the beautiful life."[27] May, accordingly, follows the classical Greek notion that attributes the aesthetic with moral virtues.

Like Campbell, May seems to be saying that the path of art, the search for beauty, and the aesthetic attitude in general, is one that leads to detachment, beyond the dualities, to wholeness. In addition, he suggests that it can refine one's nature and lead to harmonious conduct and integrity in dealing with others. In the process, he repudiates "conformist moral rules" while suggesting that the artist lives "with a greater integrity and another ethic."[28] Likewise, Campbell argues that the sociological function of myth and its ethical law is out of date.[29]

Friederich Schiller, a talented dramatist and "poet of freedom" who lived during the latter part of the eighteenth and early nineteenth century, is the authority on beauty on whom May most often relies. He wrote a series of letters to the Danish Prince, Friedrich Christian of Schleswig-Holstein-Augustenburg that have been published under the title of On the *Aesthetic Education of Man*.[30] In it, he essentially argues that education of the whole person is first and foremost an aesthetic question, an idea that comes from his interpretation of the classical ideal of Hellenic Greece. Not only does he understand beauty or the "aesthetic condition" as uniting one's active [thinking] and passive [perceptive] modes, but also the sensuous nature with the idea and reason and spirit or form with matter. The "aesthetic condition," according to Schiller, "restore(s) man to himself, so that he can make of himself what he wills."[31] Art, especially tragedy, for him, can create a condition of contentment or equipoise, harmonizing the spiritual and the physical. Art, therefore, according to Schiller, should be at the center of the educational process.

Schiller is not a concise thinker and interchangeably proposes two different theories on psychological development. In one theory, he argues that humankind can potentially progress upward in a hierarchy of three levels of existence, somewhat akin to Plato's tripartite division of humankind. They include, from the bottom up, the sensuous person who lives according to the natural appetites, the aesthetic person whose nature is refined, and finally the moral person who controls his nature using his will. Moreover, according to Schiller, it is necessary to pass through these stages in order; one must first live the physical condition, then the aesthetic, and finally the moral or rational. The moral condition in this scenario is related to reason, and, according to Schiller, it leads to freedom. In this case, the search for beauty, apparently of transitory value, is a step toward enlightenment.

In the second theory, which is sometimes mixed up with the first one, Schiller sees beauty as an end in itself, sometimes a work of reason and sometimes elevated beyond reason or a sublimation of reason. For example, he sees beauty as "the work of free contemplation, and we step with her into the world of ideas."[32] He finds truth in beauty suggesting that the ideal is to turn from "ordinary actuality to an aesthetic one."[33] In addition, "reason (can) plant social principles," but he contends, "Beauty alone can confer a social character." Finally, he observes that the enchantment of "Beauty alone makes the world happy." In this theory, beauty is not only a means to moral and rational freedom but also a glorious end in itself. Here, Schiller is no doubt attempting to come to terms with Plato's ideal, where both the good and the true are subordinated to the beautiful.

Like May and Campbell, Schiller proposes that an aesthetic education is central to the education of the whole person. In one theory, Schiller proposes that the aesthetic condition is transitional to the moral and rational. Yet overall, he comes across as presenting a view relatively consistent with that of classical Greece, which is that the moral attitude is influenced by beauty, revolves around beauty itself, or is subsumed to the beautiful. In actual Greek thought, there were four levels of ethical conduct: the *euprepès* or the outwardly decorous; the *dikaion*, the lawful or customary; the *agathon*, the good that strives toward the beautiful; and the *kalon*, the purely beautiful, the supreme standard of conduct.[34] Again, Schiller's view is somewhat similar to both Campbell and May. The government of one's conduct in relationship to oneself and others by conventional ethics needs to be replaced by an essentially aesthetic attitude.

In an article entitled *Human Nature and Aesthetic Growth*, art educator Frances Wilson makes the same claims.[35] She writes, "My experience leads me to believe that the aesthetic sense is also the moral sense, and the sense of self of being" and "of becoming."[36] She sees the "aesthetic sense" as "an integrating system" and equates it with the moral, social, and religious sense.[37] Like Schiller, she argues that it allows for a simultaneous perception of the opposites and the perception of wholeness.

Moreover, again like Schiller, she observes that the "aesthetic sense" refers to the power of imagination, a passive perceptive quality, while integrating the person dynamically in any given situation, an active quality. Wilson, therefore, praises the aesthetic attitude in a way, similar to Campbell, May, and Schiller. Like them, she sees it as the perfect governor of the conduct of life, which leads toward wholeness, and the aesthetic condition as representing the ideal, being wholeness itself.

In his pamphlet entitled *The Thought of the Heart*, James Hillman makes, perhaps, the most elegant defense of the way of beauty and an aesthetic approach to life.[38] Indeed, he considers that his archetypal approach to therapy is basically an aesthetic one and that he works therapy with an "artist's fantasy."[39] Like May and Schiller, he refers to the Greek imagination in supporting his case.

Hillman begins with mythological Greece and the goddess Aphrodite, the beautiful one and soul of the universe (*psyche toukosmou*), who creates both the perceptible world and the individual soul (Plotinus as reported in Hillman, 1984). As children of Aphrodite, observes Hillman, "the soul is born in beauty and feeds on beauty, requires beauty for its life."[40] As "sun eyed children from out of the paths of the morning star," our most primordial instinct is the impulse to beauty.[41] There is accordingly, a profound psychological need to "recover our lost aesthetic reactions, our sense of beauty."[42]

Hillman turns to R. B. Onions, who traces the root meaning of the Greek *aistheses* (to perceive, to sense) back to "taking in," "breathing" in "a gasp," which suggests full involvement of the evaluative heart and the goddess of the senses, Aphrodite.[43] He notes that in harmony with this line of thinking, for Aristotle, the organ of perception is the heart, which perceives through the imagination. Moreover, he notes that Plato perpetuates ancient Hellenic understanding in his concept of the beautiful as the divine manifestation in the immanence of the world. As Plato describes it in Phaedrus, "Beauty is…the very sensibility of the cosmos, that it has textures, tones, tastes that it is attractive."[44] By living in soul, therefore, we live in the aesthetic condition; we live in beauty.

Like all the other authorities cited so far in this paper, Hillman rejects the ethical attitude *per se* and encourages the aesthetic view as a guide to the conduct of life. He again appeals to Aphrodite as a major figure in the archetype of beauty whose primordial actions, according to him, "do not, cannot separate the aesthetic from the moral."[45] Moreover, he sees individuation coming in the Aphroditic mode, as a way that requires attending to the "signals of beauty and ugliness."[46] That is to say, the path of beauty leads to wholeness by way of developing consciousness of the aesthetic response. The aesthetic path requires an aspiration toward beauty and an understanding of what that means.

The aesthetic response is, to begin with, a day-to-day affair, notes Hillman. It is, he writes, the heartfelt response to "the value of each particular thing."[47] It is the spontaneous reaction of the heart's taste, the aesthetic reflection that comes together with sensation.[48] In the process,there is a differentiation of beauty from ugliness, a discrimination of the inner heart. The aesthetic response differentiates between beauty, being "true to one's own being" and ugliness, "when we go...over to another order."[49] The aesthetic response to ugliness, reasons Hillman, involves the soul shrinking within itself, a denying and turning away. The aesthetic response to beauty involves a feeling of harmony, agreeableness, and the expansive heart, which when spiritualized, can lead to bliss and the experience of rapture and delight at the heart of things.

To conclude this defense of the aesthetic path, I now comment on a poem by Irving Layton entitled "Whatever Else Poetry is Freedom" (appendix).[50] I refer to it as I believe it can help the reader get a direct feeling for what is meant by the aesthetic response and the legitimacy of the aesthetic attitude to life. There are several observations that I think are relevant. The first is that Layton finds freedom in poetry, which means that through the aesthetic condition, he believes that he is being true to himself.

The first and last stanzas are particularly revealing. In the first stanza, Layton exhorts the poet to give up "the trick of lying" and to be open to the authentic imagination of the heart. He subsequently opens to a series of apparently unrelated imaginative perceptions, each of which carries with it a sensuous component. These include:

> Poplars and pines [that] grow straight but oaks
> are gnarled old codgers [who] must speak of
> death, boys break windows, [and] Women [who]
> lie honestly by their men at last.

In the final stanza, the poet tells us that the voice of inner freedom comes from the revelations of "far off...impatient cadences" that tell him to "sing of lust, the sun's accompanying shadow." This brings the poet to a new sense of life as "the stillness in dead feet," gives way as "your stave brings resurrection,

O aggrievèd king."

By relying on the aesthetic response and being open nonjudgmentally to inner vision, Layton not only allows a certain beauty to shine through the word, but he also finds new intensity to life through acceptance of the lustful shadow. This example, in itself, argues forcefully for the value of an aesthetic attitude to a full life. Joseph Henderson confirms this view, observing how James Joyce liberated himself from family ties with such an attitude.[51]

The Psychological Perspective and Individuation

Without knowing what Layton means by "sing(ing) of lust" and how he assimilates this shadow quality into his life, such a bold assertion, nonetheless, raises a red flag. Indeed, there are other poems by the poet that indicate a streak of violence, or at least a repressive attitude. For instance, in one poem he coolly kills a frog, and in another, he slams a butterfly against a rock. For Layton, it does not seem to be a question of right or wrong, but of openness to experience.

His poetry needs to be seen in light of the larger context of contemporary art, where there is often little conscious discernment between the beautiful and the ugly.[52] Such an attitude is an aesthetic one that operates nonjudgmentally by way of perceptive modes of sensation, imagination, and feelings. In the process, there may be a refinement of the aesthetic attitude and increasing differentiation of the inner heart. At least for some people, this seems to be the potential. For, if Plato is right, there is a hierarchy of values of beauty, a view that is confirmed by the supreme poet of beauty, Sri Aurobindo.[53] He observes that just as "all is the Divine some things are more Divine than others," and "in the artist's vision too there can be gradations, a hierarchy of values."[54] In fact, there are today signs of a resurging interest in beauty, at least with some artists, although they still seem to be in the minority.

The reality of a hierarchy of beauty, of course, suggests that for many people, perhaps most, there is little ability to discern between levels of beauty and between beauty and ugliness. Indeed, if many contemporary artists show little interest in discriminating in such a way what, then, about the "ordinary" person? Furthermore, the world today is increasingly showing an ugly face, one of violence and destruction. Such a milieu does not encourage expressions of beauty. Indeed, the influences on contemporary people, including much of popular culture, are generally not,in my opinion, such as to elevate people's aesthetic taste.

Given these considerations, it is understandable that Jung took a somewhat disparaging attitude against "aestheticism" or the aesthetic way early on and never repudiated his position.[55] Although his understanding of aesthetics usually does not include an evaluative function—he generally relates it to the intuitive and sensation functions alone—given the reality of life, I believe his argument is still valid. In fact, I have come across one passage where Jung suggests that the aesthetic response includes an evaluative function giving his logic even more power.[56] He writes about "artistic intuition selecting and presenting its images with the help of feeling values." Despite this evaluative function inherent in aesthetic judgment, Jung writes, "Aestheticism is not fitted to solve the exceedingly serious and difficult task of educating man (as) it always averts its face from everything evil, ugly and difficult.[57]

Among those who defend the aesthetic path above, only Hillman tries to directly come to terms with the question of ugliness (and evil), basically arguing that the soul turns naturally to harmony and beauty and shrinks from ugliness (and evil) as part of the aesthetic response.[58] Presumably, May is saying the same thing when he contends that the artist is amoral but responds to life's demands with great integrity. Ginette Paris supports this argument by observing that she has noticed that people's depressions often leave them when beauty in some form returns to their lives.[59] However true this may be, Hillman's argument presumes that the individual has enough consciousness of beauty to make such judgments. As Jung says,"Aestheticism… always presupposes the very thing it should create—the capacity to love beauty."[60] And even should one have the ability, or a degree of it, the hard practical reality of daily life is not, in my opinion,conducive to making decisions based on aesthetic considerations alone. The quest for self-knowledge demands that the individual not only holds up the mirror to the shadow side of reality as well as to the true, the good, and the beautiful, but is able to withstand the conflict of opposites thus engendered. In the case of our poet, Irving Layton, for instance, it is not evident that such is the case, at least from his poetry. Indeed, Layton is but one example of many creative artists who don't appear to have a developed moral sense. Urjo Kareda, for instance, writes of Richard Wagner as "a hideous man and an extraordinary artist."[61] He calls this phenomenon "the paradox of artistic creation."[62] For the development of character, another attitude is required, and that is the ethical. "What is needed," writes Jung, "is a supreme moral effort, the greatest self-denial and sacrifice."[63] In another passage, he defends his position by arguing that "the anima believes in the Kalon Kagathon, the beautiful and the good," a primitive conception that antedates the discovery of the conflict between aesthetics and morals. It took more than a thousand years of Christian differentiation to make it clear that "the good is not always beautiful and the beautiful not always the good."[64]

Sri Aurobindo is of a similar mind when he writes, "The aesthetic motive in conduct limits and must be exceeded in order for humanity to rise."[65] He observes that the aesthetic view of life, as lived in the Athens of Phidias and Sophocles and later in the Renaissance, were short lived, essentially due to the lack of ethical discipline. He writes that "without character, without some kind of strong discipline there is no enduring power of life" and that "will, character, self-discipline, self-mastery" are indispensable for psychological development.[66] For practical purposes, the ethical instinct is just as necessary as the aesthetic for individuation.

But even that is not enough for the complex journey toward Self-realization. Art, in its origin, was a sister activity to religion, suggesting that the religious instinct requires cultivation that, in its original sense, according to Jung, means taking into serious consideration contents of the unconscious and synchronistic events.[67] Such is the view of Swiss artist, Peter Birkhäuser, who believes that the religious attitude can redeem art from its present chaos.[68] There is also a natural instinct for truth and knowledge that is aided by science and philosophy and the play of reason that seek realization. In addition, there is a natural drive for happiness and the expression of power in the business of life. What is needed, then, is an attitude that embraces all these natural impulses that make up the multifaceted psyche, the aesthetic, the ethical, the religious, the philosophic and scientific, and the search for happiness and the expression of life-power, an attitude that Henderson aptly calls the depth-psychological.[69]

The way of art can now be placed in a wider perspective. The aesthetic att-itude allows nonjudgmental openness to experience and feelings, both inner and outer. Jung points the way with his approach to active imagination, especially when it takes the form of archetypal representations. A religious or contemplative attitude is necessary to bring meaning to the experience. With an ethical attitude, one applies insights to the conduct of life. The idea, generated through experience, especially when archetypal,can enrich one's bank of knowledge and be taken up by reason. A scientific scrutiny of inner and outer events leads to truths that can be generalized, the discovery of patterns in life and improved understanding. Finally, there is also a need for the realization of both mastery and some happiness in life. The way of art, then, becomes part of a larger package, as life aspires toward consciousness. It is, then, not so much a question of the way of art, but the art of life.

****

I have examined the way of art, or the aesthetic view as proposed by several important figures. Collectively, they make a very compelling argument for its central value as a guide to the conduct of life and individuation and its goal of wholeness. In the process, they all subsume the ethical impulse to the aesthetic, a notion that goes back to ancient and classical Greece. This, however, does not take into consideration the hard,practical reality of life and the need to differentiate the moral sense from the aesthetic. In addition, there are other instincts that need to be harnessed in the service of individuation, along with a broader perspective than the aesthetic, the depth-psychological.

CHAPTER 3

The Aesthetic Attitude and the Art of Life

Abstract

In this paper, I examine the nature of the aesthetic attitude which is based on a supra-rational instinct that ultimately aims at the beautiful. I observe that it not only operates by way of the perceptive modes of intuition and sensation, but also consists of an Eros-based evaluative feeling function. Individuation of the aesthetic nature involves refining one's ability to differentiate grades of beauty and beauty from ugliness. Although cultivating this attitude is of supreme value for psychological well-being, a broader perspective is required for the sake of a more complete individuation. The art of life requires the psychological attitude, which includes the aesthetic, in addition to other perspectives of equal value.

Introduction

In this paper, I discuss the nature of the aesthetic attitude, pointing out its value and shortcomings. I begin by contrasting the points of view held by Hillman and May with Jung's more critical appraisal. I then discuss the aesthetic attitude itself, taking into consideration Western notions of beauty and ugliness and the phenomenon of modern art. I conclude that individuation requires another broader perspective, the psychological, one which embraces the aesthetic as well as others attitudes of equal value.

The Problem

Rollo May and James Hillman, two eminent contemporary psychologists, place high value on the aesthetic attitude for individuation and psychological well-being. Not only does May see art as an antidote for violence, but he also sees it as an inspiring force that counteracts feelings of insignificance.[70] Furthermore, he underscores the Greek concept *areté*, that the noble life is primarily the beautiful life, thus stressing the aesthetic attitude. Hillman observes that his archetypal approach to psychology is essentially an aesthetic one and that he works therapy with an "artist's fantasy."[71] Otto Rank seems to hold a similar view, going so far as to suggest that artists need to eventually renounce their artistic expression in favor of the creative formation of personality and life.[72]

In contrast to these views, in his early work, *Psychological Types*, Carl Jung forcefully argues that the aesthetic standpoint is insufficient in dealing with the difficult task of individuation, a view he never repudiates.[73] Although he developed a meditative process called active imagination, which includes a "picture method," he differentiates it from art in that it needs to be experienced actively and responsively, with full human concern and consciousness, and not simply passively.[74] According to Jung, the more passive approach is generally true of the artist and the aesthetic perspective which, says Henderson, "values the symbol for itself alone."[75]

In fact, at least in some cases, there is an engagement between artists and their work in terms of active feeling evaluations, although the results generally remain with the art and don't get translated into life. By feeling, I mean the rational function that responds to affective states, events, and people with evaluations of worth.[76] It includes degrees of liking and disliking that can become increasingly refined with greater consciousness. It is through feeling evaluation that artists discern what they like or don't like in their artistic productions. There is also a need for Eros or relatedness, which is to say, a fully engaged instinctual relationship between artists and their art. Art without Eros is, at best, decorative or perhaps based on some intellectual concept. At its worst, it is monstrous.

From a psychological perspective, there is, in addition, a need to interact with the imaginative process to gain awareness that can be applied to the conduct of one's life. Presumably something like this is what Rank is referring to, although by requesting artists to give up artistic expression, he is throwing away an invaluable tool for objectifying the symbol that potentially allows one to see the symbolic process supporting one's own life. The aesthetic attitude is essential to allow for necessary receptivity to experience both the unconscious and life itself. But to apply insight to life, more is needed. For one, the religious attitude in the sense of conscientious "observing," "pondering," and "taking account of," based on religion, derived from the word *religere*, is essential.[77] For another, the ethical, the aspiration for the good, which relates directly to the development of will,discipline, and strength of character, is required.

The Aesthetic Attitude: Its Value and Shortcomings

I now explore the nature of the aesthetic attitude and its value and shortcomings for the art of life, especially in the contemporary world. Although the artist best personifies the aesthetic attitude, it can, according to Henderson, be the natural predisposition of people from all walks of life.[78] It is based on a suprarational instinct that aspires toward harmony and beauty, not only in objects of art, literature, dance, etc., but in religion, thought, relationships, and general sense of being. Although of supreme value, I agree with Jung that, alone, it does not satisfy the difficult requirements of individuation and the development of consciousness. Another perspective is required, one that embraces other points of view in addition to the aesthetic, which Henderson (1984) aptly calls the psychological attitude.

The word *aesthetic* is derived from the Greek *aesthetikos*, meaning "perceptive," and from *aesthanesthai*, "to perceive," "to feel."[79] The verb to feel is normally taken to refer to feelings or emotions and not on evaluative function. The kinds of emotions or feelings involved in the aesthetic response include "being in awe of," "being astonished," "exulting in," "being enraptured," etc., by something beautiful. According to Weekly, *aesthetic* simply means "to perceive."[80] Likewise, Jung argues that the aesthetic attitude operates particularly by way of the sensation and intuitive functions, the two perceptive modes.[81] R. B. Onions notes that the word *aesthetics* has the root meaning of "taking in" and "breathing in of the world" and "gasping," which suggests the act of perceiving deeply, freely.[82] According to these considerations, the aesthetic attitude is primarily one that is nonjudgmentally open to the world through all the senses, including the sixth sense, the intuition and inner vision. Although there is a relationship to the idea, it is through feelings and not thought, or thought only secondarily. When it acts on its own, there is no sense of social duty, no ethical concerns, no reasoning. Nor does it include a reflective religious function.

These considerations notwithstanding art, a product of the

aesthetic instinct, and religion, were, in the beginning, sister activities.[83] Moreover, for the Hellenic imagination of the ancient Greeks, beauty was experienced in two ways. The first way was through experiences of the natural world. Although aesthetic interest mainly focused on the beauties of the natural world, including the human body, intense experience of earthly beauty was considered the effect of divine enhancement.[84] Such a possibility for the Greek mind is explained in that according to Platonic thought, the material world as image makes present the incorporeal divine archetype. In fact, Armstrong contends that Plato kept alive the Hellenic thought of the ancient Greeks, which was further developed by the neo-Platonist Plotinus and completely rehabilitated through Proclus. The second way that beauty was experienced was in the theophanies of the gods and goddesses themselves.

The expectation for such experiences was provided for by general awareness of "the poikilia," or one divine world, expressed variously in a hierarchy of beauty.[85] The different grades and kinds of beauty imply the need for a sliding scale of value, an important notion for purposes of this essay. It suggests that aesthetics ultimately not only involves perceiving passively, but also active Eros-based feeling evaluation.

According to our earlier discussion, based on the derivation of the word *aesthetics*, it is not evident that the aesthetic attitude involves an evaluative function of feeling. It seems rather to have to do with perception, the senses and feeling as in emotion and feelings. However, for the ancient Greeks, aesthetics was considered to be the province of the goddess Aphrodite, the "Beautiful One" and the appropriate sense organ, the evaluative heart, the seat of Eros, which comes along with imagination and sensation.[86] Furthermore, Weekly notes that through German philosophy, the word *aesthetic* now carries with it the sense of "criticism of taste," indicating the need for feeling evaluations even if aesthetics as a discipline treats its subject too intellectually.[87] Finally, "gasping" and "breathing in of the world" as root meaning of the word aesthetics, to me, suggests that the evaluative function of feeling rooted in Eros plays a dominant role.

Still, the question of whether or not the aesthetic attitude includes Eros and feeling as an evaluative function is problematic in today's world. According to the *Oxford Illustrated Dictionary*, the objective *aesthetic* refers to appreciating the beautiful according to principles of good taste, and the noun *aesthetic* refers to the philosophy of art and of the beautiful.[88] The fact that along with beauty, art is the primary subject matter of aesthetics as a discipline suggests that Eros and feeling are by definition intrinsic to aesthetics. However, according to Herbert Read, the eminent art historian, the contemporary artist does not differentiate between beauty and ugliness, at least in the meaning of these words that have come down to us from the later Greek period or the Renaissance.[89] He quotes artist Jean Dubuffet as exclaiming that the notions of ugliness and beauty are illusions,and sculptor Henry Moore as saying that, for him, power of expression goes deeper than the senses and moves him more deeply than beauty of expression. It may be that what is being said, especially in the case of Moore, is that external cannons of beauty are no longer relevant. But, in their place, there is a finer sense of inner discrimination of Eros-based feeling that is relevant.

But even Moore emphasizes the spiritual vitality in power of expression rather than the beautiful. Moreover, it is difficult to get away from the fact that much of contemporary art does, indeed, not seem to be particularly concerned with beauty. This phenomenon leads Erich Neumann to write of the "terrible beauty of modern art, which itself denies that it is beauty" and that "the beautiful is abandoned in favour of the true, of so-called ugliness."[90] Herbert Read echoes these sentiments, observing that "again and again modern artists have disowned the concept of the beautiful."[91] Neumann sums up his view of the situation with questionable praise in his paradoxical description of contemporary art as "neurotic in its rapture and 'sacred' in its neurosis."[92]

He also sees a new psychic flowering emerging from beyond the contemporary chaos. Neumann particularly appreciates the paintings of Chagall and Klee and the sculptures of Henry Moore.93 I can personally think of several other artists that reveal beauty in their work, for instance,sculptor Bill Reid and painters Georgia O'Keeffe, Tom Harris, A. Y. Jackson, Emily Carr, and others. The same observation can be made of other aesthetic expressions, for instance poetry, music, dance, and architecture.

The Function of Art

The question to address now is: exactly what is the function of art, and what is its relationship to beauty and aesthetics? Martin Heidegger arguesthat the essence of art is the *alètheia* or unconcealment of being, the becoming of truth.[94] The artist is *technitès*, where *technè* denotes a way of knowing or apprehending what is present, as revealer of truth. He also notes that beauty is one way in which truth can occur. In contrast to the poet John Keats, who writes that "Beauty is truth, truth is beauty," Heideigger seems to be saying that although beauty must express truth, there are other kinds of truth. Thus, one of the functions of art is to reveal the truth of beauty. The master poet, Sri Aurobindo, speaks even more poignantly to this point observing that the truth great art seeks is that of beauty.[95]

The latter also argues that the act of creation requires an "inner power of discrimination" which edits "in accordance with a principle of truth and beauty."[96] In addition, he observes that just as the Divine exists on all levels of being, "some things are more Divine than others," and that there is, likewise, a gradation of values in the expression of art.[97] As I suggested earlier, this same notion can be found in Plato leading him to banishing any art [poetry] from his ideal republic that does not live up to what he determines to meet the highest standards.[98]

Sri Aurobindo makes other relevant comments on the nature of art. He notes that it not only involves the expression of beauty but the "self expression of consciousness." He goes on to say that "there are not only aesthetic values, but life values, mind values and soul values that enter into art."[99] He is highly critical of modern art, however, finding it, among other things monstrous and ugly, suggesting that it is not self-contained and that it lacks inner truth of life, therefore, failing its mandate.[100] Jung expresses similar views, finding contemporary artists incapable of thinking,contemplating and finding meaning in their work, which he, too, finds "grotesque," "ugly," distorted, and "revolting."[101]

In contrast to Neumann, who sees modern artists as courageously facing the forces of chaos, both Jung and Sri Aurobindo seem to be saying that they are not producing art at all, nor are they courageously facing chaos. Indeed, in one letter, Jung writes that contemporary art is serving chaos and even performing a kind of black magic, "increasing the state of disorder."[102] In another letter, he concedes that contemporary art is a creative force that "depicts the sickness of our times" wherein lies "its educative purpose."[103]

My personal view is that, with some notable exceptions, there is still considerable truth in these assessments. Moreover, although there are signs of a resurging interest in beauty since their day,there is little indication of any new significant trends as far as I know. Indeed, in some ways it is getting worse. For example, consider some of the popular expressions of contemporary music, painting, movies, and television.

These observations, I believe, are generally valid, despite the well-reasoned argument that contemporary art is actually attempting to depict a new integral consciousness. Jean Gebser demonstrates how some modern paintings fulfil the requirements for this new emerging structure of consciousness by giving several examples of art that show "the eruption of time in painting," "a suppression of dualism," and "an a-rational and a-perspective character."[104] Cubism, for example, in the art of Picasso, is a case in point. I find his line of reasoning intuitively appealing and stimulating. This phenomenon notwithstanding, the argument for the general lack of concern for beauty in contemporary art and culture is not, in my view, undermined.

If art is fundamentally about beauty and contemporary art has little regard for it, then it is important to try and understand our traditional Western definition of what constitutes being beautiful. Hilary Armstrong contends that what he refers to as cosmic piety or religiosity has had a powerful influence on European thought and imagination by way of a certain "re-Platonizing" and "re-Aristoteleanizing" of Stoicism.[105] This has led to an "other worldly" attitude that undervalues awareness of the "poikilea"— that is, the divine manifestation in the beauties of the earth. A preference for mathematical symmetry and order developed instead. Similarly, Herbert Read notes that beginning with *Aristotle's Poetics*, through medieval Scholasticism, the Italian Renaissance, and the Enlightenment "beauty was conceived as an excellence in the proportion of things."[106]

Clearly, contemporary art has been breaking away from these traditional external impositions. Perhaps, too, there is, in some cases, an attempt,however unconscious, to discover the Divine as dynamic energy and beauty in power of expression. The extraordinary impact of the art of primal people on the modern scene attests to that possibility. However, there is no reason to believe that such art should be without form and symmetry, although it may be of a different order, imposed from within. Some primal art, for instance, Northwest coast native art and Hopi sand paintings suggests this to be the case, as does the splendid art from India.

These observations notwithstanding, there is a need to come to terms with the contemporary lack of interest in beauty and the exaggerated predominance of ugliness. Read comes to our aid by exploring the meaning of the word *ugly* in several Western languages in order to understand its root meaning.[107] He notes that the contrary to definitions of beauty given above is "turpitude" or "loathliness" related to the French *laideur* and Italian *laidezze*, which in their origin meant "dull, stupid, senseless. "The German word *ugly* is based on the Middle English *uggen* or Old Norse *ugga* or *ugglier*, which is related to fear, causing fear, dreadful, or terrible. The Western conception of ugliness, therefore, has to do with what lacks symmetry, and the deformed and grotesque, which comes along with or indicates the subjective states of mind indicated here.

Read also observes that the ugly has always been present in art, even Western art—for instance, in the Christian iconography of hell.[108] In the primitive world, where there is no antithesis between good and evil, beauty and ugliness, where spiritual force is considered immanent in nature, art has a magic function, and images are often meant to elicit terror, fear, or astonishment. As in modern art, the patterns expressed are often not symmetrical, but grotesque, and they are, according to the above observations, ugly, says Read, sublimely ugly.

Given their transcendent nature, both the beautiful and the ugly are sublime and the proper study of art and aesthetics. Both go beyond the reaches of ordinary experience of the individual ego. Furthermore, ugly objects, observes Read, that are depicted by the artist with love and care redeem the hideous by transforming it through aesthetic value while lifting it to a higher level of acceptance. In addition to the depiction of objects that are ugly in themselves, there are works of art where the deformation is not in the subject matter itself, but deliberately created by the artist. Read sees this, too, as serving a psychological need and the expression and experience of this form of ugliness also a positive aesthetic phenomenon.

We can conclude from this discussion that traditional

canons of beauty no longer apply and that the emphasis in much contemporary art is not beauty but on its contrary, ugliness. This involves, as Neumann (1983) observes,the need for the artist to experience chaos as never before. In the process,there has been an acceptance of the ugly, not only for purposes of aesthetic transformation, but for depiction of the ugly in itself. The fascination we have with the latter suggests that it, too, is sublime and beyond the ego, even if ugly.

When the ugly is transformed, for instance, when it is part of a larger aesthetic whole, a spiritual and psychological need is undoubtedly being fulfilled. This allows for shadow qualities to be integrated into the aesthetic experience and can be, in this case, the result of attaining what can be referred to as the transcendent function of beauty, which takes one beyond the dualities of beauty and ugliness as we conceive them. However, when artists deliberately create ugliness, or even when they show little or no concern for beauty, unlike Read, who argues that a psychological need is necessarily being catered to, I would rather say as "self expression of consciousness," the artist is simply showing us a mirror to our contemporary reality, a reality that is anything but beautiful.[109] We are fascinated with the art of a Picasso, much of which was not done with loving care in my estimation because we see ourselves, in however a fragmented state.

If it be true that the ultimate goal of art is the beautiful and that there are kinds and degrees of beauty, as Plato indicates and Sri Aurobindo confirms,then our aesthetic education requires learning discernment in beauty and differentiating between beauty and ugliness. This requires not only the ability to perceive nonjudgmentally as does the contemporary artist, but also Eros and differentiation of the feeling function, as I indicated earlier. Indeed, Jung allows for the possibility of "aesthetic intuition selecting and presenting its image with the help of feeling values."[110] As the traditional canons of beauty no longer apply, there is a requirement to turn within for a finer discrimination of the heart. There is a need to transcend conventional conceptions of what constitutes both beauty and ugliness.

The Path of Beauty

In their origin, art and religion were sister activities. In primal cultures, art has a magical and transformational function for both community and individual alike. Peter Birkhäuser, an under recognized Swiss artist, argues that it is precisely the religious attitude that will redeem contemporary art from its present chaos.[111] He means by that, that there is a need for artists to take into careful consideration messages from the unconscious, including through their works of art, in addition to outer synchronistic events. This requires sympathetic identification with the object of contemplation and its objectification through the art, along with a search for self-knowledge and meaning. Sri Aurobindo and his coworker, the Mother, also point to the similarity between the way of beauty and the path of yoga.[112] Indeed, in India, the way of art has traditionally been considered to be one path leading to the Divine as God of Beauty.

The common origin of art and religion can be explained by the fact that they each aim at direct experience of the archetype, the source of which, according to Plotinus, is "of one quality which keeps intact all qualities in itself, of sweetness along with fragrance."[113] In Indian tradition the material creation is based on *rasa* or "concentrated taste a spiritual essence of emotion, an essential aetheses, the soul's pleasure in pure and perfect source of feeling," the experience of which gives delight.[114] The archetypal essence of life is delight, and, says Sri Aurobindo, beauty can be defined as a self-concentrated "form of delight."[115] In other words, the realization of beauty comes by giving form to the experience of bliss or ananda. In a small way, it is the sense of contentment and satisfaction that comes while completing a creative piece of work.

The proper aspiration for the artist and for people on the path of beauty is to deepen their connection to Eros and the delight of existence and to give it form or expression in life. The archetype, however, comes not only with Eros but also with Logos, as consciousness-force it comes with the quality of differentiation and meaning. Another way of saying that is that the archetype comes with the idea, as well as the effective power of realization. In addition to the experiences of beauty *per se* and existential delight, the path of beauty can also bring knowledge and the power to transform both culture and life.

On the path of beauty, one relates to ideas subjectively through feeling. Characteristically this means that one gets excited by ideas and evaluates them according to whether one likes them or not. On this path, one can also relate to power through form of aesthetic expression. As I alluded to earlier, some art expresses more power than other art. For example, decorative art has virtually no power in it. Nor do a certain style of naive art or new age art. The art of primal people, on the other hand, generally gives form to a considerable amount of power. Indeed, it may be that power of expression is what modern art is trying to come to terms with, which explains its rather meager interest in the idea of beauty *per se*. Whatever the case may be, these reflections indicate that the experience of beauty can touch one at all levels of being, encouraging wholeness. These observations, therefore, support the legitimacy of a path based on art or beauty, an aesthetic path, especially when coupled with a religious attitude.

The Psychological Perspective

But is that enough for the task of conscious individuation? Jung argues that it isn't enough. Contemplating contents of the collective unconscious and giving artistic form to them does not mean that appropriate action follows, or that one's own life is transformed. For that to happen, it is necessary to have a developed conscience and an ethical attitude. As Jung observes, the cure of neurosis is very much a moral issue.[116] He writes, "It took a thousand years of Christian differentiation to make it clear that the good is not always the beautiful and the beautiful not necessarily the good."[117] His counterpart from India, Sri Aurobindo, takes essentially the same view and argues that, in addition to the aesthetic impulse toward the beautiful, there is another instinct, the ethical, which seeks the good.[118] Like Jung, he argues that the problematic nature of practical reality requires the realization of this instinct for self-fulfilment. Without the development of character, he argues, "There is no enduring power of life."[119] If contemporary art is truly a mirror to the reality of our society, which it seems to be, then not only the religious attitude, but the ethical must come to the aid of the purely aesthetic approach to life.

In fact, individuation requires a psychological attitude that is open to all the natural and noble inclinations in humankind. This not only includes the aesthetic, ethical, and religious instincts, but also the drive for knowledge and truth. In addition, in the business of life itself, which also seeks individuation, there is both an instinctual drive for the realization of power as well as a drive for pleasure and happiness.

****

Differentiation of the aesthetic instinct is essential for self-fulfilment of the contemporary person and the art of life. For some people, it is more dominant than for others, but it is a natural drive potentially active in everybody. It allows for nonjudgmental openness to experience, both inner and outer. Individuation of this instinct leads to ever finer appreciation of beauty and harmony and the experience of delight as the essential stuff of existence. Although the authentic aesthetic instinct aspires toward the highest value, it needs to be subsumed to the psyche's greater drive for completeness and the development of consciousness. The art of living requires more than just an aesthetic attitude. As life seeks the realization of the many-colored rainbow hues of consciousness, the art of life seeks wholeness. This requires subsuming the aesthetic attitude to the psychological perspective.

References

Adler, Gerhard, editor. 1975. C. G. *Jung Letters*. Collaborator Aniela Jaffé, translation from the German by R. F. C. Hull. Two vols, vol. 1 and 2. Bollingen Series XVC: 1:2. Princeton, N. J.: Princeton University Press, vol. 1. pp. 107–8, 225–226, 316, 469, vol. 2: pp. 482–488, 81–83, 440, 511 –12, 549, 586, 589–911 , 604–5, 629–630.

Armstrong, A. Hilary. 1987. "The Divine Enhancement of Earthly Beauties. The Hellenic and Platonic Tradition." Eranos lectures on beauty. Dallas: Spring Publications, Inc. pp. 39–73.

Ashram, Aurobindo Sri. 1970. *Art: Quotations on art from Sri Aurobindo and the Mother*. Pondicherry: Sri Aurobindo Ashram Trust.

Aurobindo, Sri. 1972. *Sri Aurobindo Birth Centenary Library*. Popular edition. 30 vols, vol. 9. The Future Poetry. Pondicherry: Sri Aurobindo Ashram Trust, pp. 330–335.

Birkhaüser, Peter. 1980. *Light from the Darkness: The Paintings of Peter Birkhaüser*. Translated by Michael Mitchell and Ruth E. Horne. Basel: Birkhauser Verlag, pp. 11 5–11 6.

Campbell, Joseph. 1986. *The Inner Reaches of Outer Space: Metaphor as Myth and as Religion*. New York: Harper and Row, Publishers, p. 122.

Coulson, J. et al. 1962. Oxford illustrated dictionary. Illustrations edited by Helen Mary Petter. London: Oxford University Press, p. 11.

Gebser, Jean 1989. The Ever Present Origin. Authorized translation by Noel Barstad with Algis Mickunas, part two: *Manifestations of the Perspectival World: An Attempt at the Concretion of the Spiritual*. Athens: Ohio University Press, pp. 470–486.

Heidegger, Martin. 1977. *Basic Writings from Being and Time (1927) to the Task of Thinking (1964)*. Edited with general introduction and introduction to each section by David Farrell Krell, general editor for this volume, J. Glenn Gray-English translation by Harper and Row, Publishers. New York: Harper and Row, Publishers, pp. 252–260.

Henderson, Joseph. 1990. "The Picture Method in Jungian

Psychotherapy." *Shadow and Self: Selected Papers in Analytic Psychology*. Willmette, Illinois: Chiron Publications, pp. 252–260.

Henderson, Joseph, MD. 1984. *Cultural Attitudes in Psychological Perspective*. Toronto: Inner City Books, pp. 53–64, 45, 7–14.

Hillman, James. 1981. "The Thought of the Heart." Eranos lectures 2. Dallas: Spring Publication, Inc., pp. 24–33. V Hillman, James, Pozzo, Laura (pseudonym) (1983). Interviews. New York: Harper and Row Publishers, Inc., pp. 30–31, 186–187.

Jung, C. G. 1974. The Collected Works. 19 vols., vol. 6. *Psychological Types*. A revision by R. F. C. Hull of the translation by H. G. Baynes. Princeton, N. J.: Princeton University Press, pp. 136–146.

Jung, C. G. 1974. The Collected Works. 19 vols., vol. 7. *Two Essays on Analytical Psychology*. Translated by R. F. C. Hull. Bollingen series XX. Princeton, N. J.: Princeton University Press, p. 213–219.

Jung, C. G. 1974. The Collected Works. 19 vols., vol. 9.1. *The Archetypes and the Collective Unconscious*. Translated by R. F. C. Hull. Bollingen series XX. Princeton, NJ: Princeton University Press, pp. 215–220, 238–243.

May, Rollo. 1985. *My Quest for Beauty*. New York: Saybrook Publishing Company. pp. 215–220, 238–243.

Neumann, Erich. 1959. *The Archetypal World of Henry Moore*. Translated from the German y R. F. C. Hull. Bollingen Series LXVIII. New York: Pantheon Books, Inc., for Bollingen Foundation, Inc. Passim.

Neumann, Erich. 1974. *Art and the Creative Unconscious*. Translated from the German by Ralph Manheim. Bollingen Series LXI. Princeton: Princeton University Press, pp. 135–148, 11 2, 11 7, 120, 126, 132.

Neumann, Erich. 1983. "Art and Time." *Man and Time: Papers from Eranos Yearbooks*. Edited by Joseph Campbell. Bollingen series XXX. 3. Princeton, N. J.: Princeton University Press, pp. 37, 24, 3–37.

Onions, R. B. 1988. *The Origins of European Thought*. New York: Cambridge University Press, pp. 74–75.

Plato. 1967. *The Republic of Plato*. Translated with introduction and notes by Francis MacDonald Cornford. New York: Oxford University Press, pp. 84–85, 321–340.

Purani, A. B. 1965. *On Art*. Publisher: Nargol (D. T. Surat): Nava Sarjan Society, pp. 75, 93.

Rank, Otto. 1989. *Art and Artist: Creative Urge and Personality Development*. New York: W.W. Norton and Company, pp. 430–431, 328.

Read, Herbert. 1987. "Beauty and the beast." Eranos Lectures on Beauty. Dallas: Spring Publications, Inc. pp. 1–38

Sharp, Daryl. 1987. *Personality Types: Jung's Model of Typology*. Toronto: Inner City Books, pp. 16–18, 49–54, 75–79.

Sri Aurobindo. 1971. Sri Aurobindo Birth Centenary Library. Popular ed. 30 vols., vol. 15. *Social and Political Thought*, part I. *The Human Cycle*. Pondicherry: Sri Aurobindo Ashram Trust, pp. 127–135, 71, 84–93.

Weekley, Ernest. 1967. *An Etymological Dictionary of Modern English*. Two vol., vol. one A-K. New York: Dover Publications, Inc., pp. 18–19.

Appendix

Whatever Else Poetry is Freedom
Whatever else poetry is freedom
Forget the rhetoric, the trick of lying
All poets pick up sooner or later. From the river,
Rising like the thin voice of grey castratos—the mist;
Poplars and pines grow straight but oaks are gnarled;
Old codgers must speak of death, boys break windows,
Women lie honestly by their men at last…
....
....
So whatever else poetry is freedom. Let
far off the impatient cadences reveal
A padding for my breathless stilts. Swivel,
O hero, in the fleshy groves skin and glycerine,
And sing of lust, the sun's accompanying shadow
Like a vampire's wing, the stillness in dead feet—
Your stave brings resurrection, O aggrievèd king.

Irving Layton (1972, pp. 58–59)

References

Armstrong, A. Hilary. 1962. "The divine enhancement of earthly beauties."Eranos lecture of beauty. Dallas: Spring Publications, Inc. pp. 39, 73.

Aurobindo, Sri. 1972. Sri Aurobindo Birth Centenary Library. Popular ed., 30 vols., vol. 5. *The Future Poetry*. Pondicherry, India: Sri Aurobindo Ashram Press, p. 333, 331.

Aurobindo, Sri. 1972. The Sri Aurobindo Birth Centenary Library. Popular ed, 30 vols., vol. 15. *Social and Political Thought*. Part 1. *The Human Cycle*. Pondicherry: Sri Aurobindo Ashram, p. 91.

Aurobindo, Sri. 1972. The Sri Aurobindo Birth Centenary Library. Popular ed., 30 vols., vol. 17. *The Hour of God: And Other Writings*. Part IV. "Education and Art: The National Value of Art."

Aurobindo, Sri. 1978. *Savitri: A Legend and a Symbol*. Pondicherry, India: Sri Aurobindo Ashram Press, p. 343.

Birkhäuser, Peter. 1980. *Light from the Darkness: The Paintings of Peter Birkauser*. Translated by Rugh Horine, Boston: Birkhauser Verlag, pp. 103–117.

Campbell, Joseph. 1986. *The Inner Reaches of Outer Space: Metaphor as Myth and Religion*. New York: Harper & Row, Publishers, pp. 119–147, pp. 112–113, p. 137, 131, 122–123, 135.

Coulson, J. et al. 1970. *Oxford illustrated dictionary*. Illustrations edited by Helen Mary Petter. London: Oxford University Press, p. 11.

Doniger, Wendy. 1990. "Origins of Myth Making Man," Daniel C. Noel, ed. *Paths to the Power of Myth: Joseph Campbell and the Study of Religion*. New York: The Crossroad Publishing Company, pp. 181–186, p. 186.

Henderson, Joseph. 1984. *Cultural Attitudes in Psychological Perspective*. Toronto, Inner City Books, pp. 45–48, p. 45, p. 47–49, p. 7–14.

Hillman, James. 1983. *Inter Views*. New York: Harper & Row, Publishers, pp. 143, 145, 108–109.

Hillman, James. 1984. Eranos lecture 2. "The thought of the heart." Dallas: Spring Publications, Inc. pp. 25–41, p. 26, 28, 31, 33, 34.

Johnston, David. 1989. *Individuation: Having It Out with the Unconscious*. Two parts, part 1. The collective psyche: *An encounter*, p. 320–321. Masters degree thesis. Montpelier, Vt: Vermont College of Norwich University, pp. 333–334.

Jung, C. G. 1974. The Collected Works. 19 vols., vol. 6. *Psychological Types*. A revision by RFC Hull of the translation by H. G. Baynes. Bollingen Series XX. Princeton: Princeton University Press, pp. 289–99, 136–146.

Jung, C. G. 1974. The Collected Works. 19 vols., vol. 9. 1. *The Archetypes of the Collective Unconscious*, section 1. *Archetypes of the Collective Unconscious*. Bollingen Series XX, pp. 289–99, 136–146.

Kareda, Urjo. "Vain demons with a baton." Toronto: *The Globe and Mail*. December 14, 1991, p. C-8.

King, Karen. 1990. *Social Factors in Mythic Knowing: Joseph Campbell and Christiangnosis*. Daniel C. Noel, ed. *Paths to the Power of Myth: Joseph Campbell and the Study of Religion*. New York: The Crossroad Publishing Company, pp. 68–80, p. 72.

Layton, Irving. 1972. *Selected Poems*. Toronto: McClelland and Stewart, Inc., p. 606, 91, 58–59.

May, Rollo. 1985. *My Quest for Beauty*. New York: Saybrook Publishing Company, p. 203, 215, 25, 17, 221, pp. 27–30, p. 238.

Miller, David. 1990. "The Flight of the Wilder Gander: The Postmodern Meaning of 'Meaning.'" Daniel C. Noel, ed. *Paths to the Power of Myth: Joseph Campbell and the Study of Religion*. New York: The Crossroad Publishing Company, pp. 68–80, p. 72.

Neumann, Erich. 1983. "Art and time." Papers from the Eranos yearbooks edited by Joseph Campbell. *Man and Time*. Bollingen Series XXX. Princeton, N. J.: Princeton University Press, pp. 3–37.

Paris, Ginette. 1986. *Pagan Meditations: The World of Aphrodite, Hestia, Artemis*. Translated from the French by Gwendolyn Moore. Dallas: Spring Publications, Inc., pp. 31–32.

Read, Herbert. 1962. "Beauty and the beast." Eranos lectures on beauty. Dallas: Spring Publications, Inc. pp. 39–73.

Schiller, Friederich. 1981. *On the Aesthetic Education of Man: In a Series of Letters*. Translated with an introduction by Reginald

Snell. New York: Frederick Ungar Publishing Co., p. 17, pp. 1–20, 15, p. 12–16, 113.

Underwood, Richard. 1990. "Living by myth: Joseph Campbell, C. G. Jung and the religious life journey." Daniel C. Noel, editor. *Paths to the Power of Myth: Joseph Campbell and the Study of Religion.* New York: The Crossroads Publishing Company, p. 13–28, p. 26.

Wilson, Frances. 1956. "Human nature and aesthetic growth." Clarke Moustakas, ed., with assistance in editing Indian papers by Sita Ram Jayswal. *The Self: Explorations in Personal Growth.* New York: Harper and Row, publishers, pp. 212–219.

CHAPTER 4

The Symbolic Life: Life as Creative Process

Abstract

This talk is about individuation and life as a creative process. I discuss the nature of the archetype and the archetypal image, and then amplify a series of my paintings in order to illustrate their meaning. They refer to the archetypal constellations of creation, preservation, and dissolution for recreation which, in the case of the individual, reflect the pattern of a creative life and the individuation process.

Introduction

I am pleased to be here with you this evening and appreciate your invitation to speak to you on what I consider to be a fascinating topic. I always find that people who are interested in astrology have something of importance to teach me. Indeed, on more than one occasion, I have gained valuable insights from astrologers both regarding my personal life and outer events. Astrologers, I find, also have the turn of mind and openness to understand the message of C. G. Jung, which I am particularly interested in, and on which I wish to base my talk.

Astrology can help clarify the nature of one's psychological blueprint and law of being and guide people toward the potential fulfilment of their life. A study of Jung can direct the individual toward an inner life and the potential conscious integration into one's daily life of the archetypal patterns documented in one's birth chart, along with the planetary transits. Gret Baumann-Jung.[120] Jung's daughter, who was a practising astrologer, documents Jung's own relationship to the archetypal constellations and planetary transits in his horoscope in relationship to significant life events. When he was seventy-two years old and Uranus was in twenty-four degrees Gemini while forming a grand trine with natal Saturn and Jupiter, for example, he dreamt of being in bed with a Uranus-like old man with a long flowing white beard. Baumann-Jung also demonstrates how Jung's most creative periods involved important transits of Saturn and Uranus.

Life as a Symbol to Be Lived

The subject I propose to speak about this evening is the symbolic life and life as a creative process. Essentially, what Jung teaches us is a way to live the symbol of our life, which is to say how to become more conscious of our life as it unravels its own myth. The American Indian John Lame Deer expresses the same idea when he says that, for Indians, life is a symbol to be lived, however true that may be today.[121]

For most of us today, life is too often a symptom rather than a symbol. Rather than living symbolically, we live and express symptoms of our complexes: our mother complex, our father complex, our power complex, our victim complex, or whatever complex is driving us at the time. Rather than symbolically expressing the mother and her nourishing and caring ways or the father and his connection to the law of life and moral and ethical values, we act in a way charged with collective opinions that miss the point or with unrelated and inappropriate sentiment. Rather than responsibly discovering our own life, we are caught in a vortex of sentiment, opinions, ambitions, and desires, or lack thereof, which, in fact, is symptomatic of alienation from our own true nature.

Our natural inclination in the Western civilization is to change institutions and influence outer events in an extroverted positivistic manner. We reform, proselytise, crusade, separate, revolt, strike, and so on, all in the name of improving the lot of oneself or one's fellow human being. Perhaps by far the most extreme experiment in this direction, at least in modern times, is the widespread Communist movement along with the short-lived wilful ambitions of Nazi Germany. Even the most dominant approach to psychology in North America today, cognitive-behavioral, is based on external impositions on behavior or of ideas and a positivistic approach to value and behavioural transformation. It is becoming painfully obvious, however, that despite the highest ideals, different approaches and different systems, *plus ça change, plus c'est la meme chose.* In a fundamental way, humans themselves do not change.

Today, of course, with our tremendous technical progress, we could be on the brink of unmitigated disaster unless humankind does change. The precarious state of the ecology and overpopulation, along with the growing power of huge multilateral corporations, immediately come to mind as areas of concern. In this connection, in her biographical study of Jung, Barbara Hannah reports a vision Jung had eight days before he died, where a large part of the world was destroyed. According to her, Jung exclaimed, "Thank God, not all of it."[122] Apparently, he takes this potential for great destruction as a real possibility.

From Jung's point of view, the road to collective (as well as individual)psychic and spiritual health depends on the psychological status of individuals, the number of individuals who make the effort to become conscious of and withstand the tension of opposites in their own natures. Individuals are called to take up the task of uniting the opposites in themselves in a long process, which involves integration of the shadow, the unlived potential that is repressed due to one's personal history, and then the contra-sexual side, the animus/anima that deepens, broadens, and elevates one's connection to oneself. It also eventually involves relatedness to the Self, a suprapersonal center of being and wholeness, with all its intrinsic opposites. This means integrating the opposites contained in the god-image itself, including qualities attributed to both the devil and the Judeo-Christian God. Should we not do this, the archetypal shadow is projected onto our "enemy" and, rather than an integration of opposites, there is the potential for an explosion of opposites outside, in the collective, in society.

The task for our leaders today is to increasingly move from a dualistic position to one of polarity. We may still choose to continue to manipulate and wilfully change outer events or institutions. But then we pay the penalty; we experience the symptom along with unrest and explosive events in a clash of opposites. A more authentic change, in tune with the deeper tendencies of the *zeitgeist*, puts priority on change within one's own society and community, while withdrawing projections from one's collective enemies.

The task for individuals is to become increasingly conscious of their own life and to consciously individuate. Ultimately, all depends on individuals who, however, can affect others essentially by the integrity of their very being and their ability to withstand the tension of opposites in their own psyche. They then potentially live the symbol and not the symptom.

The Rainmaker

Whenever he had a chance, Jung reminded his disciples of the story of the "Rainmaker," which he had originally heard from Richard Wilhelm, theman who popularized the Chinese book of wisdom, the *I Ching* in the West.[123] The story is apparently based on a true experience of Wilhelm's and goes like this:

> There was a village in China, which had experienced a drought for a long time. The villagers finally decided to call in Shinto nature priests who performed a ritual rain dance in order to get it to start raining. But nothing happened. Then, they appealed to the Buddhist monks who came and did their chants. Again, nothing happened. Next, they referred to Christian priests, who came and prayed. There was still no rain. They finally called in a little old man from another village where they had plenty of rain. He went into a small humble hut and sat for three days. It then started to snow. Wilhelm asked him what he did, and he replied, "First, I got disturbed by the conditions, then I put myself in Tao, [which is to say a state of being in harmony with the Self]. The problem here is that no one lives in *Tao*, and that is why it doesn't rain. In my village, people live in *Tao* and it precipitates appropriately."[124]

The atmosphere unsettled the old man, and it took him three days to get back into *Tao*, an inner harmony that resulted in the precipitation. In the *I Ching*, this corresponds somewhat to Hexagram 61, Inner Truth, 9 in the second place. According to a commentary on this line attributed to Confucius, "The superior man abides in his room. If his words are well spoken he meets with assent at a distance of a thousand miles." Influence on others in this way of thinking is a function of one's relationship to the Self and state of consciousness and not on outer activity.

In the same vein, I can recall an elderly disciple of Jung's by the name of Dr. Hans Fierz telling me how he treated his schizophrenic patients following Jung's counsel. He said he entered into the chaos of the individual's madness, became unsettled himself, and that only by doing this could he help bring any order out of the situation. He almost totally disregarded intellectual or positivistic, extroverted solutions including that of the medical model. The way to proceed became apparent for him, he said, only by going into the chaos, illuminating it, and then taking appropriate action. The emphasis is then on individual healers and their inner contact with the springs of life, the archetype, especially the archetype of the Self. And this is not only for their own salvation but also for that of their fellow (incapacitated) humans.

The Times We Live In

From one point of view, as I indicated, *plus ca change, plus c'est la meme chose*. Human nature has not changed. From another perspective, however, it seems that in different periods of our history and perhaps also in our own lives at different times, different aspects of human nature are stressed. For example, we see in Imperial Rome, the emphasis laid on power; in ancient Greece, aesthetics and reason; in ancient Egypt, the spiritual and the occult; in the Middle Ages, Christian mysticism, the occult, and moral rectitude; during the Renaissance, a return to Greece and the beginnings of scientific inquiry, the study of nature, and so on down to the purely materialistic and utilitarian age we are gradually coming out of as we enter the age of information. As you would say, we are at the beginning of a new cycle altogether, the Age of Aquarius.

Although we are at a relatively early stage in this New Age, there are, as you know, an increasing number of signs that we are indeed witnessing the birth of something new. The emphasis now seems to be on the development of consciousness. On the negative side, we see destruction and dissolution everywhere: wars, inner-city violence, potential ecological disasters, extensive family breakup, neuroses, the blind search for new values, drug epidemics, chaotic art forms, power struggles on the political front, and a blatant rise of false prophets and dark cults. On the positive side, we are witnessing a tremendous rebirth in spiritual seeking, the revival of the mantic arts, and now, new and more integrated and meaningful art forms as well as interesting new technology. In addition, there have been definite advances made by women while, collectively, men are showing increasing interest in developing more self-understanding. There are as well increasing indications of a developing racial equality. Finally, there are people from all walks of life who are becoming open to and realising spiritual experiences that are changing their lives in a healthy way. There are more and more integrated men and women, more seed people, as the astrologer Dane Rudhyar calls them.

What does this mean to each of us? It means that the whole collective unconscious is in turmoil. And that means that your unconscious is in turmoil and my unconscious is in turmoil. Jung found that each of us has not only a personal unconscious that is related to our own personal history and personal problems, but also a collective unconscious that relates to our neighbors, our fellow country-folk, our ancestors, and to humankind in general. What I am saying is that, at that level, the psyche is being stirred up thanks to a profound transformational process taking place today. There is a profound metamorphosis of the gods and the instinctual nature taking place in our time.

Evidence for the existence of the collective unconscious is the similarity of motifs found in myths, religions, and fairy tales around the world and throughout history. Another proof is that in dreams, there are typical motifs that are identical to many myths, religious stories, and fairy tales. Consequently, we can gain some understanding of our dreams by amplifying them with, and understanding this material that has been produced by the collective unconscious. I know you understand the collective nature of the unconscious because astrology is grounded on this principle. Humans act in typical ways. If we are consciously in tune with oneself at the archetypal level, we live symbolically. We are then in touch with the archetypal source of life.

On the Archetype and the Archetypal Image

Before going into the concept of archetype, I would like to tell you of a dream that really illustrates very nicely what I am driving at, and it will at the same time, I believe, be an interesting introduction to the idea of the archetype and archetypal image. This was a dream that seven different Hopiwomen are reported to have had the same night, during the crisis at Wounded Knee, a few years ago, in 1963.[125] In their tradition, if a dream appears to seven different people, or seven times to the same person, it is what they call a "true dream;" it is prophetic. It is what many primal people call a big dream and what Jung refers to as an archetypal dream. In this case, the Hopi medicine people believe it to be relevant not only to all Hopi or all Indians (First People) but to all of us, at least here in North America.

Here is the dream:

> A magnificent Indian chief, who is wearing a beautiful feathered head-dress, rides up on a powerful white Appalachian horse. His long black hair falls in braids to touch the earth below. He carries a staff with an eagle carved on top while an eagle soars above, flying in the same direction as the chief. The chief rides on, and all the dreamers and other people begin to follow after him. They go through a contemporary North American city with large skyscrapers. As they pass by the buildings there is a huge conflagration but some people are able to come through and follow this great chief. As they did, they began to wear the costumes of the ancient people of the countries of their origin—Indians [First People] wore Indian costumes, people with ancestors from Celtic countries wore the costumes of the Druids, and so on.

The chief in the dreams is an archetypal image, a symbol of a spiritual leader. The staff with the eagle carved on top symbolizes his spiritual authority and relationship with the eagle. The eagle, which, in fact, sees at a distance in considerable detail, symbolizes the Word or Logos, which is to say spiritual discernment and meaning. The feathers, also related to the eagle, represent knowledge, and the white horse, purified or spiritualized dynamic energy. The conflagration is the fire of purification, where much is necessarily destroyed. And, finally, the people represent all of us, the ordinary people, some of whom are able to withstand the required purification and follow the spiritual master and then live in a much more natural manner, in touch with their natural instincts, which is far from the way we live today.

This is an example of an archetypal dream of marvelous beauty and of great portent, I dare say. Its collective nature is clearly illustrated by the imagery and the meaning we can easily take from it. One can see that it is not only meant for Hopi but for all of us.

The fact that no less than seven women had this dream at the same time is another remarkable illustration of the collective nature of our minds. At this level, human consciousness, if only indirectly through the image, is touching the archetype. Consciousness goes beyond the personal.

The human mind at a certain level is collective. We are each an individualized expression of this collective unconscious, organized around the individual Self, which is the Self of all. The road to salvation for the individual (and for society) depends on individuals taking up the cross of their life and becoming more conscious of how archetypes mold their lives,live their lives. In this way, life becomes symbolic and is lived in a relatively conscious symbolic manner.

Not only does this process transform the individual, but others are also affected in turn. Individuals in touch with the healing source of life, and integrating some of it in their own life, will have a healing effect on others too, whether it be directly or indirectly. An example of this is Jung himself,who lived the symbol of his life in an exceptionally conscious manner. His psychology is now having the most extraordinary effect on others in all areas of life and in all disciplines.

Now, what is an archetype? First of all, it is necessary to distinguish between the archetype-in-itself and the archetypal image. The archetype-in-itself is imperceptible; it typically cannot be perceived or represented and is only potentially present. It is an invisible point of energy, which rests in the unconscious and belongs to what Jung refers to as the psychoid realm. This means that the archetype is based on a transcendent factor which is as much trans-physical as trans-psychic in nature. There are two poles to the archetype, a spiritual pole and a dynamic pole. In this regard, Jung writes that archetypes are "formal factors" responsible for not only the way we apprehend the world but for "patterns of instinctual behaviour."[126] [127]

Although the following examples simplify matters too much, I hope they are suggestive to the reader of how an archetype functions—a mother inclined to be nurturing apprehends the world in a nurturing, motherly way and acts accordingly; a father inclined to be good-protective perceives the world in a protective-good fatherly fashion and acts accordingly. Archetypes are conscious-energy systems of dynamic readiness for action. Animals and birds, fish and plant life all fit into a fixed pattern of life—for example, the fixed migration of birds. They have living dispositions. There are typical actions and reactions of the species. This is no less true of human beings. We apprehend the world and act typically in a way that humans do everywhere and have done so at all times.

With his realization that the archetype is *psychoid*, Jung was able to explain the phenomena of what he called synchronicity, which is to say the experience of meaningful coincidences. The significance of the fact that there is both a spiritual and physical and dynamic dimension to the archetype is that it can affect us in such a manner that we consciously experience its effects in time, in this physical world. Indeed, archetypes are experienced as coming with both the power of transformation and destiny. As such, we can speak of original acts of creation or, if you will, of grace directly affecting our life. In this regard, the constellation of the archetype, according to Jung, is an act of creation in time.[128] Life itself then becomes truly creative, a creative process. Otherwise, life is largely based on unconscious learned behavioral patterns driven by the complex and our personal history, at least from a quantum or truly holistic point of view.

We can experience the effect of an archetype through synchronicity. By that I mean, causally unrelated events that dovetail in a meaningful way for the observer. One example is when you dream something, and it really happens. Another is if you dream of something happening in another part of the world and it happens, or if you dream about something that relates to a future event. Here we have inner and outer events coinciding in a meaningful way.

Another example is two or more external causally unrelated events coming together in a meaningful way for the individual. For instance, you decide to go downtown shopping at Eaton's. On your way there, you meet someone who is out for a walk, who has some vitally important news for you. The coincidence of meeting each other is meaningful. A final example in the same vein is that you experience, as if by chance, an event that affects you to the quick in an uncanny way. For example, you are downtown and unexpectedly see a clown, and he has an uncanny, inexplicable emotional affect on you. The same event could happen and only elicit a minor interest. We would not talk of synchronicity in the latter case. The constellation of the archetype, which comes with intensity and a charge of energy, and which is reflected in the experience of synchronicity, always has an emotional content.

I have spoken, then, of the archetype-in-itself and its effect in time, which we can experience through meaningful coincidences, that is, to say synchronicity. Moreover, our daily expressions, our typical, actions, reactions and aptitudes, and ways of understanding are a manifestation of the archetype. Yet in this latter case, I do not speak of experiencing the archetype, as it is here simply a question of living and acting in a normal human manner, a just-so story. Nothing creative is happening.

For the sake of clarity, we may divide the archetype into two poles. The readiness to act in a certain way, the innate disposition, we may call instinct, which is one pole of the archetype. We experience it as a physiological dynamism. The instincts may enter consciousness as an image or as images. This is the spiritual pole. In this case, we speak of the archetypal image. It is the instinct's perception of itself. When the archetype is constellated, we potentially experience both instinct and image.

As an illustration of an archetype image, take my painting over here—the third panel where we have an Image of God the Creator. It is, of course, not the archetype-in-itself; it is not God the Creator, which is unknowable and not perceptible, but an image of Him, thrown up by the waters of the unconscious.

It is as if the light of consciousness indirectly encounters the archetype and makes it visible it through the image. One can only describe and understand the archetype through the effect it has on one personally. Awareness of the archetypal image that is constellated in one's life at any given time allows consciousness and acceptance of the direction life is taking (I might add, if we like it or not), along with the power of transformation.

The archetypal image is, in this case, a symbol. The word *symbol* is derived from the Greek word *symballein*, meaning "to throw together," as if to say by an ego-transcending synthesizing process. A true symbol then is the best possible representation of something which, in itself, is unknowable. A symbol in this sense of the word must be distinguished from a sign, which is a fabrication representing something else, for instance, a company or a product.

The archetype, which in itself is not representable, is molded by an individual and society's experiences and consciousness, and given form. So archetypal images that come to me, and which I express artistically or otherwise, will be different from your images expressing the same archetype-in-itself. The images from one culture and from different times in history will differ from another. Yet due to the collective nature of the archetype, there will at the same time be an underlying similarity in theme and meaning.

Although in one sense, individuals affect the image of the archetype, the archetype molds us. These archetypal images can be experienced in dreams. For the individual, it can then be symbolic, a living meaningful symbol of the archetype. The more consciously we let the archetype mold our lives, the more we are in conscious touch with the living well of life, the more we live symbolically or, perhaps better said, the more we are lived symbolically and our life becomes creative.

In order to understand dreams, Jung devised a technique he called amplification. We amplify the images and themes of our dreams with material (a) from personal associations of the dreamer and (b) in cases when the archetypal image is clearly expressed, with material from myths, fairy tales, religion, spirituality, astrology, and so on. This procedure can help individuals to understand what is happening in their life at any given time, what archetype is moving them, living them. When the dream is clearly archetypal, there is a message that is meant for the collective as well as strictly for the individual. But only individuals can consciously assimilate its meaning in their life.

****

For the individual, the symbolic life is precisely depicted here in these images. It is accepting the cyclic rhythm of life, the periods of creation, of preservation, and of destruction or, perhaps better said, dissolution for re-creation. For institutions and for the economy, it is the same, accepting what nature gives and not forcing it with wilful, unrelated planning. This is accepting life.

45

By becoming more conscious in our lives, we not only accept life but we have consciousness-life. Of course, we don't have to be artists to do this, but we can all potentially assess the divine source of life and participate in its creative unfolding. Life then becomes a symbolic adventure, an adventure in consciousness.

References

Baumann-Jung. 1975. "Some reflections on the horoscope of C. G. Jung." Translated by F. J. Hopman. In *Spring: An Annual of Archetypal Psychology*. New York: Spring Publications, pp. 35–55. [Original paper delivered in German at the Psychological Club Zurich in October, 1974].

Erdoes, Richard, Fire/Lame Deer, John. 1972. *Lame Deer: Seeker of Visions*. A Quokka Book. New York: Pocket Books.

Genesis 1:1–5. 1952. RSV. The Holy Bible. New York: Thomas Nelson & Sons.

Hannah, Barbara. 1976. *Jung: His Life and Work: A Biographical Memoir*. New York: Bantam Books Inc. (p. 128).

Heline, Corinne.1977. *Sacred Science of Numbers*. Los Angeles: New Age Press, Inc. pp. 27, 64.

I Ching, the: Or Book of Changes (1976) C. F. Baynes, (Trans.) Princeton, NJ: Princeton University Press.

John 14:12. 1952. RSV. The Holy Bible. New York: Thomas Nelson & Sons.

Jung, C. G. 1970. *Alchemical Studies*. R. F. C. Hull (Trans.) vol. 13, Bollingen Series XX, Princeton University Press. p. 95.

Jung, C. G. 1975a. "The Transformation Symbolism in the Mass." In *Psychology and Religion: West and East*. R. F. C. Hull (Trans.) vol. 11, 2nd ed. Bollingen Series XX Princeton, NJ: Princeton University Press. p. 240.

Jung, C.G. 1975b. "Synchronicity: An Acausal Connecting Principle." In *The structure and Dynamics of the Psyche*. R. F. C. Hull (Trans.) Vol. 8, 2nd ed. Bollingen Series XX Princeton NJ: Princeton University Press. pp. 419–531.

Matthew 16:18. 1952. RSV. The Holy Bible. New York: Thomas Nelson & Sons.

Plato (1967). *Timaeus and Critias*. Translated by Desmond Lee. Markham, Ontario: Penguin Books Canada Limited. p. 61.

Shinnah, Oh. 1977. Visions: Side one, 382–440 (tape recording). Four Corners.

von Franz, Marie-Louise (1972). *Patterns of Creativity Mirrored in*

Creation Myths. New York: Spring Publications. Pp. 123–124.

CHAPTER 5

The Ecology of the Self

Reflections on a Series of Four Paintings
Entitled *The Turning Point*

Abstract

This essay is about ecology of the Self. First, I show how the interrelationship between the individual and the community is essentially ecological. By way of illustration, I amplify a series of four paintings entitled *The Turning Point*. They demonstrate how the experience of the Self involves transformation over space and time. They also indicate the fact that by way of the Self the individual does not merely act on "the ecology" but is contained within ecological harmony.

Introduction

The purpose of this brief essay is to engage in reflections and amplifications on a series of four paintings entitled *The Turning Point* from the point of view of the ecology of the Self. I begin with a discussion on the meaning of the word *ecology*, following which I reflect on the nature of the Self and its representative symbol, the *mandala*. I then amplify the meaning of the images depicted on each of the four panels.

The constellation of the archetype that relates to these paintings has had a far-reaching effect on the artist's personal life. For reasons of propriety, however, I will leave such references out of the discussion except to say that, synchronistically, it involves a change in profession from college professor to therapist and a physical move from one side of Canada to the other. More important to this essay is the study of how the Self is profoundly ecological in nature and that experiences of the Self can be both transformative and bring one into harmonious alignment with ecological demands.

Ecology: The Individual and the Environment Regarding the Word *Ecology*

Webster 's complete definition takes the following form:

1. A branch of science concerned with interrelationship of organisms and their environment esp. as manifested by natural cycles and rhythms, community development and structure, interaction between different kinds of organisms geographic distributions, and population alterations;

2. The totality or pattern of relations between organisms and their environment; and

3. Human ecology.[129]

In essence, this definition suggests that ecology has to do with the integral pattern of interrelationships between organisms and their environment, the whole and its parts. From the point of view of this essay, it is noteworthy that this includes both human involvement and community development. In addition, as Miller and Drexler observe, a natural patterned system, which is implied in the meaning of the word *ecology*, is a spontaneous order that emerges as a result of individual atomic forces.[130] I will refer to both these points later when discussing the paintings.

As the definition of ecology includes the interrelationship of organisms and their environment, it is interesting to uncover the meaning of the word *organism*, especially as it relates to humankind. The complete definition according to *Webster's* is:

1. Organic structure;

2. An individual constituted to carry on the activities of life by means of parts or organs more or less separate in function but mutually dependent; and

3. A living being.[131]

As the definition of organism includes the living (human) being, it suggests that the individual is, in essence, not simply concerned about or studies ecology or acts upon "the ecology," but more profoundly, is an integral part of the ecology. Accordingly, the question to be addressed is how individual human beings fit in harmonious interrelationship with a complex multitextured environment, which is as much spiritual as physical.

In order to discuss the nature of harmonious ecology from a human angle, it is necessary to make assumptions on what constitutes individuals in their essence. According to Jung, the archetype of the individual is the Self, which represents psychic totality.[132] It is, psychologically, a union of all possible opposites, of the conscious and unconsciousness, of Logos and Eros, of good and evil. Particularly relevant to this discussion and the ecological interrelationship of the individual and community is the fact that the individual Self is, in Jung's words, "as much one's Self and all other Selves, as the ego."[133] He also observes that "individuation" or the fulfilment of the Self in time "does not shut one out from the world but gathers the world to oneself." The implications are that by living in harmony with the Self, the individual lives in ecological balance.

Although, for most of us, this can only be a distant goal, a goal of a lifetime and an occasional experience, such an observation can, I believe,give direction to one's efforts. Such a view places humankind in ecology and does not consider people as mere actors upon "the ecology." A movement toward authentic ecological harmony can only ultimately be effective with both individuals and community seeking to live according to dictates from the Self and, not as is the case in today's consumer culture, where "lower level" desire rules.

Turning Point 6

Amplification on the Paintings: *The Turning Point*

The symbol par excellence of the Self is the *mandala*. "It is," writes Jung, "the self representation of a psychic centripetal process."[134] To be genuine,it is a structure that spontaneously emerges from the unconscious, indicating a direct affinity with the word *ecology*, as previously indicated. Elsewhere, Jung writes that the mandala is "formation, transformation, eternal minds eternal recreation, which is the self."[135] Thus, a direct experience of the unconscious by way of a spontaneously produced *mandala* indicates a potentially consciously lived creative transformative process engineered by the Self. In such an instance, one is organically contained ecologically.

The four paintings entitled *The Turning Point*, I believe, symbolize such an experiential potential (appendix). The artist saw the images in a dream,which he then painstakingly reproduced as faithfully as possible. The first panel represents the cover of a book, while the last two panels are reproductions of the last page and inside cover at the back of the book. The second panel is a painting of one part of the pictures at the end of the book,which "lifted off the page to take up all his inner vision.

To begin with, since the images are found on the cover and in the book, it means that they come along with knowledge, the symbolic significance of a book. Starting with the first panel, I will now amplify each of the images to find meaning in them. C. G. Jung's name is on the bottom left-hand corner of the first painting. He is a man of great spiritual wisdom who observes that the archetype, as the fundamental building block of reality, is psychoid, meaning that, in its essence, it both transcends and embraces spirit and matter.[136] Moreover, Jung (1968, p. 215) notes that it is "fairly probably…that psyche and matter are two different aspects of one and the same thing."The appearance of his name at the bottom left side of the panel suggests the potential for insight and meaning now to be found at the "lower end" of the archetypal spectrum, which is in relationship to the physical world.

The other name, which appears on the top left-hand side of the first panel,is that of Fritjof Capra, a physicist. He has written two popular books, one entitled *The Tao of Physics* and another, *The Turning Point*, a title which relates directly to the book in the dream. He shows how the study of physics, in addition to other disciplines, has come to the point of acknowledging a unitary reality.[137] The knowledge contained in the dream book, therefore, is concerned with the nature of this reality. The fact that Capra's name is on the top implies that the study of matter or the physical world is on the ascendant, again, suggesting meaning that directly involves the physical world.

According to David Bohm, both quantum and relativity theory are grounded on the assumption of "unbroken wholeness," whereby the "implicate order" expresses itself in the "explicate order," with the whole being enfolded in each of its parts.[138] He sees mind and matter as being acausally interrelated, mutually enfolding projections of a higher order.[139] Bohm, Capra, and other physicists have, accordingly, come to a similar model of psychic reality, as did Jung.

The color of this panel and a dominant color in all the panels is violet,considered to be the "royal color" as it is often worn by kings, queens, and popes. Esoteric literature suggests that it has spiritually transformative properties. Likewise, Jung chooses violet to represent the spiritual pole of the archetype.[140] As he observes, it is a synthesis of blue and red that implies the "readiness for action" as the physical end of the archetypal pole is also taken up (p. 413).

The V shape is actually reminiscent of the trajectory taken by colliding subatomic particles and in itself is aesthetically deeply satisfying. Here, I refer the reader to the chapter entitled "The Cosmic Dance" in Fritjof Capra's book *The Tao of Physics*.[141] Moreover, as a spontaneously ordered structure, it is, in its essence, ecological according to Miller and Drexler, as discussed above. In other words, the image suggests a transformative process that affects the individual at the core of being and that concomitantly affects interrelationship with the community and more generally the multileveled environment.

The title of the dream book, *The Turning Point*, in itself, is suggestive of transformation and change. Interestingly, Hexagram 24 of the *I Ching*, also entitled *The Turning Point* has a commentary that is directly relevant to the theme of this essay. It goes as follows:

> After a time of decay comes the turning point.
> The powerful light,that has been banished, returns.
> There is movement, but it is not brought about
> by force...The movement is natural, arising
> spontaneously. For this reason, the transformation
> of the old becomes easy. The old is discarded and the
> new is introduced.
>
> Both measures accord with the time; therefore,
> no harm results...Everything comes of itself at the
> appointed time. [142]

According to Miller and Drexler's observations, referred to on page 4, the natural, spontaneous quality of the transformation implies ecological balance. Moreover, its "easy" nature "that accords with the time" indicates a harmony with "natural cycles and rhythms: indicative of ecological "at-one-ment," according to the definition of the word *ecology*. Authentic transformation, the Hexagram implies, comes about primarily by being harmoniously contained in ecology and not by acting upon "the ecology."

When the dreamer saw the picture portrayed on the second panel, he heard the word *mandala*, indicating it is a genuine symbol of the Self, his essential nature and unique personality. The circular hole at the bottom of the *mandala* indicates openness to the ground of being and the re-creative energies of the collective unconscious. By way of amplification, the alchemist Gerhard Dorn referred to the *spiraculum aeternitatis* or air hole through which the Self enters time.[143] The color turquoise surrounds the dominating violet. Like the latter color, turquoise is a synthesis, this time of green and yellow. It, too, is a color with spiritually transformative properties. Indeed, it has been held sacred by many people, including some native North Americans, Tibetans, and the ancient Egyptians.[144] The *mandala's* vertical shape stresses a link between spirit and matter.

The third and fourth panels are identical and contain a multiplication of the individual *mandala* along with the symbolic V shape. As I indicated earlier in the dream, the single *mandala* form was "lifted out" of the pictures depicted in the third and fourth panels. The many *mandalas* together suggest the interrelationship of many Selves, or the Self in community, with each Self connected to each other through the ground of being.

The identical picture portrayed in the third and fourth panels are, of course, themselves *mandalas*. As they each consist of twenty (20) individual *mandalas*, this number is qualitatively significant. Numerologicaily, it is the number two (2) raised to a higher power and symbolizes the rhythmic polarity of life.[145] The two panels together consist of (40) *mandalas*, which symbolize the Self (4) raised to a higher power. The *mandalas*, therefore, each represent the individual Self in a community of many Selves, living in alternating rhythms of polarity. The natural rhythms indicated here, again, relate the paintings to the meaning of the word ecology.

I am also reminded of Jung's observation that each Self is paradoxically both individual and all other Selves (as well as the ego).[146] The V-shaped symbol on these two panels indicates that the transformative process taking place not only affects oneself but, at a profound level, interrelationship with the community. That is to say, the transformation depicted here is based on the ecology of the Self.

The fact that the last two panels are identical suggests that this process is just beginning to become conscious. This is based on the phenomena of double motifs which, according to von Franz, generally refer to the fact that a content from the unconscious divides in two as it approaches the threshold of consciousness.[147] Along with the "air hole" alluded to above, this also indicates an interrelatedness between a timeless general acausal orderedness and synchronistic events that take place over space and time, what Jung defines as acts of creation in time.[148] These considerations emphasize the fact that the transformative process depicted in these paintings is not only initiated by the Self but takes place in linear time.

****

I have tried to show how ecology is profoundly related to individuals in their interrelationship with a complex multileveled environment. Transformation toward or within ecological harmony comes through experience of the Self. What ensues is a far-reaching spiritual transmutation that affects individuals and their interrelationship with the community in linear time, with repercussions that involve both the spiritual and physical aspects of life.

In keeping with the nature of the individuation process, which is a life-long endeavor, there is no conclusion to this paper. One can, however, come to a turning point, when individuation begins to consciously embrace a wider world. Experiences of the Self seem to more meaningfully include the physical world. The ego as purusha begins to more consciously recognize itself as being contained in a greater Self. Synchronistic experiences multiply, and the ego begins to be capable of functioning as an active witness to the intelligent designs of the anima, the archetype of life.

Appendix

Picture of a Series of Four Paintings entitled: *The Turning Point*

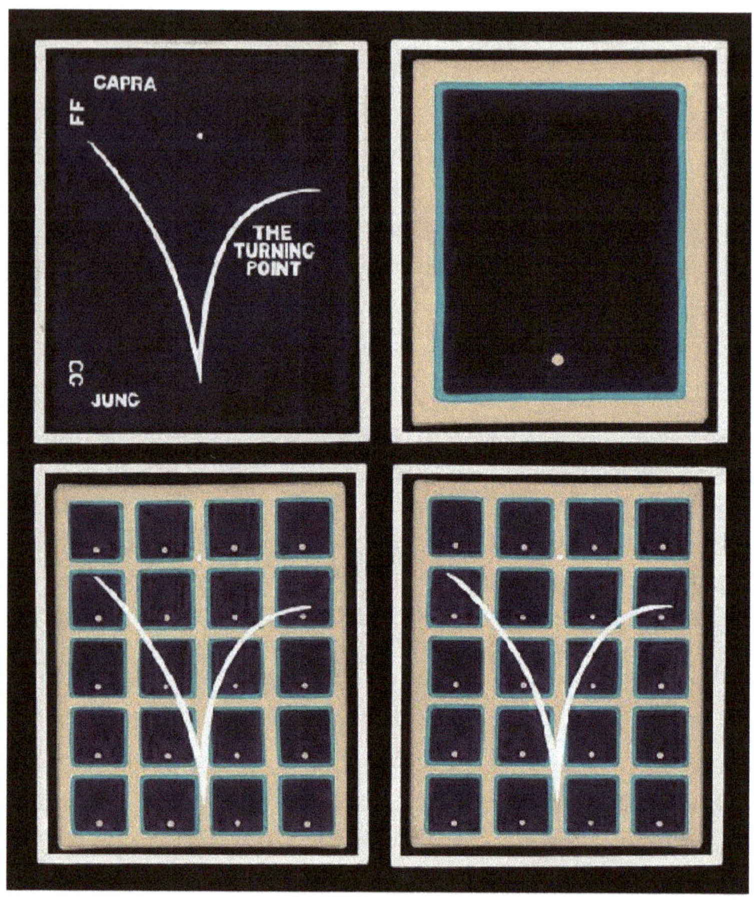

Reference

Capra, Fritjof. 1983. *The Turning Point: Science, Society and the Rising Culture*. Bantam Books, New York: Bantam Books, Inc. passim, p. 211 –233. Johnston, David (1990).

The I Ching rendered into English by Cary F. Baynes, forward by C. G. Jung; preface by Helmut Wilhelm. Bollingen Series XIX. Princeton, N. J.: Princeton University Press, 1989, p. 97–98.

Jaffée, Aniela, ed. 1979. C. G. *Jung: Word and Image*. Bollingen Series XCVII. Princeton, N. J.: Princeton University Press, p. 77–78.

Jung, C. G. 1971. The Collected Works, 2nd ed., 19 vols., vol. 6, *Psychological Types*, 11 parts, part XI Definitions, translated by R. F. C. Hull. Bollingen Series XX. Princeton, N. J.: Princeton University Press, p. 460.

Jung, C. G. 1971. The collected works, 19 vols., vol. 8, The Structure and Dynamics of the Psyche, 2nd ed., part III *On the Nature of the Psyche* translated by R. F. C. Hull. Bollingen Series XX. Princeton, N. J.: Princeton University Press, p. 226, p. 215, p. 211 –213. Jaffe, Aniela, ed. (1979).

Johnston, David. 1989. "Individuation: Having It Out with the Unconscious Part" II. "Having It Out with the Unconscious: A Personal Account."Master's degree thesis. Montplier, Vermont, pp. 213–413, 443–444, 487, 330.

Poncé, Charles. 1991. "The Ecology of Desire." A talk given at the Pacifica Graduate Institute. Carpinteria, Calif, June 15, p. 16.

von Franz, Marie Louise. 1980. On Divination and Synchronicity: The Psychology of Meaningful Chance. Toronto: Inner City Press Wilhelm, Richard (1967) translation.

Webster 's Third New International Dictionary of the English Language. 1966. Springfield: G. & S. Merriam Company, publishers, entry "ecology," p. 720.

Webster 's Third New International Dictionary of the English Language (1966). Springfield: G. & S. Merriam Company, publishers, entry "organism," p. 1590.

PART II
Images

CHAPTER 6

Images and Amplifications of Selected Paintings

Jung developed concepts and models which show an astonishing similarity to modern physics.

— M. L. von Franz

Since psyche and matter are contained in one and the same world,and moreover are In continuous contact with one another and ultimately rest on irrepresentable transcendental factors, it is not only possible but fairly probable, even, that psyche and matter are two different aspects of one and the same thing.

— C. G. Jung

…consciousness may well be an essential aspect of the universe that will have to be included in a future theory of physical phenomenon.

— F. Capra

The significance of the parallels between the worldviews of physicists and mystics is beyond any doubt.

— F. Capra

After a time of decay comes the turning point. The powerful light,that has been banished, returns. There is movement, but it is not brought about by force…. The movement is natural, arising spontaneously. For this reason, the transformation of the old becomes easy. The old is discarded and the new is introduced. Both measures accord with the time; therefore, no harm results…. Everything comes of itself at the appointed time.[149]

— *I Ching*, Hexagram 24

The images of the unconscious place a great responsibility upon a man. Failure to understand them, or a shirking of ethical responsibility, deprives him of his wholeness, and imposes a painful fragmentariness on his life.

— C. G. Jung

Often people approach the unconscious with and inner utilitarian or power stand point. They want to exploit the unconscious….

Such a person does not notice that he is deceiving himself.

— M. L. von Franz

Nothing in the human psyche is more destructive than unrealized,unconscious creative impulses.

— M. L. von Franz

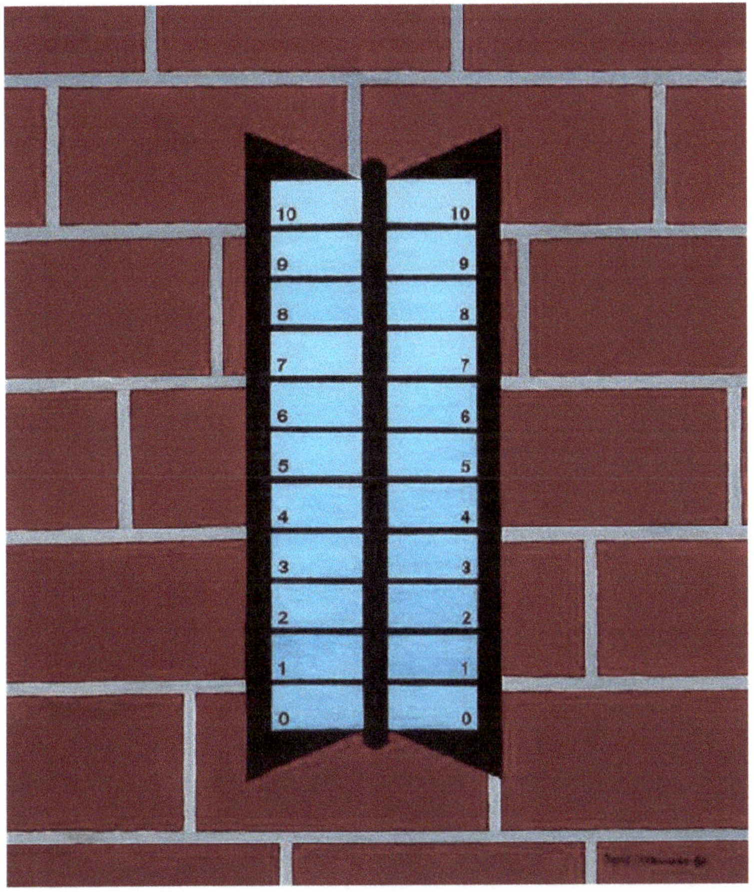

The butterfly is a symbol of the psyche or soul and represents the "breath of life."[150] After a period of gestation in a chrysalis, the caterpillar emergestransformed as a beautiful winged creature, the butterfly, suggestingtransformation and rebirth. The story of Eros and Psyche recounts howPsyche is considered the most beautiful of women, so beautiful that she is worshipped as a goddess in place of Aphrodite, making the latter envious.[151] Aphrodite consequently arranges things so that Psyche becomes initiated into a heroic quest, which ultimately culminates in her being united by love with Eros, the son of Aphrodite.[152] In this image, through analogy, one can say that the butterfly as psyche or the instinctual breath of life drawn by love, has landed on the red bricks of Eros.

There are other interesting and relevant amplifications on the butterfly image.[153] Some four thousand years ago in Minoa and Mycenae, there is evidence of a goddess related to the butterfly or being symbolized by it.[154] The tomb of the double-edged ax, the labyrs, at Knossos is the shrine of this goddess, where the double-ax is an emblem of the goddess and related to the butterfly.[155] The underground dwelling of the goddess is the labyrinth, the maze through which the hero and heroine must find their way to the center, which symbolizes the center of being. Legend has it that the sweeper of the labyrinth at Knossos created the maxim "know thyself."[156] Rather than follow ego-related desires, following the prompting of one's soul leads to self-knowledge and a life directed by the Self. This interpretation is supported by the fact that in some places, in southeast Italy, during the sixth millennium BCE, the chrysalis and emerging butterfly symbolized new life after death and regeneration.[157]

The vertical position and unusually long length of this butterfly suggests spiritual aspiration, as does its blue color, where blue has values of coolness, detachment, devotion. The bricks of Eros are red, a hot color, which imply desire, passion, and relatedness.[158] The horizontal direction of the bricks suggests passion and desire for life or in the play of life. As the image of the butterfly consists of horizontal rectangles, its qualitative spiritual influences take place in the field of life. Each rectangle contains a number from zero (0) to ten (10), which is indicative of the nature of the different influences. There is a parallel between this image and the mystical *Kabbala*, which is represented by the Tree of Life, which contains ten centers of life and power known as Sephiroth.[159] Not the quantitative, but the symbolic and qualitative value of numbers are most significant for purposes of this discussion.

In their qualitative aspect, numbers do not add up arithmetically in the sense that 1 plus 1 = 2, but each number symbolizes an essential universal quality. Thus, one can speak of the value of oneness, twoness, threeness, fourness, etc., and not of numbers that are composed of one, two, three, or four units. According to Pythagoras, numbers symbolize the elements of everything under the sun.[160] For Jung, number is the most fundamental expression of the archetype in both spirit and matter and the archetype of order which has become conscious.[161] Likewise, Sri Aurobindo's spiritual colleague, the Mother, recounts an experience she had of numbers. She is recorded as saying they represent principals of conception (origination) and realization.[162]

A brief discussion of symbolic and qualitative value of the numbers from zero (0) to ten (10) follows. With some exception, the essential nature of all things is expressed by these numbers as, exceeding 10, another series begins. Theosophical reduction reduces the double digits to single digits—for example, 15 reduces to $1 + 5 = 6$, and the number 12 reduces to 3, given that $1 + 2 = 3$.

Zero (0)
A Feminine Number

Sri Aurobindo writes that "nothing can arise from nothing. *Asat*, nothingness is a creation of our mind...out of its own incapacity it has created the conception of a zero." "But," he asks rhetorically, "what in truth is this zero?" He responds, "It is an incalculable infinite."[163] Indeed, the word *zero* has its beginnings in the Sanskrit word *sunya*, which means void or empty with the sense of swollen womb, or pregnant potential.[164] This understanding may date back to Vedic times, some six to eight thousand years ago. In India, over time, the truth of the zero, for the most part,became ignored, as the spiritual goal became the quest for the Transcendent, *That*, or *nirvana*, a void, the extinction of all opposites and total cessation of all movement.[165] The world became perceived as an illusion.

The Arabs transmitted the zero to Europe sometime during the twelfth century around 11 20 CE.[166] Sunya became *sifri* in Arabic, *zephyrum* in Latin, and zero or cipher in English.[167] In the Western world, the practical and quantitative aspects of numbers, including the zero, dominated thought. The zero allows for multiplication of value, and since the age of reason,when it is placed before the one, it allows for negative as well as positive numbers. Spiritual reality itself became regarded as an effective illusion and the qualitative aspects of numbers were repressed. The result is science and technology, for the most part today, at the service of humankind's inflated ego.

Among the Mayans and other Indians of the Americas, the earliest known hieroglyph for the notation zero came in the third century CE. There is some evidence to indicate that its roots lie in Olmec culture and that the concept of the zero dates to some 1500 to 3000 BCE.[168] The word *lubay* means "blown out, extinction."[169] The word *zero* has roots in the word *lub*, which means "end of journey and place where the burden rests.[170]" It suggests the completion of a circle of life and return to the primordial space, now with full awareness.

Taken together, the original east Indian view and the Mayan concept of zero point to the paradoxical coincidence of beginning and end, of birth and death. The western European understanding seems to have enumerative and practical value with immense implications for everyday life. Presumably,the essence of the number zero is contained in all these views, although the deeper more quantum truth seems to have been understood by the ancient east Indians and Mayans.

One (1)

One (1) symbolizes the *Logos* in the manifestation, the *Purusha* of Hindu philosophy.[171] It represents unity and the beginning of evolutionary unfolding, individualization, self-expression, and initiative.[172]

Two (2)

Two (2) symbolizes the Feminine, Prakriti in Hindu thought. Two (2) symbolizes duality and, with greater awareness, polarity and alternating cycles of experience.[173] The *Logos* is manifest through the power of two (2).[174]

Three (3)

The number three (3) is dynamic and symbolizes process, the unfolding of the archetype over time.[175] Jung observes that "Three is the unfolding of the one (1) to a condition where it can be known-unity become recognizable."[176] The power of three (3) brings insight.

Four (4)

The number four (4) has the symbolic value of concretization and karmic limits, therefore implying that it is realized through pain and suffering.[177] With the realization of the four, insights are no longer rarefied, but give way to creative realizations in time and space—"realizations in the act of becoming."[178] Pythagoras calls the number four (4) the symbol of the eternal principle of creation, while St. Martin refers to it as the universal number of perfection and the world creation.[179] Sri Aurobindo regards the *Supermind* as the supreme unitary source of multiplicity, Truth-consciousness with effective power of realization, with the symbolic value of the square or four (4).[180] For Jung, psychic wholeness, which includes grounding experiences in material reality, is also symbolized by the number four (4).[181] Like Sri Aurobindo's *Supermind*, it represents the *unus mundus*, which has a direct link with the primal one (1).[182]

Five (5)

The number five (5) symbolizes the Self emanating from behind the heart center. It represents Leo, the fifth sign of the Zodiac, which governs the heart.[183] Western esotericism identifies the number five (5) as the resurrected Christ. It is the centered four, the quintessence, and the inner Christ.[184] Don Juan's injunction that there is only one path, the path with heart, indicates its symbolic value.[185] Self-knowledge through life experiences, including both joy and sorrow, reflects its significance.[186]

Six (6)

The number six (6) can be represented as a hexagram and the six-pointed star, the interlaced ascending and descending triangles.[187] Well-known western religious examples are the Star of David and the Seal of Solomon.[188] The image is also significant in Tantra as well as in alchemy, where it represents the union of fire and water, and male and female in harmonious generativity.[189] It is an essential aspect of Sri Aurobindo's symbol as well as other spiritual leaders.[190] The Mother observes that for Sri Aurobindo, the six-pointed star symbolizes *Sat* (existence), *Chit* (consciousness), which comes with force, and *Ananda* (bliss) as the descending triangle, and the answering upward directed triangle, human material aspiration, light, life and love. Here, it symbolizes the union of the human and the divine.[191]

Seven (7)

The number seven (7), made up of the trinity (spirit) and the quaternity (form), symbolizes the individuation process.[192] It is the sum of the number four (4) plus the number three (3) and refers to archetypal realization in space as the individuation process unfolds over time, where the goal is wholeness, the attainment of completion. The primordial significance of the law of seven (7) is suggested by the fact that solidifying salt molecules first appear in a triangular or pyramidal form and subsequently as a square or a cube, where the triangle has the same significance as the number three (3) and the square as the number four (4).[193] Psychologically, these amplifications indicate that insight and imagination are directly experienced as related to the psyche of the participating individual.[194] An individual consciously directed by the qualitative power of seven (7) experiences insistence for archetypal realization to be experienced over space and time. The individuation process can then ensue, life become more conscious, and the goal potentially realized. The goal of the individuation process is wholeness, symbolized by the number four (4).

Eight (8)

The number eight (8) has the same symbolic value as the lemniscate, which represents eternal and continuous motion and the infinite.[195] It signifies eternal energy in the manifestation and can either be experienced as a sense of freedom and expansion of being or regressive degradation and chaos,depending upon one's state of awareness.[196] It represents intuition and the freedom that comes from being guided by the center of being and wholeness, the Self.[197]

Nine (9)

The number nine (9) governs evolution over time and symbolizes matter and cosmic knowledge.[198] It has traditionally been regarded as "serpent power," the kundalini, Shakti Consciousness-force and wisdom in nature.[199] Nine-month human pregnancy and birth are based on this nine-powered cycle of time. Norelli-Bachelet (Thea) regards nine (9) as the seed of the Transcendent in evolution.[200] She observes that there is a nine-year cycle that governs potential psycho-spiritual transformation over time as described in the Gnostic Circle.[201]

Ten (10)

The number ten (10) consists of the "masculine" one (1) and the "feminine"zero (0).[202] It symbolizes equality between the masculine and feminine principles, primordial will, and the pregnant womb, which is represented by the pillar (1) and the zero (0).[203] The decade is considered perfect and embraces the whole nature of number and represents totality.[204] St. Martin holds that ten (10) is the image of the Divinity itself.[205] It represents the summum bonum of creation, God in the manifestation.[206]

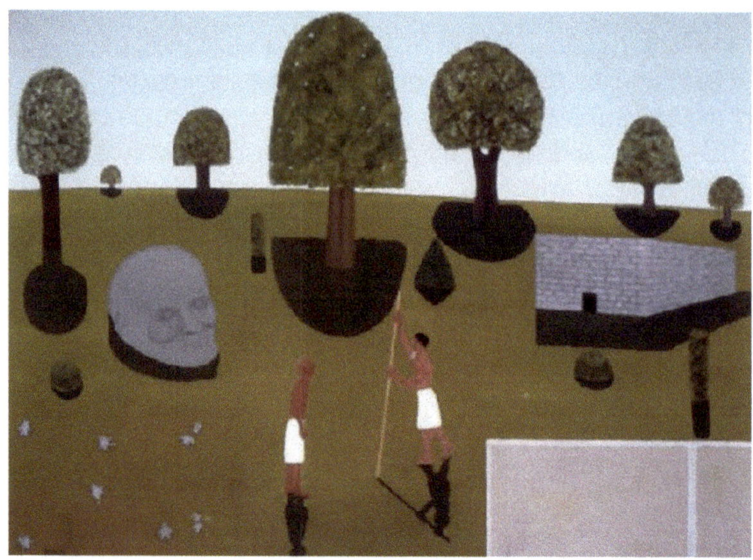

The scene depicted in this image was "discovered" in a dream halfway between "Ottawa" and "Montreal." This psychic space suggests that the inner Egypt is found through a synthesis of the intellect and the duality of life, including shadow, which is depicted in the image. As the capital of the country, Ottawa represents the governing head of Canada, while Montreal is the place where the duality of life is well represented, given its English-French bilingual nature as well as the many different ethnic groups that live there. At the time of the dream, it was the city in which I had lived more than anywhere else.

Egypt represents the occult and hidden side of the personality, which links the psyche to an historical period of great antiquity, according to credible sources, with the "First Time" (*Zep Tepi*) dating at 11 ,450 BCE.[207] To discover inner Egypt means to become conscious of aspects of the polytheistic psyche, which the ancient Hebrews left to follow their monotheistic deity, *Yahweh*. This departure by the Hebrews led to rejection of the golden calf and the Egyptian realm of the mother goddess. The golden calf is a symbol of *Horus*, the divine son of the Egyptian goddess *Isis*, whom the Israelites continued to worship in the wilderness during the early part of Exodus, inciting the wrath of their leader, Moses.[208]

For some scholars, Egypt is the cradle of Western civilization;

for others, it represents another long-lived civilization altogether. In an important Egyptian creation myth, the earth and sky are separated by their father, the air god, Shu, bringing discernment of the sky goddess as Nutt and the earth god as Geb.[209] In sharp divergence, Greek mythology depicts the sky deity is a male god, Zeus, and the earth deity as a goddess, Gaia. The Egyptian choice of a masculine earth god in Geb indicates a relatively different psychology and order of civilization than the one found in ancient Greece,which is generally considered to be one of the principal bedrocks of Western civilization. In harmony with its mythology, the Greek experience and the glory of Greece involved an upward aspiration for light and conquest of the instinctual psyche, respect for reason and aesthetic values, and the quest for ideal beauty and truth.

A male earth god in Egypt, in contrast to the Greek way, points to concretization of ideas, where, ideas in ancient Greece, and generally in the West, have been typically spiritual or mental and intuitive. For one example, especially at the end of the third millennium and the end of the Old Kingdom, at the beginning of the Middle Kingdom, Egyptians became invested in the occult and immortality of the dead in a somewhat material way.[210] Their mythology included hybrid figures of animal/human-like gods and goddesses, and there were associated animal cults. Their afterlife journey, with which there was an enormous investment of religious thought and energy, was depicted as taking place in the underworld.[211] Rather than seeking immortality while alive, elaborate rituals were conducted for realizing immortality in the afterlife, although, to begin with, only the pharaoh and, then, members of the royal family. As early as the Old Kingdom (2686–2125 BCE), the elite also expected to live beyond death,and if they could afford it, they too partook of rituals to ensure immortality. Yet life in the world and a just social order, established by the goddess Maat, was also appreciated and desired.[212] All these considerations put emphasis on being established instinctively on the earth and in the earth and an afterlife of immensely long duration, millions of years, along with projected awareness of the gods and goddesses in harmony with the (animal) instincts.[213]

Although the order of Egyptian civilization seems quite opposed to the values and attitudes attributed to Western civilization, there has been striking influences on the Western mind from the beginning. Exodus, the founding myth of the Jewish people, primarily involves Moses leading the Jews out of Egypt. Moses was raised as an Egyptian by Bithiah, the daughter of the pharaoh Ramesses I, who saved Moses, as a newborn Hebrew male child from being drowned under order of the pharaoh Thutmose II (1492/3–1479 BCE). Later, in response to the similar threat of persecution of male children under two by the Roman Emperor, Herod,Joseph took Mary and Jesus and fled for refuge in Egypt. According to Matthew 2:14–15, 19–20, God's angel, who counselled Joseph to flee to Egypt with his family and then to call his Son, Jesus, out of Egypt, was fulfillment of the prophecy suggested in Hosea 11 :1, where God is reported to have said, "I called my son out of Egypt."[214] Egypt, in other words, has made a major imprint on the Western religious mind.

With Akhenaton as pharaoh of Egypt from 1353–1336 BCE,monotheism, possibly henotheism, was established in Egypt although it was short-lived, with a return to strict polytheism in 1336 BCE during the reign of his son, Tutankhamun. With Judaism and Moses, like with Akhenaton's Egypt, there was a monotheistic God, although early Judaism was henotheistic. In the case of the story of Mary and Jesus, there is a direct parallel between it and the narrative of Isis, the Egyptian goddess, and Osiris, her divine son-god. Especially the religious thought of the New Kingdom (1600–11 00 BCE) had a strong influence on Christianity.[215]

Otherwise, there is evidence for Egyptian influence on Greek architecture, sculpture, and thought, including on Plato's theory of forms,thanks to the efforts of the Ptolemy pharaoh, Psamtik I, who, likely, arranged for the transmission of Egyptian philosophy to the Greeks.[216] In addition, the major source of esoteric subjects, such as alchemy and hermeticism, and those taught in the school of Pythagoras, find their roots in Egypt. Despite the apparent divorce between the Egyptian mind and the West, there is a deep need today to assimilate Egyptian influence into contemporary Western thought and life values, especially alchemy and hermeticism, which permeates the psychology of C. G. Jung, especially in his alchemical treatises. Egypt is truly the undervalued cradle of Western civilization and represents other worldly values and the search for immortality.

At the outset, rejection of its Egyptian pagan connection by the Jews was probably more like suppression than repression, and instinctually in harmony with the demands of the times, psychologically, in order to gain further consciousness and active will in harmony with a superior force. Contemporary individuals need to return to that psychic geography of the soul, although this time with greater consciousness and willpower that has been gained since then. Over time, the initial suppression became repression, which was further exacerbated in Christianity especially Protestantism. The contemporary individual must descend into this realm of the psyche responsibly, as there is always the danger of identifying with unconscious impulses and instincts, while being swept away into a neo-paganism. A glance at the contemporary world, including elements of popular culture should convince one of this danger.

The little clay dolls in the image, most of which are dismembered, represent the souls of the dead. Some myths speak of God creating the first humans out of clay.[217] Moreover, the broken dolls as such symbolize a real person and in many ancient cultures, such figures, as depicted here, were to act as a symbolic substitution for the corpse.[218] Dismemberment, as indicated by the broken dolls, suggests death and a return to the womb.[219] The far building on the right consisting of stone bricks is the place where the dead are buried.[220] The black door represents death or the unknown. As the building is made of stones, it is a symbol of the Self. The fact that the building is long rather than high suggests that the direction of the psychic energy involved in these aspects of the psyche is in the horizontal—that is, in instinctual life—rather than in the vertical direction. By becoming aware of these elements of the psyche, one lives a more intense, deeper life. The ancestors of the soul are then allowed to live through the contemporary person and concerns.

Similar in appearance to the stone head venerated by the ancient Olmecs, the stone head depicted here represents the spirit or awareness of the earth.[221] The young man is an Egyptian, and his concrete beard indicates his royal status and rulership in life.[222] The ancient pharaohs wore false-beards of such a shape, as indicated in ancient paintings and statues. The fact that it is concrete suggests that it is like stone, a symbol of the Self. In addition, the concrete beard, like the concrete building in front of the image, suggest that the nature of the pharaoh's concerns have to do with hard daily reality. He is depicted penetrating the earth with a pole or rod, suggesting active phallic generation.[223] His probing generates understanding of the spirit of the earth. The staff or rod was often depicted in the *Old Testament* as a symbol of guidance imbuing the holder with the quality of leadership. Likewise, in Egypt the pharaoh's symbol of authority and rulership was a shepherd's crook.[224] The crook, in fact, was a symbol of the god, and the pharaoh was considered the incarnation of Horus or Osiris.[225] The older bald man, also Egyptian, is a wise old man and represents meaning, insight, and wisdom. His hairless head indicates the sacrificial nature of his life as a priest of the Mother.[226]

In the young man and the old man, there is an impressive symbol of the two principle dimensions of life, the priestly and the kingly man's relationship to God and his relationship to life. The fact that they are together suggests these two principles are working in harmony, unlike in the disastrous split that we have known for centuries, and for which Christ's only answer is—and could only be at the time he lived—"Render therefore to Caesar the things that are of Caesar's, and to God the things that are Gods."[227] The path of individuation today, however, does not permit such a compartmentalization of life.

Midway Through Life: Initiation

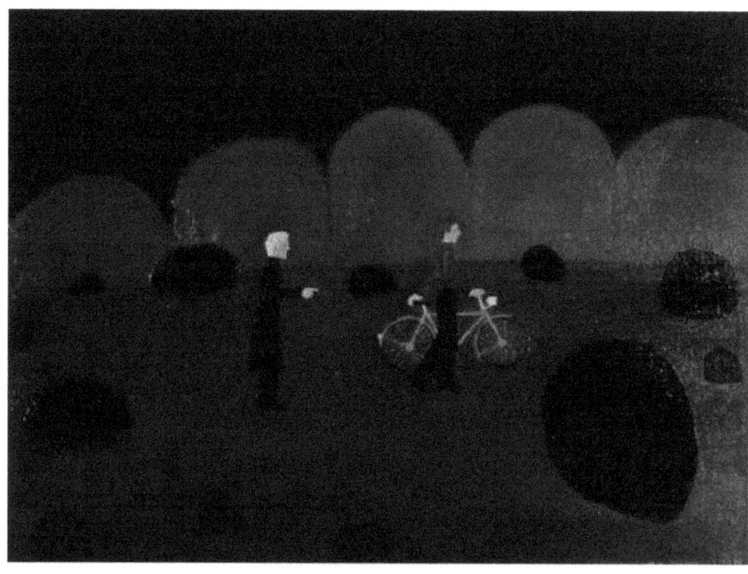

In this image, one is reminded of Dante and Virgil, his spiritual guide, as described in *The Divine Comedy*. The first canto of Book I, Hell, begins with the lines:

> Midway this way of life we're bound upon, I woke to
> find myself in a dark wood, where the right road was
> wholly lost and gone.[228]

Here, one is in a dark underworld, a similar place to Dante's dark wood.

As Jung insists, the individuation process really begins in earnest only when the individual arrives at the zenith of life, after which one's efforts can turn from principally extroverted considerations to inner culture.[229] The older shade-like man is a Virgil-type figure who points the direction that individuals must go in their inner quest. It is through the dark underworld, or unconscious toward the right—that is, toward consciousness. Conscious individuation requires that one becomes more aware by meeting different aspects of oneself in the unconscious and integrating them to consciousness.

The older man points the way with the forefinger of his right hand. The right hand indicates conscious direction, while the forefinger, according to palmistry, is said to be ruled by Jupiter, the sign of the guru and leader.[230] The white hair indicates wisdom, suggesting he is a wise old man, while his black outfit indicates his identification with the unconscious and the "unknown." His shade-like appearance also suggests his identification with the underworld, the unconscious.

The younger man, a contemporary-looking individual, must travel alone through this darkness on his path of self-discovery.

One does not become conscious by worshipping "beings of light," but by lighting up the unconscious. As one reads in John 1:5, "The light shineth in darkness and the darkness comprehended it not."[231] The deepest need of our psyche in its darkness is to comprehend it by the light that shines in its midst.

The bicycle is an appropriate vehicle as it is both contemporary and indicates the solitary nature of the pursuit. The fact that one must pedal a bicycle or walk on foot, as in the image, indicates that individual effort and time is required in order to become conscious. As the wisdom of Luke 21:19 relates, "By your endurance you will gain your lives."[232] Conscious individuation leads to a widening and deepening of the personality, unconscious individuation to a hardening. The blue color of the bicycle suggests the spiritual nature of the quest. Blue is a cool color, the color of the sky, and considered to be the color of many spiritual leaders.

The roundish hills of stone suggest that this is the country of the Self. Despite the darkness and the general feeling of desolation, it exerts a powerful magnetic attraction to the psyche. The hero, represented by the contemporary-looking man, appears to move with confidence in the direction indicated by the spiritual guide. It is also interesting to note that his head as apex and two arms from a triangle, which can be extended to the earth, indicating vertical aspiration for knowledge.

Mephistopheles

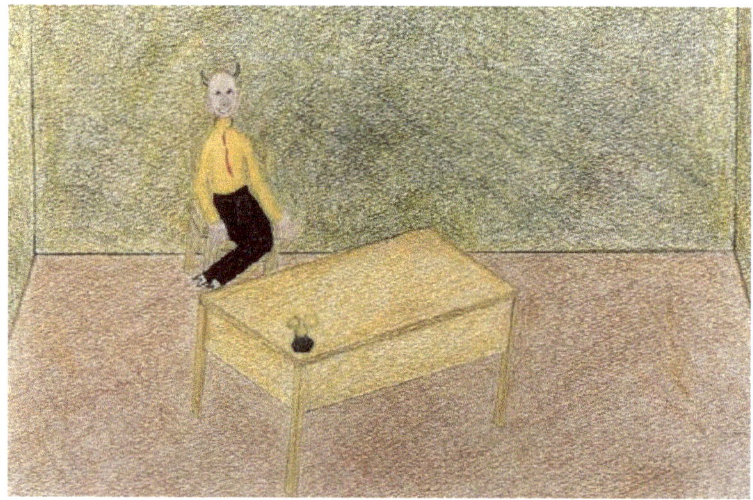

Here, in this image, is a cunning-looking fellow with horns, a lopsided lunar smile, a red lunar-shaped tie, and animal hooves. He symbolizes a collective shadow figure. This image emerged during the time I worked as a sales representative for a modest-sized computer payroll company. Sales encourages opportunities to fudge facts and to avoid telling the full truth, even if one doesn't lie outright, and one is constantly tempted to give in. The standard teaching for sales people involves educating the evaluative feeling function in the service of the power principle. Courses in the art of selling teach sophistry, sophisticated argument techniques with the sole purpose of "closing the sale." Successful salespeople, typically, have both empathy and the ability to "feel into" the collective aspect of the potential client's psyche, as well as "ego drive," the will to power and ambition to be on top, to win.

In many sales positions, like the one I filled, the job definition requires making a considerable amount of "cold calls" in order to ferret out potential customers. This activity often requires intervention into other people's private space, something I felt very uneasy about doing, even though this is considered normal sales practice. Ultimately this led to my departure from the computer company and eventually finding a job selling life insurance.

Before taking on this assignment, I had the following dream:

> I see a cluster of trees surrounding a low, narrow
> rectangular shaped one-story building. It is darkish.
> I take an ax and then chop down all the trees from
> about two feet from the roots. I contemplate the
> scene and do not like the feel of what I see.

The low, narrow rectangular building informs me symbolically of the nature of the work involved. It indicates that the work is primarily extraverted (outside) in the horizontal axis of life at a relatively low level of inspiration. According to the dream, I use the feeling function to evaluate the work environment. Swinging an ax suggests an active effort at discernment. The ax has traditionally been a symbol for a god or goddess, especially related to the labyrinth, which can be taken as representing a challenging path of life. The suggestion of these symbolic realities is that discernment comes from the Self, one's center of being and wholeness.

In another dream I had at the time, the following transpires:

> I see a picture that I have drawn in colored
> pencil, the image of which is reproduced above. In
> the image is a man with a bald head, two horns
> and a lopsided grin, sitting behind a desk. Three
> yellow flowers are placed on the top right-hand
> side of the desk. He is wearing a yellow shirt, a
> red tie consisting of two crescent shapes, and black
> pants. He has animal hooves.

The image of this figure represents a shadow figure for me. The horns, as well as the double crescent-shaped tie, suggest a Mephistophelean-type individual. Red indicates Eros relatedness, and the yellow shirt,illumination. With the right attitude, following the ways of Mephistopheles,who "does evil but engenders good" brings consciousness. A Luciferian figure, who is the bearer of light, he can guide one to greater awareness. The animal hooves indicate an undifferentiated standpoint based on animal instincts which, for humans, translates as the power principle. The lunar indications and bald head indicate receptivity. Since the insights and understanding received are used in the power principle, it is expressed as charm and cunning as depicted by the lunar-shaped crooked smile.

It is noteworthy that the image of Mephistopheles is based on an archetypal and collective shadow. He is not a personal shadow figure,although the dreamer has a personal relationship with him. During the individuation process, there comes a time that one is required to deal with the collective shadow. The individual aids and abets the collective shadow through the personal shadow, which takes many forms based on personal history. It can express itself, for instance, as concupiscence, manipulation, greed, lying, pride, envy, narcissism, and so on.

When I was selling life insurance, the attitude promoted by management was totally in the service of narcissism. I was astounded at how I was asked to begin the job by producing a list of one hundred (100) friends,acquaintances, and relatives and calling them up to sell them insurance. I have learned that this is typical of many sales jobs that rely on personal contacts and referrals. The common advice was, "If potential clients don't buy from you and they 'need' insurance, then they are not genuine friends." The sales commissions, as is typically the case, are arranged to encourage putting the emphasis on some products and not others. It basically has to do with what is more profitable to the company and not what is best for the customer. The sales person can learn to manipulate figures and emphasize certain facts in such a way that the customer does not realize the truth. One creates confusion as necessary to make the sale. One learns the art of sophistry and uses extraverted feeling, to "read the customer," to empathize in order to satisfy the power drive and earn money.

Scott Peck makes observations on "evil" forces that are inimical to a healthy lifestyle that, to a degree, fit the characteristics of many sales jobs. His list includes the imposition of one's will upon others, creating confusion, lying, including half-truths, as well as the use of "seduction, cajolery, flattery, and intellectual argument" aimed at human weakness (called in marketing textbooks, "needs") and, particularly, stimulating fear.[233] Peck notes that people who are identified with these "evil" qualities are coherent and self-possessed, holding down responsible jobs, "apparently functioning smoothly in the social system."[234] It is no wonder that the United States currently (2018) has a president who fits these characteristics. Business is driven by a large shadow, of which its leaders and educators are blithely unaware or else consider essential marketing practice. It is considered perfectly normal to conduct business in the way we do, and there is, consequently, considerable reluctance for the business world to examine its conscience in any depth.

The Philosopher

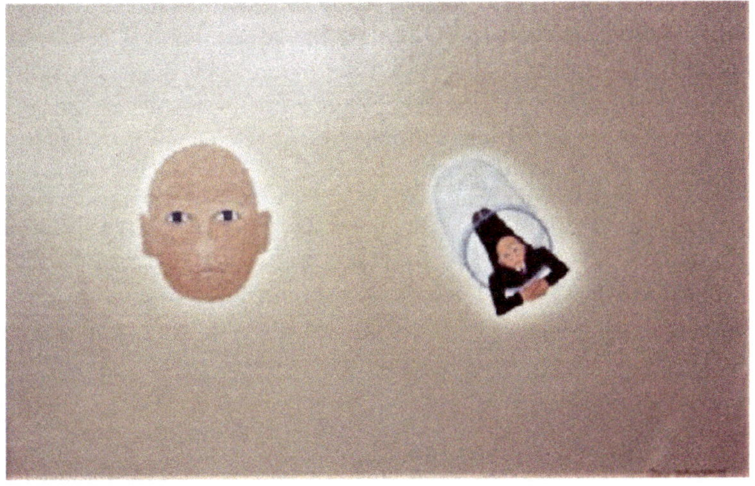

The alchemists considered the head, especially the male head and brain, to be the seat of the *anima intellectualis*.[235] It represents Logos, understanding insight and consciousness.[236] The fact that the head in the painting is completely hairless indicates its spiritual nature and the necessary sacrifice of the old ego-oriented thoughts represented by hair. Shaving off the hairs is associated with "dying to life" and spiritual transformation.[237] Monks of many religions and sects have their heads shaven or tonsured to symbolize the sacrifice (death) of worldly ways in deference to a spiritual life.[238] Initiation rites into the mysteries for both men and women have often included shaving off the hair.[239] Many heroes emerge from their trials having lost their hair.[240] In this image, the same kind of *sacrifice* is suggested, indicating a necessary *change* in attitude from worldly ambition to seeing life as a spiritual quest for consciousness.

The little man in the jar reminds one of the alchemist's *filius philosophorum* or son of the philosopher, a manifestation of the Self.[241] The Upanishadic verse that describes "The Purusha who is seated in the midst of our self" as "no larger than the finger of a man" further amplifies the significance of this figure.[242] The jar or vessel is a feminine symbol that is both a container and like the womb gives birth, in this case to consciousness and meaning.[243] The arms and hands, representing active nature form the base of a triangle that points upward and slightly to the left. The union of the right and left hands suggest the interrelationship between the conscious and unconscious.[244] Both the arms and the hands representation, with the hands having a generative significance as well.[245] The triangle, with arms as base, indicate aspiration upward for consciousness, in the realm of action and generativity. Moreover, the base is roughly rectangular in shape, suggesting that the horizontal nature of the activity is where meaning and understanding come.[246] The man's suit is brownish red, indicating his instinctual Eros nature.[247]

Consciousness and meaning come through an active generative life, not in world denial. It is, however, through vertical aspiration that consciousness and meaning is brought into life. The leftward pointing apex (the head) of the triangle suggests that consciousness still resides in the unconscious, the direction toward which the aspiration mounts.

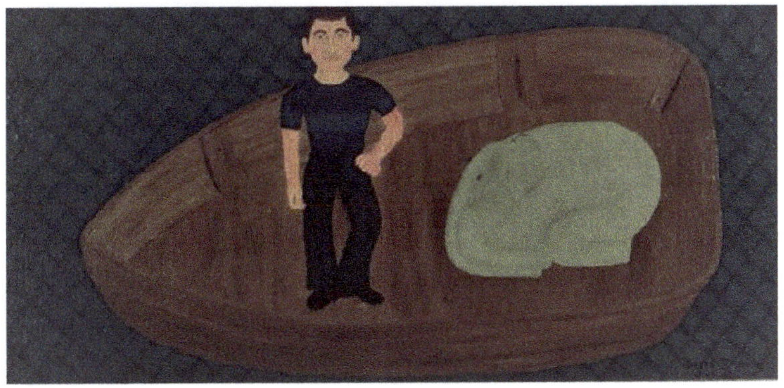

The Physical Mind and Sensation Function

This is an image of a "low browed" man and an apparently sleeping elephant curled up in a brown boat that is moving toward the left. The background water contains a curious net like effect.

I will begin my amplification with the low-browed man. In Sri Aurobindo's epic poem *Savitri*, book 2, canto 10, *The Kingdoms and Godheads of the Little Mind*, the following passage is marvelously apposite:

> First, smallest of the three, but strong of limb
> A low brow with a square and heavy jowl
> A pigmy thought needing to live in bounds
> Forever stopped to hammer fact and form
> absorbed and cabined in external sight,
> It takes its stand on nature's solid base.
>
> A slave of a fixed mass of absolute rules It sees
> as law the habits of the world
> It sees as truth the habits of the mind
> In its realm of concrete images and events.[248]

The "low brow" seems to an image of what Sri Aurobindo calls the physical mind and related to what Jung refers to as the sensation function. The brown color of the boat supports this amplification. This color points to the earth and is related to both the physical mind and the sensation function.[249] The horizontal blue stripe and blue pants imply that there is an element of spiritual will as well.[250] The horizontal direction of the stripe indicates that there is a force of will related to involvement in physical life.

The rectangular horizontal shape of the painting itself reinforces emphasize on the horizontal direction of the psychic energy. The movement is directed toward the left, into an aspect of the unconscious that has to do with will and the physical world.

The vehicle that carries the psyche is a boat. In ancient Egypt, the boat was considered a living female being, a goddess. The goddess Isis was often represented with a boat on her head, suggesting that she was the boat.[251] She was, in fact, depicted as fighting for Horus, the son god, in his journey through the underworld ensuring his resurrection.[252] Like Horus, the deceased was considered to travel in the boat of Ra, the sun God, in his journey after death.[253] This belief suggests that the psyche is carried by the Mother goddess, or the Self, and not the personal ego.

To be in a boat in one's dreams means that one has a certain protection in one's journey into the unconscious. Inner efforts and sacrifice in life and discernment have forged a boat cut from the tree of life and knowledge. The boat in this sense is the result of the development of a philosophy of life that protects the ego against inundation by the waters of the unconscious— that is, from being dragged down into the unconscious. This boat, fabricated by inner work, now protects and assists one in the present journey within.

The curled-up sleeping elephant gives further indication of the nature of the journey into the unconscious. The elephant symbolizes strength, firmness, longevity, wisdom, and the earth.[254] In the Indian *Kundalini chakra* system, an elephant is portrayed in the muladhara *chakra*, the base of the spine *chakra* found at the sacral plexus between the anus and the genitals.[255] *Muladhara* means root (*mula*) support (*adhara*).[256] It is the physical *chakra* where the spiritual energy is most condensed. It governs a materialistic world view, ruled by hard facts.

According to Ajit Mookerjee, the deity of this *chakra* is the lord of the gross physical, that is, the material world.[257] Jung describes the *muladhara* as the root support of the world where the gods are asleep while the ego identifies with consciousness.[258] This may explain why the elephant is asleep in this image. He observes that it refers to our conscious world, the most banal place, the day-to-day life of appointments, obligations, duties, bus tickets, the cause and effects of life.[259] Jung contends that *muladhara* is the place where humankind is the victim of impulses and lives in the unconsciousness of participation mystique.[260] Here one is entangled in the world through the roots of daily life.

It is a common error for many spiritual seekers, especially intuitive types,to want to leave behind this area of the psyche as too mundane. But this attitude leads to spiritual inflation and a neurotic provisional life.[261] As in a provisional life, there are no deep attachments formed; there is no possibility of true detachment either.

According to Jung, despite its heights, our conscious Western culture is still fundamentally based on *muladhara*.[262] As long as the ego is identified with external consciousness, it is blindly caught up in the external world and lives in the personal or *sthula* aspect of the psyche—that is, in the reality of cause and effect.[263] As one's viewpoint widens and includes elements of the impersonal psyche, the *sukshma* aspect, the collective unconscious, one can begin to realize that the conscious external ego is entangled in the world of causality.[264] Moreover, carried by the force of the archetype and synchronicity, one can, at times, be opened to the *sukshma* aspect of the psyche, including the subtle physical world.

Another aspect of this painting to consider is the net-like effect found in the water. According to Greek mythology, the "net of heaven" spans earth and heaven, and by it, the goddess, Themis, maintains world order and the laws of the universe from which there are no escape.[265] Likewise, in Indian mythology, *Purusha* creates the world through his *Shakti-Maya* by making limits, order, and universal laws.[266]

Overall, the image suggests that the psyche is meant to become more cognizant of the fixed laws of life pertaining to the physical world, the world of the *muladhara chakra*, and the world of the "low brow," the "little mind," the physical mind, and the sensation function. It may also suggest a move into the subtle physical world, or the physical world in its *sukshma* aspect. Like the elephant, the physical world in its *sukshma* aspect appears somewhat "eternal," fixed and solid like the elephant, while the *sthula* aspect appears transitory and illusory.[267]

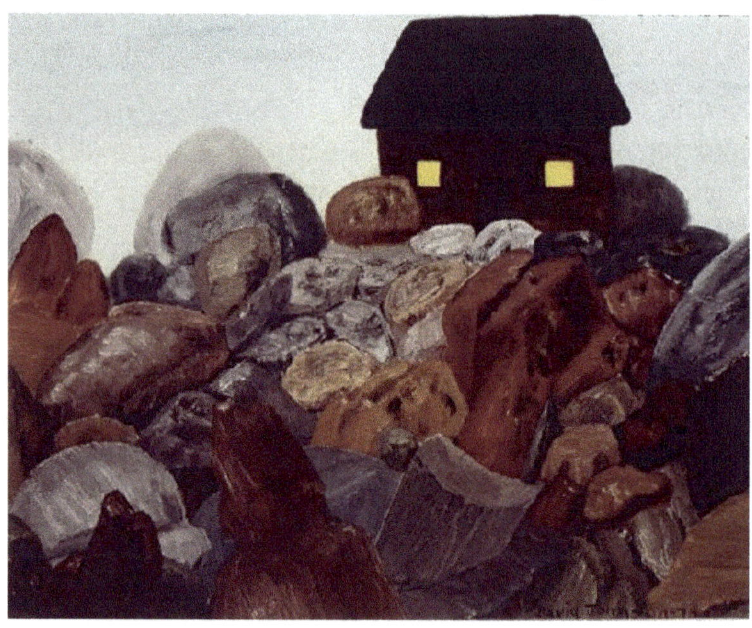

In this image, there is a wooden house lit up from within, stationed on a field of rocks. Stones and rocks are a symbol for the Self.[268] They are experienced as enduring and relatively unchanging over great periods of time. For the alchemists, the stone was considered to be *incorruptible*, while reconciling all opposites and was the sought-after goal.[269] The *lapis philosophorum* (philosopher's stone) was correlated with Christ and was believed to contain within it, soul, body, and spirit.[270] In 1 Corinthians 10:4, Christ is identified as a spiritual rock from which the water of life springs.[271] And to his disciple, Simon, Jesus says, "And I tell you, you are Peter, and on this rock I will build my church"[272] The name Peter, that of the first vicar of the Church, etymologically means "a rock" in Greek.[273] In the Old Testament, there are liberal references to rocks as a symbol of the Self. For instance, in Genesis 28:22, one reads, "And this stone which I have set for a pillar, shall be God's House"[274]

After emerging from their first home, the protective cave, the primitive first dwelling was the tomb, built for the souls of the dead.[275] Following that, human's sought protective dwellings for living souls in trees, then houses with pillars made from trees, and, finally, simple houses on the earth.[276] This house is square, symbolically suggesting materialization and connection with the solid earth yet separation from perfection of the whole.[277] Psychologically, the house represents protection, shelter, and security in the sense that a religious faith, philosophical conviction or *weltanschauung* gives one protection against the chaos of opinion in life. In this case, the house, a log cabin, is made of wood. This indicates that it is made from pieces of the tree of life and knowledge—that is, the house has been built through sacrifice and discernment.

The house also represents the human personality, with each room relating to different aspects of the psyche. The house itself can also symbolize parts of the psyche, especially in this case, the head, the seat of consciousness. The two windows are like eyes, the roof like the top of the head, and the door like the mouth. The light seen through the window (eyes) indicates consciousness and understanding.[278] A symbolic head, the overall indication is meaning and consciousness. The black roof indicates unknown thoughts that may potentially become conscious. In support of this, a light is appearing on the left, forecasting that consciousness is emerging from the unconscious and beginning to light up the rocks or the Self.

This image was constellated in compensation for a shaky and difficult period of outer chaos. Overall, this is a psychic representation of a house or worldview built upon the solid foundation of the rocks of the Self. This house of discernment and consciousness gives protection and security. There are still unknown thoughts, but light or awareness is coming from the left, the unconscious.

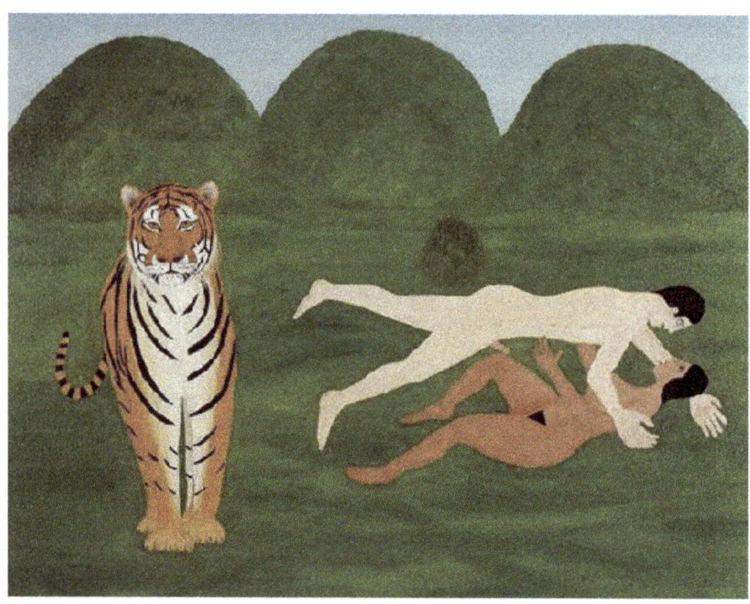

A member of the cat family, the tiger, which is found throughout Asia, is feared because of its reputed ferocity and cunning.[279] A carnivorous animal, it is normally found in the valleys, often near swamps, waterways, and woodlands.[280] The tiger has also adapted to life in some rocky, mountainous areas.[281]

The symbol tiger represents what, in the West, is referred to as the "Terrible" or "Destructive Mother." In India, there are tiger caves that belong to the goddess Kali, she who dances the dance of destruction.[282] According to popular depiction, she is a fierce-looking goddess who stands on the corpse of her consort, Shiva, while slaying the ego of desire.[283] Yet she not only slays, she succors and nourishes the generation of new living form.[284] Moreover, she gives courage and strength while hastening one on the path towards spiritual freedom and independence.[285] In the words of Sri Aurobindo, "Therefore with her is the victorious force of the Divine and it is by grace of her fire and passion and speed if the great achievement can be done now rather than hereafter."[286]

In India, she is one of the most popular goddesses and is worshipped by millions. In that country, there is a much greater acceptance than in the West of the natural cycle of life and the mysterious interrelationship of life and death. We tend to deny the stark reality of death and try to conquer it along with everything else in nature. The results are psychologically devastating, as life, too, is affected and not fully lived.

That many aspects of the illusory ego are slayed on the path of individuation goes without saying. One's conscious attitudes and direction in life is inevitably myopic. Conscious individuation means a gradual shifting of the axis from the ego to the Self. The ego becomes relativized and increasingly transparent to the unconscious, the mother of all consciousness. With integral yoga and the individuation process, one becomes an increasingly conscious instrument of the Divine Mother or the Self as the real doer of works.[287]

As there are three hills in the painting the symbolic number three (3) is significant. It is dynamic and symbolizes process and insight, which, here,signifies disintegration of ego, creative transformation, and the fixing of new form.[288] Through the archetypal number three (3), a link is formed between the transcendent One and the manifest world.[289] The three hills,therefore, have the same symbolic significance as the tiger—that is, the disintegration of the old and illusory aspect of the ego to allow for a new principle to be given birth. The psyche is depicted here as being in a state of transformation.

As three figures are in the valley, the process of transformation is taking place in life, not on some lonely mountaintop of the spirit. The quest is for consciousness-life, not simply consciousness or unconscious life. The man,representing the masculine principle, is falling, presumably from a plateau that is too high; perhaps he is living too much in the intellect. This descent potentially results in the consummation of the coniunctio with a dark woman, who is rising to meet him with open, receptive arms. This dark woman represents an earth anima, aspects of the soul that are presently unconscious, but which appear to be aspiring for consciousness. Receiving and being impregnated by the spiritual "masculine principle," or Logos,will result in the birth of a child of discernment. The fact that the inevitable position for the consummation is horizontal supports my earlier contention that psychic energy is moving in the direction of life.

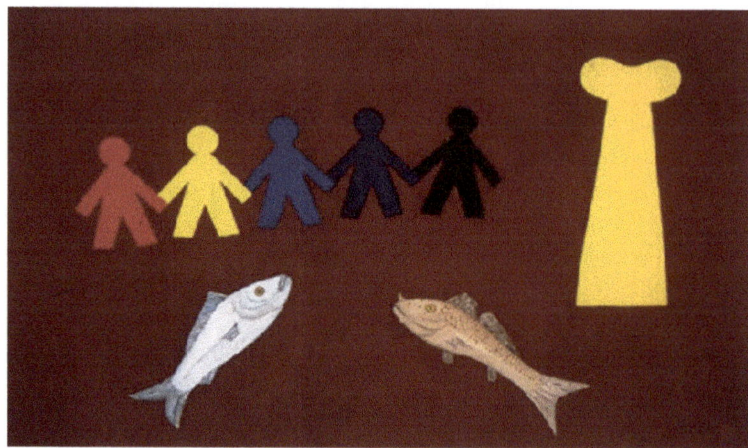

In both Western esoteric tradition and eastern spirituality, man is considered to consist of several subtle "bodies," in addition to his gross material frame.[290] Some commentators describe it as one subtle body with psycho-spiritual energy concentrated at different subtle centers known as *chakras*.[291] These "bodies" include the vital or life body and the mental body, perhaps related to the red and blue figures in this painting. There is also a subtle physical body. The colors attributed to the different *chakras* are typically red for the *muladhara* (root) chakra, yellow for the *manipura chakra*, green for the anahata (heart) *chakra*, blue for the *visuddha* (throat) *chakra*, purple for the *ajna* (third eye) *chakra* as well as the crown *chakra*, along with white.

The color green is often attributed to the sensation function, blue to the thinking function, and red to the feeling function.[292] A fourth figure is yellow, the color often related to intuition, and sometimes the thinking function.[293] Blue is also considered to be the color of the spirit, while red represents the libido and Eros— that is, relatedness.[294]

The violet or purple figure suggests spiritual transformation.[295] It is a synthesis of red and blue, Eros and Logos.[296] Violet is the "royal color," worn by both popes and royalty. In esoteric tradition, it is considered to have transformative power.[297] Jung attributes violet to the spiritual pole of the archetype and red to the instinctual pole.[298] This relates to the fact that the archetype is a "formative principle of instinctive power."[299]

As there are five (5) figures in this painting, it is interesting to amplify the numerological significance of the number five (5). In esoteric Christianity, five (5) represents the Christ person, the one who, through consciously suffering the opposites in life, becomes spiritually transformed.[300] The individual moved by the archetype of the life of Christ gradually becomes more conscious and in harmony with destiny.[301] It represents the star of individuality like the astrological sign Leo and the planet Venus.[302] Five (5) is also the number of Mercury, the quintessence or subtle substance of all things.[303]

The two fish point to the two poles of being: the spiritual pole and the earthly instinctual pole, depicted by the blue fish and the brown fish respectively. Their position suggests two sides of a triangle, pointing upward, indicating aspiration for consciousness. It is interesting to note that the brown fish is also a unicorn. Jung indicates that a unicorn is a demonic, divine nature power with relations to the "holy spirit," the horn suggesting a creative spiritual quality.[304]

The background color is brown with what appears to be a yellow keyhole with a kidney-shaped top. The kidney is the organ with the function of cleansing the blood and would, therefore, embody the symbolic value of purification of Eros. In Chinese tarot, the power of action is attributed to the kidneys.[305] The color yellow in the form of a keyhole indicates that intelligence and consciousness can be found in the instinctual earth symbolized by the color brown.[306] The psychological earth is a symbol for the alchemical *coagulatio*, which allows experiences to be related to the ego and earthly reality.[307] According to Edinger's interpretation of certain myths, it is promoted by action.[308] This image, therefore, suggests that the key to illumination and psycho-spiritual transformation is found through active participation in all levels of life.

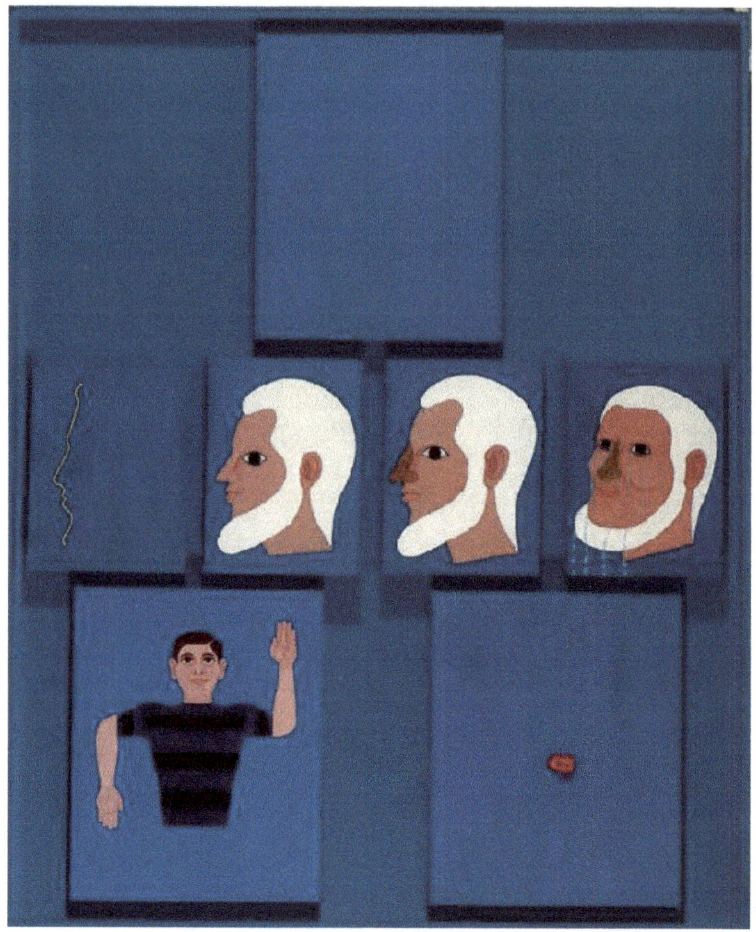

First, take the color blue, which is the background color for all the paintings and the color of the first panel. Blue is regarded as the color of the spirit and represents intuition or spiritual will.[309] The Virgin Mary is often shown wearing a blue cloak, designating her as a sky goddess.[310] Krishna, the Indian god, and his consort Radha have a blue body.[311] Masters of different spiritual movements say that they can be experienced through a blue light.[312] Blue is the color of both the sky and water and, therefore, all-embracing, pointing both upward and downward. For the alchemists, there is a "heavenly or divine water," indicating the similarity between water and spirit.[313] Water pertains to the alchemical *solutio*, representing dissolution, birth, and generation, while the blue sky represents the spirit.[314] This amplification should help us to understand the meaning of the first panel,but also the whole series of paintings. The principal idea suggested by the color blue is that of a spiritual all-embracing background for dissolution and potential birth and generation.

The second panel has a yellow outline of a face in profile on a blue background. In Genesis 1:1–5, one reads,

> In the beginning God created the heavens and
> the earth. The earth was without form and void,
> and darkness was upon the face of the deep, and
> the Spirit of God was moving over the face of
> the (blue) waters. And God said, "Let there be
> (yellow) light", and there was (yellow) light.[315]

The "Spirit of God" moves "over the face of the waters" to manifest the creation.[316] Yellow is the color of the illuminated mind and of consciousness.[317] It is the color of the sun and of light. In the creation myth according to *Genesis*, the advent of light comes after the creation of heaven and earth. It, therefore, represents the dawn of consciousness. Thus, the idea of creation and consciousness is profiled in the second panel.

The third panel has a figure of a bearded head, with an eye that reminds one of an Egyptian painting. The amulet of the "Eye of Horus" in Egyptian mythology represents either the sun, or the moon, or Ra and Osiris, respectively.[318] In other words, it represents the deity. It reminds one of a fish's eye, which, like the eye of God, appears to be always open.[319] Thanks to a transparent film over the eye, it appears open even in the dark depths of the sea.

Regarding the head itself, the later alchemists maintained that the secret lies in the head, which is "a synonym for the arcane or transformative substance."[320] For the ancient Egyptians, it was the "Covered Temple," a symbol for the Self.[321] Thus, by gaining access to the symbolic head, the seat of consciousness and wisdom, one can solve inner problems.[322] In *Timaeus*, Plato contends that "the human head is the image of the world"and therefore, contains the divine secret.[323]

With a little imagination, one can see that the beard and hairline around the ear form the omega (Ω). In his essay, *Transformation Symbolism in the Mass*, Jung notes that for the alchemist Zosimos, the sought-for "round element" is the letter omega (Ω).[324] This symbol may well be interpreted as the head, since the Liber *quatorum* also associates the round vessel with the head."[325] He then says that "probably all these ideas go back to the 'head of Osiris', which crossed the sea and was therefore associated with the idea of Resurrection."[326] Osiris was an Egyptian Christ-like figure, the Divine Son of Isis, a dying and resurrecting God. Curiously, this head I have painted has an Egyptian flavor, and it is "floating" on the blue (waters).

With perhaps a little more imagination, one may see that the beard and hairline forms something like the symbol OM, which, in Hindu thought is "the word," the seed sound for creation.[327] "The Word" or Logos has a similar meaning in Christianity. In John 1:1–5, one reads,

> In the beginning was the word, and the word was with God, and the word was God. He was in the beginning with God. All living things were made through Him, and without Him was not anything made that was made. The light shines in the darkness, and the darkness has not overcome it.[328]

In the image on panel three, then, there is reference to meaning and creation through the word by the Deity or the Self. This is an image of "God the Creator."

On panel four, there is a mutation as the nose turns into a piece of earth, possibly a stone. The nose is often considered to be the seat of the intuition, the faculty which links one to the unknowable.[329] The motif of "the stone that is not a stone" is well-known in alchemy, representing the mysterious "man."[330] Here it is a nose, relating it to Zosimos's notion that the stone is the "head-element" itself.[331] The stone in alchemy is a symbol for the Self. Jung says that "The lapis (stone) signifies the inner man"... the freeing of which is the goal of the alchemical procedure.[332] In Judea-Christian tradition, the rock is an important symbol for God, for example, the Lord as the Rock of Salvation.[333] Jesus says to Peter, "On this rock I will build my church, laying the foundation for Christianity."[334] Peter, Christ's vicar on earth, has a name meaning stone. In the choice of matter as a symbol of God or the Self, there is the clear idea of preservation. After the act of creation, there is the need for preservation. This, therefore, is an image of "God the Preserver."

On the fifth panel, there are four streams of water, four tears from the eyes of the God Image. In number symbolism, four (4) symbolizes materialization and truth-consciousness, spirit and effective realization.[335] It partakes of the same qualities as the cross, karmic limits, intensity, and pai and suffering.[336] A common theme in creation myths found throughout the world involves the Creator crying.[337] One often finds it, for instance, in North American Indian creation myths.338 In an account of a Winnebago myth, one reads, "His tears fall down and form the lakes, and then he begins to wish….He creates everything from wishing"[339] In an Algonquin tribe, the story goes, "In the beginning there was nothing but water. On the water was a boat and in the boat a man who cried because he had no idea of what his fate would be. The Moshush Rat came out from the water and said, 'Grandfather, why do you cry?' And then she fished up the earth for him.[340] In this myth, the creator God cries out of anxiety, as he does not know his fate. For purposes of this amplification, what is most noteworthy is the fact that there is a resultant creation, the earth.[341]

A major procedure in alchemy is the operation known as *Iiquefactio* or solutio, the turning into liquid in order to undo or dissolve "differentiated matter "into its original undifferentiated state, the *prima materia*."[342] The alchemists observed that "matter" is often hardened or solidified in a "wrong way," as is one's ego.343 They, consequently, found the need for "matter" to be dissolved in order to find the philosopher's stone. Von Franz observes that, "This sheds light on what crying means, namely it effects an "abaissement du niveau, mental" (lowering of the conscious attitude)through which the creative contents of the unconscious can breakthrough"[344] From the point of view of the individual, this dissolution eventually leads to creative activity, and rebirth, a new attitude. The image on this panel, then, is that of "God the Destroyer," better said, "God the Dissolver."

One should not forget that there are four (4) tears, and, in its essential qualitative value, four (4) means truth-consciousness.[345] Various motifs of the number four(4) frequently appear in creation myths throughout the world.[346] Depicted here is not personal destructiveness that comes from an egotistical personality but dissolution that originates from a transcendent source. Both the cause and effect of the dissolution is related to one's inner truth and the Self's teleological impetus toward wholeness.

On the sixth panel there is a *swastika,* which, here, is human and,therefore, potentially conscious. The *swastika* is a sun or moon symbol found throughout the world, for example among aboriginal North Americans, in pagan Germany, and, to this day, in India.[347] It is often depicted as revolving from left to right in the direction of the movement of the sun, representing a movement toward creation and consciousness.[348] In this case, it is revolving toward the left, toward the unconscious, toward dissolution. A counterclockwise swastika known in Sanskritas as a *sauvastika* symbolizes the moon, night, and the feminine principle.[349] This symbolism suggests that the dissolution of ego attitudes leads to Eros and relatedness, a fact that is confirmed on the seventh panel. Dissolution follows logically from the message on the fifth panel. (The *sauvastika* should not be confused with the Nazi use of the swastika, which was a perversion; the latter was depicted as tilted counterclockwise, with the hooks facing clockwise. As, in fact, happened, this symbolism promotes gross destruction and not dissolution of ego attitudes and values and the development of Eros, like the *sauvastika.*

The *swastika* is a form of the cross. If the three preceding panels represent the "Father God," this panel represents the "Son," in a sense, the individual who is the cross, who carries the burden of personal life, even when it leads to "dissolution of ego attitudes and values." This eventuality,in fact, is an integral part of the demands of the individuation process. The color of the sweater is also significant and generally fits the developing theme. There are two sets of alternating horizontal stripes, one set brown,the other blue. As indicated earlier, blue is related to spiritual values such as intuition, devotion, and divine will.[350] Brown represents the earth, the alchemical *coagulatio,* which suggests the potential for relating these symbols to the ego and to life.[351] The following panel reinforces this notion.

Christianity is the "religion of suffering," of "God" through His "Son,"taking on the "cross of matter," that is of the Divine's descent into the darkness (of the unconscious) to bring deliverance through His resurrection. As Jung argues, however, we have let Jesus carry our cross for the past two thousand years, repressing our own responsibility to do so.[352] Today we must each take up our own cross. This requires consciously embarking on the path of individuation and the symbolic life. In astrology, the

Ascendant,Descendant, Nadir, and Mid Heaven form the cross of one's life. In accordance with this symbolic reality, individuation means becoming aware of personal and archetypal influences through life experience and introspection.

Finally, on the seventh panel, one sees the results of the dissolution of consciousness. The light of consciousness, the Logos, the Word, creation no longer exists. There remains a red splotch of blood, which symbolizes undifferentiated Eros. Blood is the symbol for the feminine principle or Eros, the "great binder and loosener."[353] Christianity, the religion of the cross, is also the religion of love, of the blood of Christ. In alchemical tradition, the blood contains the seat of the soul as well as the Holy Spirit.[354] One reference by the alchemist, Senior (Ibn Umail), even depicts the soul itself as remaining in the water like in this image of the seventh panel–as "therein consisteth all life."[355] Similarly the ancient Vedic scripture of India, *Mandala Eight*, Sukta 43, the *Viruna Angirasa*, verse 9, reads:

> In the waters, O Fire, is thy seat, thou beseigest
> the plants; Thou becomest a child in the womb and
> art born again.[356]

The Jerusalem Bible rendition of the first letter of John 5:7–8 reads, "There are three witnesses in heaven: the Father, the Word and the Spirit,and these three are one; there are three witnesses an earth: the spirit, the water, and the blood."[357] Reference to the "witnesses on earth" suggests the need to bring the reality of the metaphysical trinity into life and the material world.

On the last panel. One is left, then, with the matrix of the feminine,wherein lies the seeds of rebirth and of recreation. One is left with the Holy Spirit which creates ever anew as well as the individual soul, which brings the creation into space and time, the here and now. With blood, life becomes full bodied and animated and, in the words of Jung, "the devil no longer has an autonomous existence but rejoins the profound unity of the psyche."[358]

I am reminded of the words of Jesus as recorded in John 14:12 in reference to the action of the Paraclete, the Holy Ghost. He says, "I tell you most solemnly, whoever believes in me will perform the same works as I do myself, he will perform even greater works."[359] Creation, perhaps, evolves in a generally ascending spiral of consciousness, allowing works to become "greater." After suffering the pain of ego dissolution, one is left with the seeds for a new cycle of creation. By consciously accepting even the difficult periods in one's life, one can look forward to new creative living, grounded in the here and now.

These panels depict a synthesis of the creation cycle, with the trinity of the Godhead expressed in two different ways. Firstly, there are images of the Father God as Creator, Preserver, and Destroyer. In Hindu mythology, the Triune Godhead—Brahma, Vishnu, and Shiva—represent God as Creator, God as Preserver, and God as Destroyer.[360] In astrology, the same principle is expressed in the cyclic rhythm of the Cardinal, Fixed, and Mutable points.[361] Secondly, there is the Father (panels 3, 4, and 5.), the Son (panel 6), and the Holy Ghost or Eros (panel 7), which resembles the Christian Trinity.

There are seven different panels. Seven (7), which consists of four (4) plus three (3) is the number that symbolizes the individuation process. The number three (3) represents the rhythmic flow of psychic energy being related to the manifestation of the archetype, time, and destiny.[362] It is, says Jung, "an unfolding of the one to a condition where it can be known."[363] It, therefore brings insight and knowledge.[364] The number four (4) represents both consciousness and materialization.[365] The step from three (3) to four (4) turns one's mind away from mere abstract knowledge and insights to participation in "realizations in the act of becoming."[366] Thus the fact that there are seven (7) panels neatly expresses the rhythm of creation and the experience of synchronicity over space and time. It represents the individuation process and the symbolic life.

The symbolic life is gained by conscious acceptance of its cyclic rhythm, the periods of creation, of preservation and of dissolution for re-creation. This engagement means accepting life in all its goodness, as well as its painful trials and tribulations. And by concomitantly becoming more conscious through the process, one not only accepts life as it is, but there is "consciousness-life."

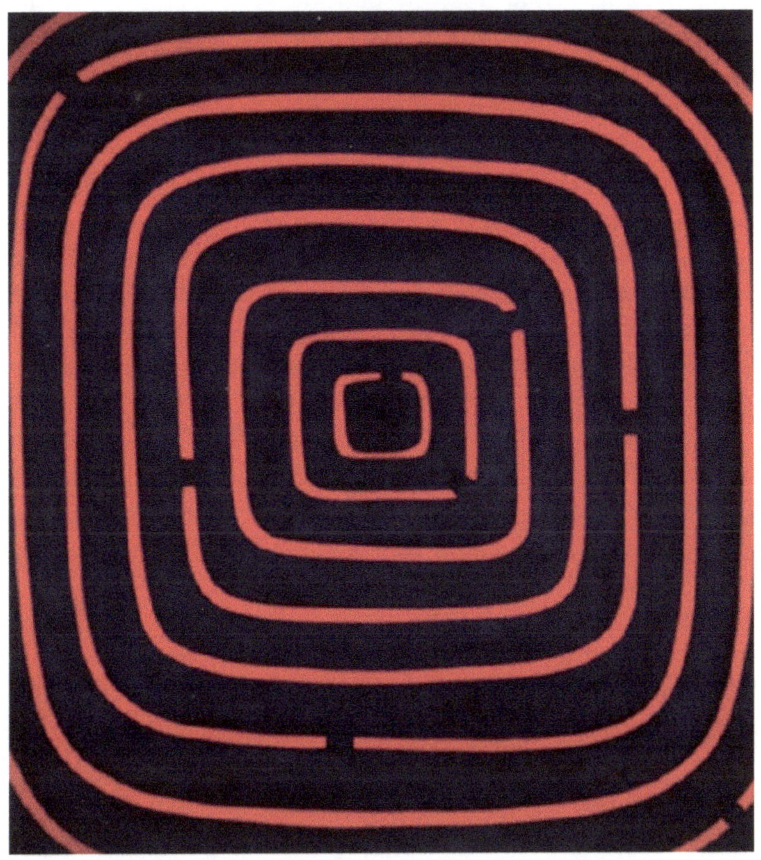

This simple-looking image represents a labyrinth. The labyrinth is a symbolic representation of a "rite of passage," an initiation into one of the major transitions in life, including spiritual initiation into the "mysteries," which necessitates psychological death and resurrection.[367] Initiation is derived from the word *inire*, which means to enter, to go into.[368] The word *labyrin* is possibly derived from the word *labyrs*, which means a two-headed ax, an ancient symbol for a god or goddess.[369] Eliade, however, argues that it is more likely derived from the Asiatic *labra/laura*, meaning "stone, cave," suggesting the underworld.[370]

The center of the labyrinth has traditionally involved spiritual significance and included such symbols as a rose, a crescent moon, a swastika, or a cross, all indicating spiritual values.[371]

In the story of Theseus, a minotaur was found in the center,

95

a beast, half man and half bull, which Theseus was required to kill, and then find his way out.[372] The minotaur represents a person's lusts and passionate nature of which one has to become aware and master in order to discover the spiritual center.

The labyrinth can also be understood as a journey through the underworld, the land of the dead, as indicated above.[373] It is the place for the journey of the hero and symbolic sun that shines during the night. It represents the "heroic quest," a journey into the dark night where one no longer knows in which direction to go, where there are obstacles, wrong turnings, and in this case, since there is no symbolic center, even no certainty of the exact goal. It is the seeker who becomes initiated into and treads the labyrinthine path, the son or daughter returning to the Mother —"the Mother who is the matrix which allows the labyrinth of the phenomenal world to come into being."[374]

The hero Odysseus, on his return from the Trojan wars, comes upon Aiolia, the death isle of the magician sorceress, Kirke (Circe).[375] Here, Odysseus forgets his purpose for a year, beguiled by seductions and enchantments. So it is, in one's spiritual journey, when one comes to the point that the external paraphernalia, rules and dogma, even the physical guru, no longer represent what is necessary for one's psycho-spiritual development. Spiritual rules, let alone rules of society, are no longer binding. At this point, one is very easily subjected to rationalizations and excuses, in the final analysis, one's own.

The only guidance that one has in this case is from within, most profoundly from the Self. In one's confusion, one must turn to the inner light again and again. I am reminded of Dante, when he says, "In the middle of the journey of our life I came to myself within a dark wood where the straight way was lost."[376] Redemption comes not from escaping the phenomenal world. It is, in fact, precisely there where one finds one's way to the center.

In the story of Theseus, it is the worldly Daedalus, technician and craftsman who builds the labyrinth and who gives Ariadne the thread with which Theseus finds his way out.[377] A similar motif can be found in Goethe's Faust, where Mephistopheles leads Faustin to life and greater awareness, after being cooped up in his study.[378] Through the ways of the world and life, one can become more aware, as long as one has the appropriate attitude. Being initiated, entering and going through the labyrinth teaches one to accept what has hitherto been rejected in one's life.

In addition, according to the legend of Theseus, the anima (Ariadne) helps Theseus find his way.[379] Psychologically, this means that through the anima a man gains conscious entrance into the collective unconscious and becomes guided by the intelligence of nature. Ariadne gives Theseus the thread by which he finds his way out.[380] The thread symbolizes destiny and indicates that going through the labyrinth takes one into its more conscious realization.[381] In a book entitled *The Way of Wyrd*, the seeker is required to learn to jump along luminous inner threads that he envisions.[382] A deeper sense of destiny means being directed by the Self and not the psychological complexes.

One may well ask if this process does not lead one to being blindly caught in life, in the *kleshas* (destructive emotions and mental states),without the possibility of any exit. There is always this danger. Through introspection and insight, however, one can become conscious of one's destiny and life. This is quite different from the life of the irresponsible individual blindly lost in a sea of desire and instinct. When one conscientiously travels through the labyrinth, one is moving in a circular fashion around the center, the Self.

The alchemists call this process the *circulatio*.[383] Psychologically, it allows one to repeatedly experience an unconscious complex from all sides,leading to consciousness and awareness of a reconciling transpersonal center.[384] The labyrinth's sacred nature also suggests a certain protection for the seeker, in that it is believed that only the initiate can enter.[385] Asin the case of Aeneas, certain sacrifices have first to be made.[386] Protection today comes through consciousness and symbolic thinking.

At this point, it may be relevant to quote from Francis Thompson's haunting poem, *The Hound of Heaven*.

> I fled him down the nights and down the days.
> I fled him down the arches of the years
> I fled him down the labyrinth ways
> Of my own mind; and in the midst of tears
> I hid from him...[387]

> From those strong feet that followed,
> followed after...[388]

They beat—and a Voice beat More instant
than the Feet—"All things betray thee, who
betrayest Me."[389]

"Ah, fondest blindest, weakest,
I am He whom thou seekest!
Thou dravest love from thee, who dravest
Me."[390]

This is a beautiful poetic rendering of one man's individuation process and his experience of the labyrinth. In the final analysis, something like this is the goal of every seeker, relating the path to the *labyr*, the sacred ax, symbol of God.

The background for this image of the labyrinth is a deep blue. Blue symbolizes faith, devotion to a higher will, guiding intelligence, and loyalty to the will of God.[391] Pale blue is the color of *ananda*, or bliss, of Krishna, Sri Aurobindo, the Virgin Mary and other spiritual personalities.[392] Deep blue is the color of the higher mind—that is, the philosophic, synthesizing mind.[393] Red, the color of the labyrinth itself, represents the alchemical *rubedo* and symbolizes the libido, life, Eros, the "great loosener and binder."[394] Deep red symbolizes divine love.[395]

This labyrinth then depicts a union of Eros and vitality with the will and the higher mind. This suggests how the seeker can find his way through the maze and around the obstacles, as well as the goal. The goal is the higher mind and being directed by a higher will, while the obstacle is following personal will, especially inflated by the constellation of an archetype. In addition, the goal involves connection through Eros, while the obstacle is the ego-persona and desire, again, especially when inflated by the archetype. By what means does one find the way to the goal? By being consciously related to the Self, along with an attitude that recognizes the ego's relativity and its subordination to the Self.

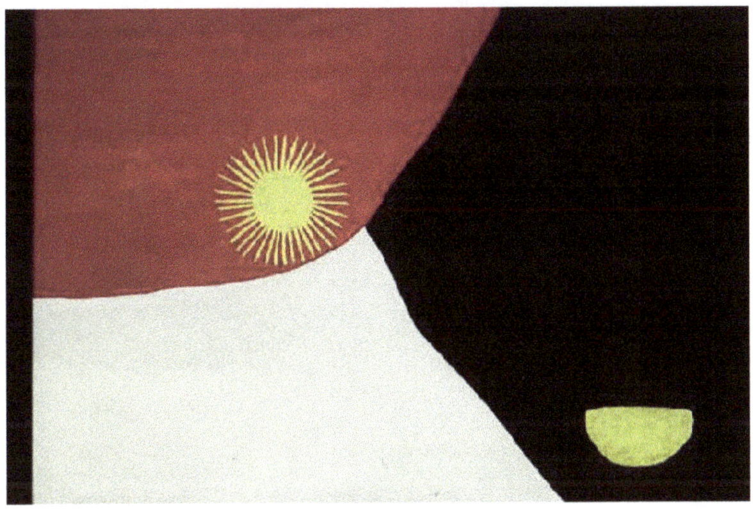

Esoteric literature indicates that the psyche consists of different colors, through the emanation of different colored auras.[396] The color gray is generally not mentioned at all, and the color black, and even red, is often evaluated negatively. But these evaluations are in error, based on a limited understanding of human psychology.

In alchemy, there is said to be two lights: revelation from above and the light of nature, the *lumen naturae*.[397] Sri Aurobindo refers to *Prakriti* or nature as consciousness-force.[398] Individuation can be defined as the process of finding consciousness in life. The principal colors of the Earth Mother are red and black.[399] In a broad sense, red is Eros, that is relatedness to both one's instincts and to the community, while black represents the unknown and is also often considered a primal feminine color. The red area in the painting contains a golden sun, suggesting that the highest value and consciousness can be found in Eros.[400] The black area contains a golden moon shape, suggesting that the highest value is to be found in the descent into the dark yin of the psyche with her natural lunar rhythms. This is in keeping with the fact that the Earth Mother is often depicted as related to the moon.[401] The gold of consciousness can be found by making this descent.

Finally, the color gray indicates a coming to awareness and acceptance of concrete reality—that is, acceptance of the physical world as it is. Given that the Greek goddess of wisdom, Athena, is gray-eyed, gray also suggests wisdom. Introverted intuitive personality types are divorced from the earthy and concrete aspect of the psyche, which they consider inferior. For them,only with a long and earnest struggle can it become, at least to some degree,assimilated to consciousness. This is very difficult for sensation-oriented people to understand as their psyches are naturally riveted in concrete reality. For the intuitive person, however, as inferior, the sensation function comes with the weight of the shadow and the collective unconscious.

Master

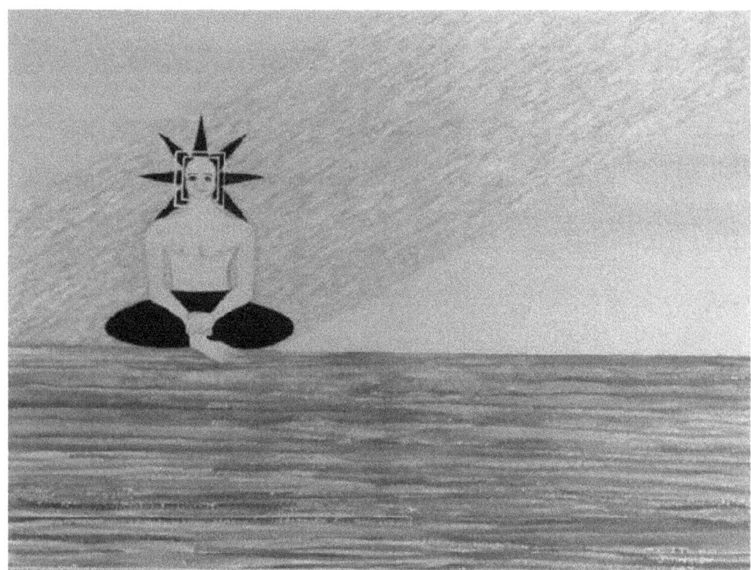

This is an image of a painting done by the wise old man within. As a water color, it suggests that mainly feeling and intuition were involved in creating the image. A body of water represents the unconscious, the mother of all consciousness.[402] Its blue color signifies spirit.[403] That the figure is sitting on the water indicates self-mastery, especially of the emotional life,and that the conscious and unconscious are in harmonious relationship. As amplification, the well-known image of Jesus walking on water presents itself. The first part of the conscious individuation process is "having it out with the unconscious," what Jung refers to as *auseinandersetzung mit der unbewusstsein*.[404] This undertaking eventually leads to more transparent relationship between the ego and the unconscious. The ego continues to have rights and obligations, however relativized, as it becomes more open to the energies from the unconscious.

The diagonal trajectory of water in the image suggests reconciliation of the forces of life (horizontal) and spiritual aspiration (vertical). The Egyptian pharaoh, who was venerated as the incarnation of God, is sometimes depicted as the diagonal of the sacred triangle, the essence of which is contained in all right-angle triangles.[405] The many-colored nature of the flow of water suggests the spirit Mercurius as *omnescolores*. Or the play of colors in the *cauda pavonis*, the peacock's tail.[406] The subtle variations in color require the application of feeling.

The vertical nature of aspiration, as suggested by the seated position of the figure, which forms a triangle, indicate that the flame of human aspiration leaps heavenward. The brownish-red bottom indicates Eros at an instinctual level.[407] Thus, the vertical aspiration has an instinctual base that flames from the bottom up. For the contemporary individual, there must first be a long descent of consciousness in order to *arrive* at this position. Striving too hard or forcing the process of individuation is a psychologically dangerous practice. The alchemists observe that too much heat (willful effort) can spoil the transformative process.[408] One has to learn to flow with the psyche, and that requires "time, balance and patience."[409] There is a natural rhythm of ascent and descent as well as a rhythmic going within and extraverted going without.

There is a double slightly rectangular shaped white halo depicted around the head. The head is symbolically the center of meaning and understanding.[410] The slightly longer vertical axis indicates that the emphasis is primarily on the vertical dimension (of aspiration) and the horizontal direction (of life) is secondary. The square-like shape suggests the need for the aspiration to be directly related to concrete experience. The square is a feminine symbol signifying matter and truth-consciousness.[411] The need to draw ethical conclusions from dreams and active imaginations and to realize them in life is implicit in this idea. The double nature of the halo indicates that this relationship is becoming conscious.

Finally, there is also a seven-rayed star-like configuration surrounding the head. The number seven (7) signifies completion, attainment, and emergence into a more conscious order of being.412 It is the number of individuation and of the spiritual master. The seven (7) rays themselves indicate penetrating insight into the nature of things. As the color is reddish-brown, it implies that this penetration is both instinctive and Eros related.

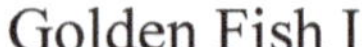

Golden Fish I

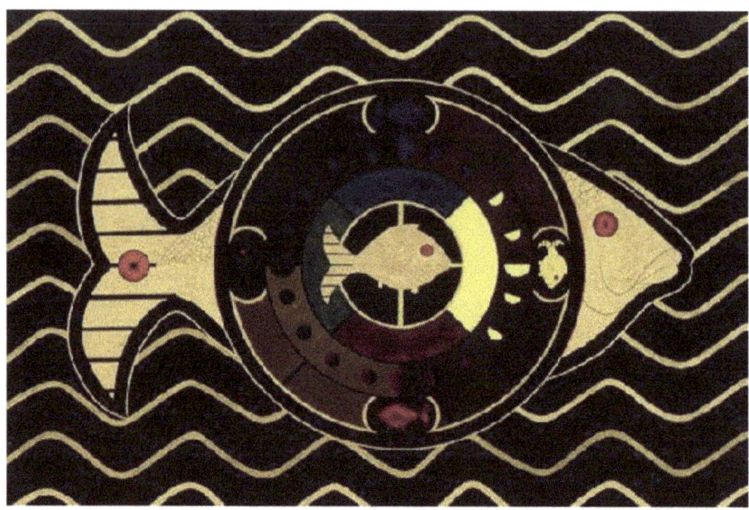

According to historical evidence, fish cults date back at least six thousand years, with the fish originally representing a goddess.[413] A historical sequence of events begins with the Syro-Phoenician goddess *Atargatis*, who was sometimes portrayed as a fish.[414] She had a son called Ichthys, also depicted as a fish, who later evolved into the Babylonian god Ea-oannes.[415] Since 200 BCE at Alexandria, Christ, too has been portrayed as a fish and called *Ichthys*, the fish that comes out of the depths.[416] For Christians, *Ichthys* (or *Ichthus*) has taken on the meaning of *Iesous Christos Theos Huis Soter* (Jesus Christ, son of God, Savior).[417] Although Christian and other traditions see the fish as representing a male god, they are all essentially sons of the Mother, and ultimately take part in Her nature. The fish, therefore, is either a feminine symbol *per se*, or masculine, which is not divorced from the feminine.

At the center of this image is a small golden fish on a cross against a black background. The obvious amplification is that of the sacrifice of Christ as fish, with the cross symbolizing the opposites contained in the Self. The fourfold nature of the cross gives it the same significance as the number four (4), a feminine number, symbolizing materialization, wholeness, and truth-consciousness.[418] The sacrifice to the Mother has a realistic dimension that takes place in daily life and responsibilities, either professional or domestic.

In Edinger's account of the Christian myth, Jesus represents the paradigm of the individuated time and space-bound ego.[419] Strong in its own ego identity, it has found its way back into relationship with the all-encompassing Self and is now "operating under" its aegis.[420] The Christian concept of *kenosis* or emptying psychologically means relinquishing the inflated identification of the ego with the Self. This allows one to be filled with energies from the deeper psyche. The black center indicates that behind the cross lies the unknown and mysterious depths of the psyche, out of which comes creation from its fullness. The gold color of the smaller fish and the cross suggest its high value and its relationship to the larger golden fish. As king of the metals, gold is an apt color for a fish depicting the divine son, "King of kings."

The large golden mother fish contains a mandala that not only includes the small fish on a cross against a black background but also the four colors, green, red, yellow, and blue equally partitioned around a circle. In addition,there is, as well, an outer circle of four earth-brown colors. The first four colors symbolize wholeness, representing the basis for the four functions of consciousness. Yellow, on the side of the fish's head, or consciousness would be related to the superior function of intuition; red to an auxiliary function, feeling; blue to a second auxiliary function, thinking; and green to the inferior function, sensation, found on the side of the fish's tail, or the unconscious.[421]

The black stripes on the fish's tail point to the primitive stripe motif, which, von Franz suggests, represents the need for order and differentiation of chaos.[422] It is through the inferior function that the individual experiences the collective unconscious. The concomitant chaos in one's life requires an experience of the Self, along with an ego capable of assimilating that experience in order to reestablish order in the psyche. Order is reinstated,this time at a more conscious level.

The relatively large size of the second fish and its function as container indicates its more cosmic and feminine nature. The gold color indicates its high value. In Orthodox Christianity, importance is laid on the cosmic or universal Christin addition to the personal time-bound historical Jesus that tends to be emphasized in the west. In the Eastern tradition, "Christ is true God and true man, one person in two natures, without separation and without confusion."[423] Thus, Western Christianity concentrates on the "suffering humanity" of Jesus, whereas orthodox Christianity sees both the "suffering humanity of Christ "and a "suffering God."[424] This larger fish,then, is symbolic of the greater Self, whereas the smaller one represents the time and space bound potentially individuated ego.

The different brown colors suggest a differentiation of the psychological earth—that is, the instincts. In this image, they encircle the four functions,whereas, psychologically, they would be more appropriately located inside the four functions, and more central. The viewer should note that the earth is not any of the four functions themselves not even the sensation function,but could be called something like psychological substance, related to the alchemical process of *coagulatio*.[425] It allows for each of the four functions to be potentially connected to the earth, the instinctual ground and conscious to the ego.[426] There are also four smaller fishes, each by its color related to one of the four functions and wholeness. In Jewish symbolism,the fish are the faithful who swim in the waters of the Torah. Similarly, early Christian converts were understood to be fish, while the apostles were designated as "fishers of men" who believe in him.[427] Here, the fish are contained in the mandala and the large fish, born by the Mother, potentially her sacred servants in life.

As students of depth psychology, we are all fisher people (of the unconscious) like Christ's early disciples. Fish represent a complex of energy and value for which the conscious ego in its askesis is fishing. Related to the fish is the fishes' eye, or *scintillae*, the alchemist's sparks of consciousness.428 Like the eye of God, the fishes' eyes appear to be open even in the depths of the sea. They are, therefore, an apt representation of the light of consciousness and intelligence in nature, and particles of light in matter. By comparison, revelation from above represents universal truths,but they do not help the individual in his or her personal struggle for consciousness in life. Centers of intelligence in the unconscious illuminate one's struggles in the ignorance, "where the darkness comprehendeth it not."[429]

The "eye" mandala on the tail is also relevant. In fact,

many fish have a camouflage eye on their tail to confuse and protect them against predators. The mandala on the fish's tail offers somewhat the same kind of protection,a protection through the Self and consciousness, as order is brought into the inferior function.

The background for the whole painting is deep blue-black with wavy golden lines, which suggests the cosmic background of the image: reflecting the traditional idea that the individual psyche is a microcosm.[430] In addition to the wavy lines, this image also has a series of sixteen dots that form a circle, four of each of the colors found on the inner circle on one half and black on the other. It is interesting to compare this image with the findings of contemporary physics, where the nature (particles) of subatomic matter is sometimes seen as waves and at other times as dots.[431]

The gold color of the wavy lines relates them to the golden fish, whereas the colored dots relate them to the different functions of consciousness along with the shadow side of each of the functions. Together they represent background and foreground, potential reality (waves) and actual reality (dots). As the lines have abasically horizontal thrust, as does the fishes' direction, the image is concerned mainly with life as expressed through the individuating ego in the world.

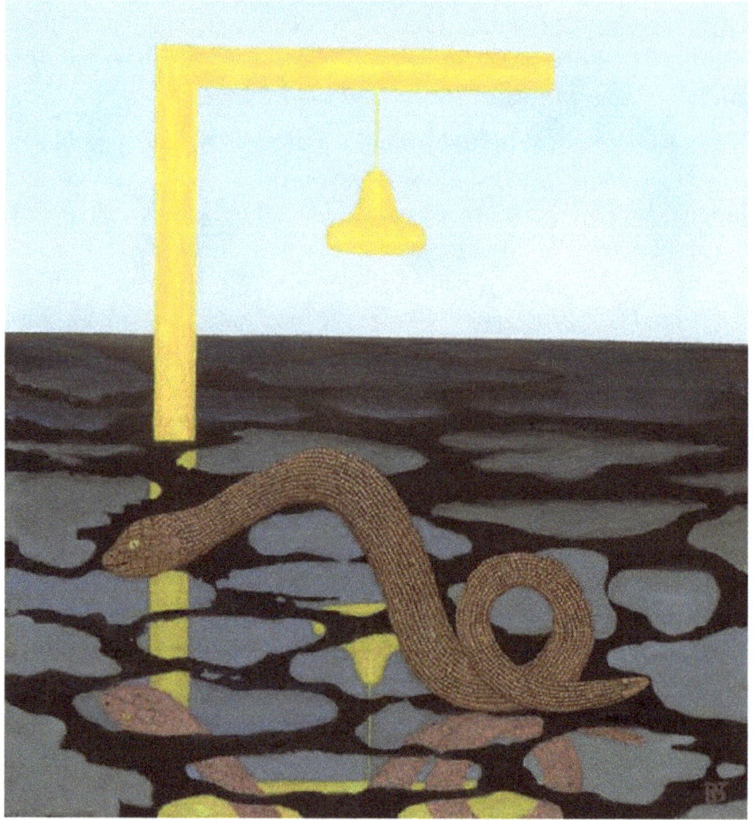

In this image, a serpent moves toward the left on a muddy earth with puddles of water. Behind the snake, there is a right angle or two-sided square with a pear-shaped plumb and line hanging from the center of the horizontal axis. There is reflection in the puddles. Each of these aspects of the painting warrants amplification.

Mud is the result of the mingling of earth and water and indicates what the alchemists called the *solutio*.[432] A union of two elements produces a third, which is, psychologically, new consciousness. The Gnostic quest to liberate spirit from matter is also relevant.[433] Mud, therefore, suggests entering the collective unconscious to find new life.

The snake is a complex symbol, sometimes representing forces of good and at other times of evil.[434] Various traditions depict it as allegory for both the devil and Christ. At times, it is understood to represent the watery magical power of the Earth Mother, symbolizing wisdom. The oracle of Delphi in ancient Greece kept a snake.[435] Representing the dark chthonic world of instinct, it is associated with the temptation of Adam and Eve against God's will. Yet the serpent promises them that by eating of the fruit from the tree of knowledge, "your eyes will be opened, and you will be like gods, knowing good and evil."[436]

In one Gnostic tractate, the serpent is depicted as being both wild beast and instructor.[437] Based on John 3:14, the Gnostics conceive of Christ as Logos and the healing serpent, while St. John himself is associated with the symbol of a serpent standing in a chalice also representing the Logos.[438] Asclepius, the "god of Doctors" in ancient Greece has a snake as his familiar.[439] He, in fact, has many similar attributes to Christ. In northern (Scandinavian) mythology, the hero is depicted as having snake's eyes, while in Greek mythology, the soul of the hero becomes a snake.[440]

These projections onto the snake are, in part, due to its distance and alienation from human consciousness, like God, and, in part, due to its ability to regenerate a new skin after casting off the old one. Due to this latter quality, the serpent has taken on the symbolic meaning of rejuvenation or regeneration.[441] Accordingly, some Christians consider it to be an allegory for St. Paul's "putting on the new man."[442]

In this painting, the tail is firmly situated on the muddy earth, forming a circle. The tail in a circle symbolizes wholeness and the necessary protection of consciousness as well as, in this case, rootedness on the earth. The reddish-brown snake symbolizes Eros. It is phallic, penetrating and masculine on the outside and feminine on the inside. This suggests that one must be open and receptive to life in order to truly give. The serpent way depicted here is directed mainly in the horizontal, that is. It leads one into life, although in a fashion that one would never choose with one's conscious intelligence. The serpent path is beyond dogma and the accepted structures and conventions of contemporary civilization. Without the protection of consciousness, however, following this path can lead into unconsciousness.

To follow the serpent gives consciousness and knowledge through life experience. This does not mean a blindly instinctive and sensual life, but it does mean going into areas of life that otherwise might be considered taboo. The reflections in the puddle add to this meaning. Following this path means going through conflict and at times experiencing chaos, in order to become more aware of the tension of opposites in one's nature. Becoming conscious of Eros allows one to differentiate these opposites.

The right angle or two-sided square is a symbol dear to the masons and had symbolic significance in ancient Egypt and elsewhere.[443] It partakes of the general meaning of a square and the number four (4) and has to do with limits and concrete materialization. In Egypt, many of the gods and goddesses are depicted seated on a two-sided square.[444] It is one of the symbols for the "great" god *Ptah* and means "builder."[445]

Ptah is the greatest of the old gods of Memphis (Egypt). He is a smelter caster, a sculptor, a master architect, and designer of everything that exists in the world.[446] The supplicants address Ptah by saying, "Thy feet are upon the earth."[447] Ptah tells the deserving deceased, "you have stablished your house firmly."[448] Hence the right angle is associated with being firmly planted on the earth. The worshippers also say of Ptah, "Thou makes the earth to bring forth fruit, and gods and men have abundance."[449] By being firmly established on the earth, one is effective and productive, not simply living in a spiritual or intellectual world of abstractions.

At the center of the horizontal axis a pear-shaped weight or plumb hangs from a plumb line. It is a symbol held sacred by the masons.[450] The plumb line is used to raise perpendiculars, putting the emphasis in height and depth. As it is located at the midpoint of the horizontal axis, it also suggests balance and right, measure, justice. Along with the vertical axis of the right angle, it suggests the aspiration for self-knowledge, influx from the spirit,and self-transcendence. Both the pear-shaped plumb and the two-sided square are "feminine" in form.

They are, however, masculine on the inside, as indicated by the golden-yellow color, signifying illumination. Thus, the two-sided square and plumb and plumb line together symbolizes Logos, the spirit of civilization, and the spirit of the times. They also represent the creation of forms where life can expand and make itself secure.

Overall, the image depicted here suggests both Logos and

Eros—that is, spirit, order, civilization and self-transcendence, as well as desire, which leads toward self-knowledge through conflict and opposition, that is by becoming aware of the opposites in the psyche. It is a symbol of consciousness-life. The path requires both community and solitude, in both places where Eros and Logos can be found. But life becomes reversed: one finds creative imagination and abundance in solitude, while in community, one seeks abstinence.

Violet Woman: Impressionism

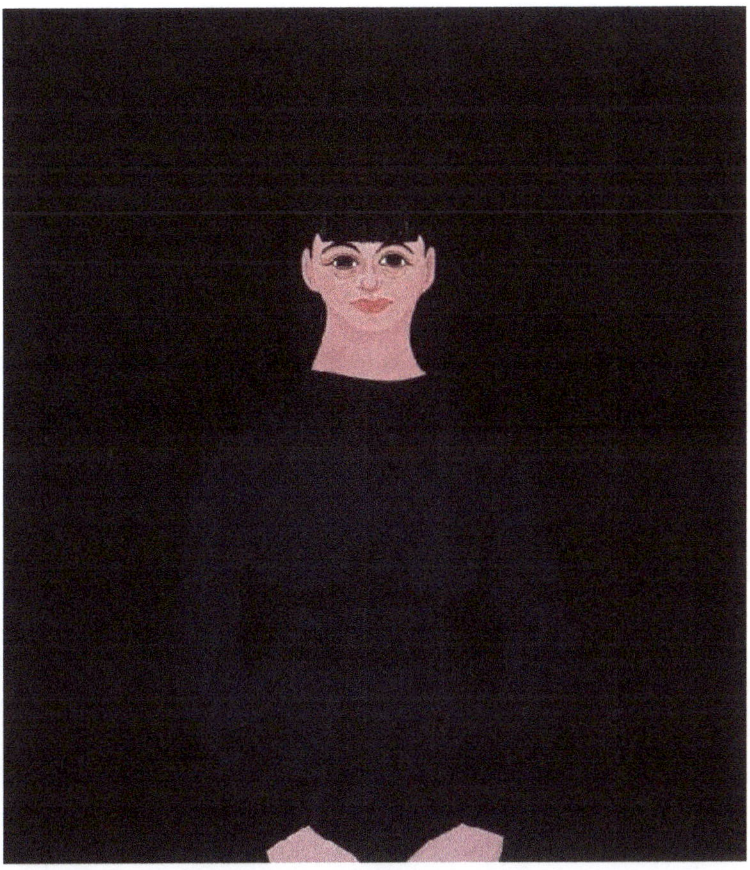

There are two things that immediately strike one about this image: (a) that it is done in the impressionistic style and (b) that a violet or purple hue permeates most of the painting. The woman symbolizes an aspect at the anima who, when internalized, for a man is the mediatrix to the unconscious.[451] The area of the unconscious she reflects is suggested by the style of the painting, the color, especially the dominant color, and the general appearance of the woman. The anima or the archetype of life itself is "She who must be obeyed" an expression taken from the novels of Rider Haggard.[452] Should the Anima not be obeyed, violence is done to one's own nature and objectively to women as well.

Impressionism as an art style flourished in the late 1800s, especiallyin France.[453] In essence, the impressionistic artist attempts to be faithful to subjective impressions rather than preconceived forms and colors that, in fact, correspond little to retinal reality.[454] They consider light and color, and not form, to be the most important visual reality and depict the image in a diffused subjective manner.[455] Such a way of seeing the world seems to relate to the diffused awareness of what Erich Neumann refers to as the matriarchal consciousness.[456] There seems to be a decided emphasis on the brain's right cerebral hemisphere where intuition and sensation are located,as well as introversion and the synthesizing mind.[457]

The impressionistic artist attempts to capture the subjective atmosphere and mood or impressions that are discrete and transitory like the Buddhist notion of *samsara*.[458] Impressionism, therefore, suggests a subjective turn,an introversion and an abstraction from so-called extroverted "reality." The rational choice of color and attempt to depict the mood of the moment indicates the predominance of the feeling function, the ability to move into the "atmosphere" of the moment the intuition, and fidelity to the actual sense perceptions, sensation. Given the diffused integrative vision of the impressionistic artist, Eros also appears to play a role.

Besides the emphasis on the evaluative feeling function, the left brain seems to be devalued. Its analytical, Cartesian intellect plays little or no role as perspective is virtually nonexistent.[459] The image of the woman is the locus of perception and form itself dissolves into the background.

In this painting, the color purple or violet dominates. Both these colors have a profound spiritual significance. In one alchemical treatise, the "Son of the wise "is clothed in red and purple.[460] Joachim of Flora sees himself as a bridegroom clothed in a purple garment at the last judgment.[461] The alchemist Khunrath associates Venus with the color green, which changes into an intense purple, at which time the philosophical tree blossoms.[462]

The pre-Celtic god of the Alder tree and god of healing, Bran, was reputed to have worn royal purple.[463] In the Kabala of Jewish mysticism, the color purple relates to an aspect of the Shekina hand, the Divine presence.[464] On being initiated, the Roman vestal virgins were given a headdress bordered with purple.[465] Purple is known as the royal color and is worn by kings and queens.[466] Astrologically, it is the color of Sagittarius, which is sided by Jupiter or Zeus.[467] Esoteric groups see violet as the color of freedom and spiritual transformation, and purple as the desire to serve God and the power of peace.[468] Jung chooses ultra violet to depict the color of the spiritual pole of the archetype and red as the instinctual pole.[469] Violet is made up of red and blue, suggesting the true spiritual pole of the archetype has formative power. It is a marriage of instinct, often expressed by the color red, and spirit, which on its own is usually depicted as blue.

The woman appears open and sensitive. Her brown eyes suggest instinct and earth, her gray sweater, the urge to concretize her feelings, that is to be aware of them in concrete experiences of life, and her blue skirt, a spiritual standpoint.[470] Her gray hair falls straight down in front, indicating a need for a descent to a lower center of awareness.

Overall then, the symbolic stress of this image is to take one away from the extroverted mode into a more subjective and introverted way of intuition, sensing and evaluating the moment, a moment that the artist is connected to in Eros. It also suggests a spiritually transformative influence that requires a descent to a lower level in the psyche. Both extroversion and the analytical cartesian mind are devalued. The world takes on something of a "relative reality" in the Buddhist sense. This image, therefore, compensates for an ego too much attached to the extroverted world of samsara and relating to the world in a too conventional manner.

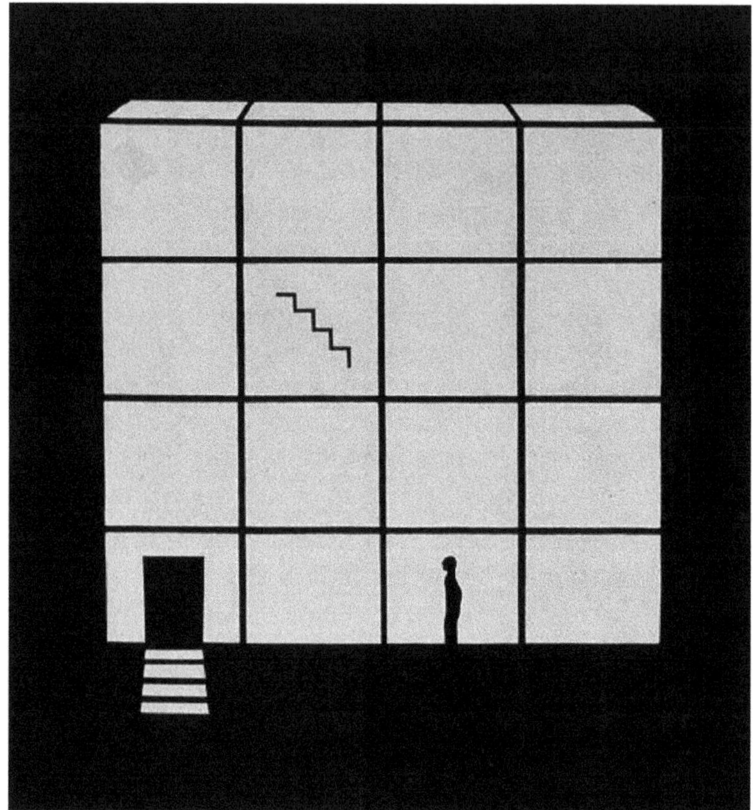

This image consists of night, with a square of white light, consisting of sixteen (16) independent cubes of white light. Within the square, there is a black staircase and a black man, while a black-and-white staircase leads to a black door where one enters the white square. In addition, there is a splash of turquoise on the upper left corner of the square.

A square has the same significance as the number four (4), a feminine number that means manifestation, the earth, truth-consciousness, and wholeness.[471] In *Kundalini yoga*, the physical chakra, the *muladhara*, has four petals and is the foundation for the growth of the "mother flame," according to Western occult literature.[472] The symbolic color of this chakra is white. The white light, according to Sri Aurobindo, is the "light of the Mother (the Divine consciousness)."[473] It contains all other colors and is the source from which they can manifest. White is pure consciousness, from which, together with force, all life grows.

White is purity and wholeness,the power of Divine truth.

With the white light, one becomes conscious of the black man. Egyptian mythology depicts the inhabitants of the netherworld as black.[474] In Rome,they were also depicted as black and called *inferi*, and *umbrae*, referring to shadow figures.[475] According to Plato, dream images are like shadows as dark patches against light and lead one to a reversal of the ordinary view of life.[476] In Lucian's dialogues, in the descent into Hades, the dead are prosecuted by their own shadows, which makes life in the " upperworld" seem "as if it had been a dream."[477] A relationship with the black shadow means connection with "death", that is anon-ego related reality. It implies consciousness of greater depth in life.

There are two sets of stairs, one inside the cube that is black, and one that is black and white that allows entry into the cube via a black door. Various staircases and ladders often appear in dream material concerning "death."[478] von Franz suggests that this may point to a gradual connection between body matter and psyche.479 This interpretive amplification appears to agree with my previous discussion on the white cube and black men. There is a connection between the black staircase and the black man. These staircases lead one down into the netherworld and soul essence, the home of the black man. The staircase has four (4) levels, each making a right angle, numerologically, suggesting its connection with the material world and concrete realization.[480]

The other staircase also has four steps, again suggesting a connection with the material world. Black and white indicate the widest duality. It suggests the *Tai Chi*, the Chinese sign of the two fishes, one black with a white spot and one white with a black spot. One enters the cube by climbing these steps of duality, consciousness and depth. The black door in the white cube is like the black center in the white fish and indicates depths. One climbs by the staircase of duality, and by going through the darkness and depth of the psyche, one enters the white light of the Mother consciousness.

As there are sixteen (16) sets of cubes, this number is also significant. The number sixteen (16) is formed by multiplying four (4) times four (4). It consequently carries a similar, although higher power, of the number four (4), which refers to truth-consciousness, and connection with material reality. In the words of Sri Aurobindo, "We shall see that what exists is not world at all but simply this infinity of spirit in which move the mighty cosmic harmonics of its own images of self-conscious becoming."[481] With full realization of the qualitative number four (4), this understanding becomes conscious and the heavens are brought down to earth.

There is, in addition, an influence represented by the color turquoise on the top left-hand corner of the cube. The ancient Egyptians considered it to be sacred to Isis and Osiris, while it is held sacred to love goddesses who unite through desire.[482] Many North American Indians and Buddhists hold turquoise to be sacred and of high value.[483] The Apaches believe that turquoise can be found at the end of the rainbow.[484] In a Navaho myth, the ancestors of the hero see the Sky Father descending and the Earth Mother rising to meet him.[485] Where they unite on the top of the mountain, a small turquoise figure is discovered.

These amplifications indicate that the color turquoise reconciles and transforms opposite principles. The green of life and personality is mixed with the blue sky of spirit, a sacred *coniunctio*, leading to the transformation of both spirit and life. As the dab of turquoise is on the left-hand side of the cube, it indicates the transformative influence is still somewhat unconscious. Yet it also indicates that with the white cube as foundation and a corresponding deepening of consciousness of the psyche,the result can be a transformative influence in life.

Soulbird

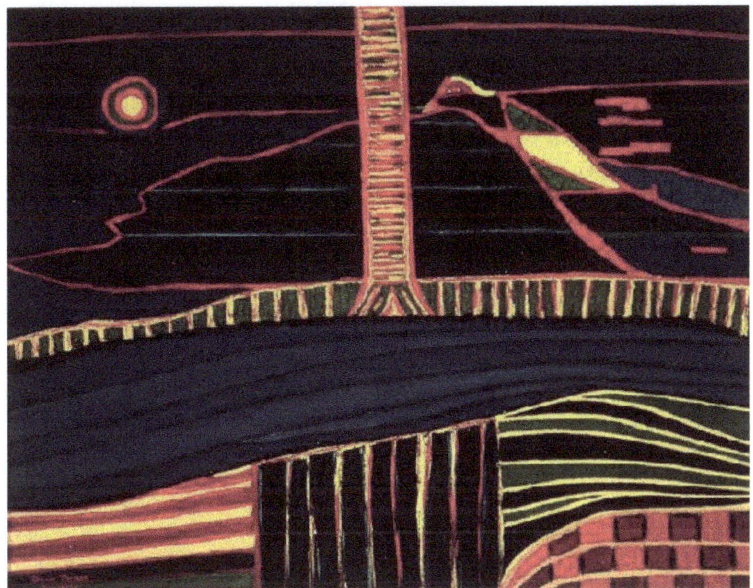

This image is a picture of one of the few paintings of mine that is done in the extroverted mode. The image, with its bright colors, captures an emotional explosion in the sense that expressionistic art does. In this case, the emotional state of mind was constellated due to an outside event, essentially pleasurable but laden with unconscious conflict. The many vertical and horizontal lines indicate that the tension is essentially due to a confrontation between the (vertical) spiritual dimension and the (horizontal) involvement with life. Painting this emotional state helps to objectify it and clarify it to consciousness.

As creatures of the air, birds represent thoughts. Given the bright colors depicted here, they represent thoughts laden with emotions and feelings. As it is night, a deeper, unknown part of the psyche has been constellated. Both the flight of the bird toward the left and the flow of the river in the same direction suggest that the unconscious is currently being stirred up.[486]

The turquoise color of the river suggests the spiritually transformative nature of the experience. Turquoise was a color of the highest value for the ancient Egyptians, as it is by many North American Indians.[487] The turquoise stone is sacred to Isis and Osiris, the Lady and God of the turquoise.[488] It represents the union of male and female, spirit and life.

The central tree pole indicates a vertical movement a connection between the earth, the river of life, and the heavens. The tree has been linked with several concepts, including that of being the midpoint or axis around which everything turns, the symbolic center.[489] It symbolizes the mother from which all life is born and represents containment, fertility, and rebirth. The tree is also symbolic of the phallic, the masculine principle of procreation.[490] Erich Neumann writes about a legendary light tree of the night sky, the soul tree of resurrection through which every creature who dies enters eternity in the form of a star.[491] Jung shows how the philosophical tree of alchemy is directly related to all life process in general as well as the individuation opus.[492] According to Manichean doctrine, the pillar of glory is the perfect primordial man.[493] For the ancient Hebrews, the Lord is a pillar of guidance as fire by night and cloud by day.[494] In Egypt, the *djed* pillar is called the spine of the god Osiris, and it contains the sun, as Ra, which resurrects each morning.[495]

The implications of these amplifications are that the whole being is centrally involved in the situation that resulted in this image. Despite the conflict-ridden, emotion-laden situation, the image indicates the possibility of creatively emerging with new awareness. Life potentially does not just happen, but there can be a gain in consciousness by taking it seriously and not avoiding emotional conflict.

Soulscape

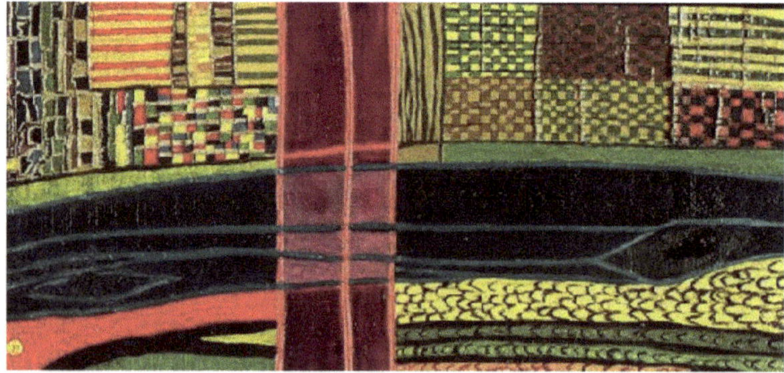

This is an image of a painting psychologically related to the previous soulbird image and a movement into a more introverted state of mind, a stepping back and abstraction from the emotion-laden experience. As the painting rests horizontally, the main thrust continues to be on the involvement in life. The emphasis on detail, which include lines and squares, gives evidence of the psyche's intense efforts to put order into its emotional condition.

The central axis on the horizontal arm is blue, the color of the spirit and Logos, while the central axis on the vertical arm is red, the color of Eros and the color that Jung attributes to the instinctual pole of the archetype of relatedness.[496] The suggestion in this image is that Logos or meaning is discovered in life experience, and that there is Eros and instinctual relatedness to be found in the vertical dimension, that is in the heights and depths of the psyche. The central square is violet, the royal transformative color, a result of the synthesis of red and blue, Logos and Eros.[497] The square shape suggests an insistence on realizing this transformative effect in life which comes through both the emotional experience itself and the psyche's reflections upon itself.[498]

The Man in the Grey Flannel Suit Hanging Loose

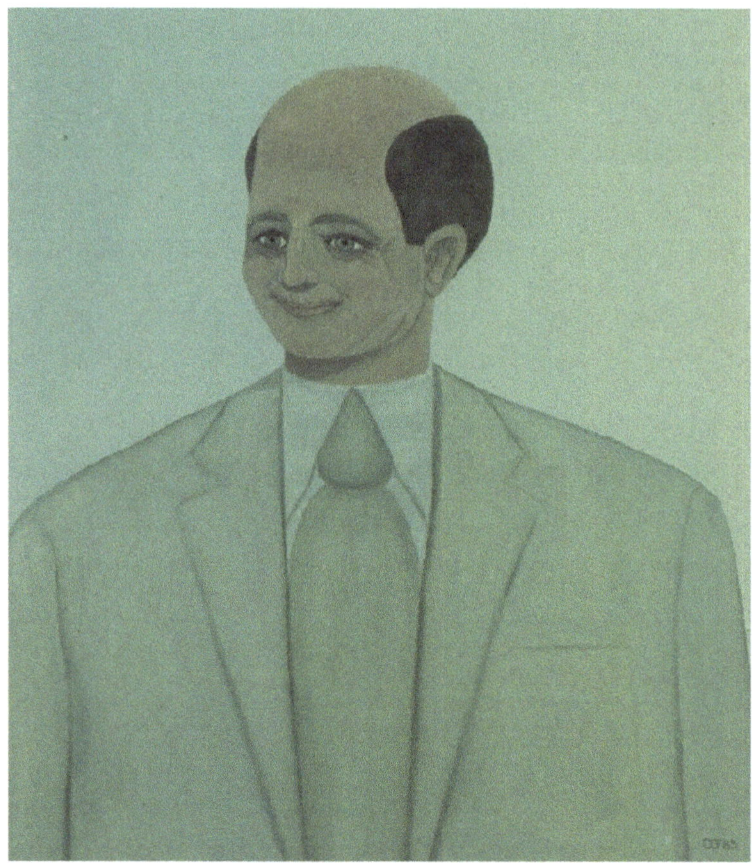

The man in the gray flannel suit represents the businessman. The all permeating gray, which include the color of his eyes, his suit, his tie, and his skin hue, point to the prime importance of this color and to the psychological meaning of this image. Gray is the color of concrete, which suggests hard, concrete reality.

Athena, a goddess with gray eyes, was given birth through parthenogenesis by Zeus, jumping out of his head fully armed and fully clothed. The head in alchemy relates to the arcane substance, suggesting that Athena's birth-womb is the seat of *Logos* and spiritual meaning.[499] She is known to be clear sighted and to give wise and useful counsel.[500] She is the goddess who inspires the useful crafts, whether they be domestic, political or military.[501] During the Trojan War, she counselled the winning Achaeans (Greeks) on strategy and tactics. She is associated with the hero Odysseus, whom she aids and guides on his return home.[502] She is, in fact,helpful to many hero figures and the heroic nature in all of us. These amplifications are suggestive of the appropriateness of the color gray to symbolize the business man, the arch "realist," who today conducts his business with astute strategy and tactics, not unlike his military brothers.

This image of a relaxed businessman is, in many ways, compensatory to the way most, if not all, business is run today. Contemporary business,which is increasingly of an international nature, is extremely competitive. At best, conduct is based on a pragmatic ethic, with very little philosophic or psychologically redeeming underpinnings. In contrast to this image of a relaxed individual is the reality of the constant drive for increased productivity and profits. This is largely behind the increasing stress found at work and does not encourage the businessman to "hang loose" as portrayed here.

Science, technology, and business represent the central focus in our present culture. We have all been party to the creation of an exceedingly complex yet exceptionally one-sided civilization. The present system of civilization has developed to the point of surpassing humankind's limited understanding and moral capacity. It serves mainly to bolster the appetites and cajole the inflated ego. Ethics today needs to be more conscious than ever due to the enormous long-term impact of today's decision-making.

Given these considerations, it is very difficult to see where the "man in the grey flannel suit hanging loose" fits in today's business world. Once again, one can be reminded that any great transformation begins with the individual. Institutions (civilization) change when humankind changes. The individual businessperson can only start from where he or she is on the path of the individuation process. One should not be blinded to the narrowness of the business life, its essentially one-sided concerns, its conscious misuse of psychology and the arts, and its general drivenness. Business' generous philanthropic side, which is commendable, does little to alleviate the collective shadow of the business world. Individuation means deepening and broadening one's cultural horizons; it means sincerity and unity of purpose, something that the individuating businessperson must struggle with and reconcile to current business practices and demands, or eventually find his or her way out.

White Man Swimming in Green Water
And Waves with Brown and Blue

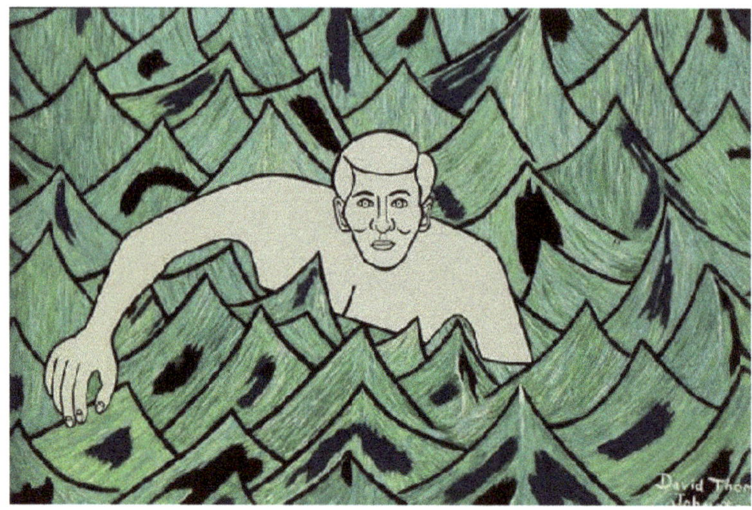

Swimming or entering a body of water psychologically means entering a new element—that is, it indicates the potential coming to birth of new awareness. It is equivalent to the alchemical "solution or baptism" and indicates cleansing and rejuvenation, death of ego and rebirth.[503] The act of swimming suggests expertise, that the psyche can make its way through and not be overwhelmed or drowned by the new contents from the unconscious. The individual is pure white, which suggests purity.[504] As white is the essence of color and reflects heat and all colors, it indicates openness and receptivity.[505] This does not mean passivity, as by swimming the figure is playing an active role. His rectangular shape suggests emphasis is on the horizontal—that is, on life.

The waves are principally green, which is the color of life, vegetation, hope, and healing.[506] (The waves carry in them an intense brown and an intense blue, brown being the color of the earth, representing the alchemical *coagulatio* and blue the spirit.)[507] The suggestion in this image is that the new attitude to life that is welling up from the unconscious comes with coolness and spiritual detachment and can be related to the ego through the instinctual earth. The waves emerge forcefully and pointedly, indicating a thrust from the unconscious toward consciousness. In physics, the wave function symbolizes potential being, which, when it collapses, becomes actual being. Not only consciousness is indicated in the image, but assimilation and realization in concrete reality.

The Mother of Alchemy

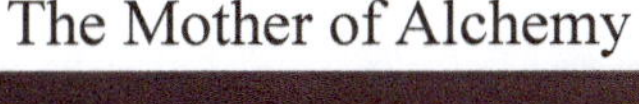

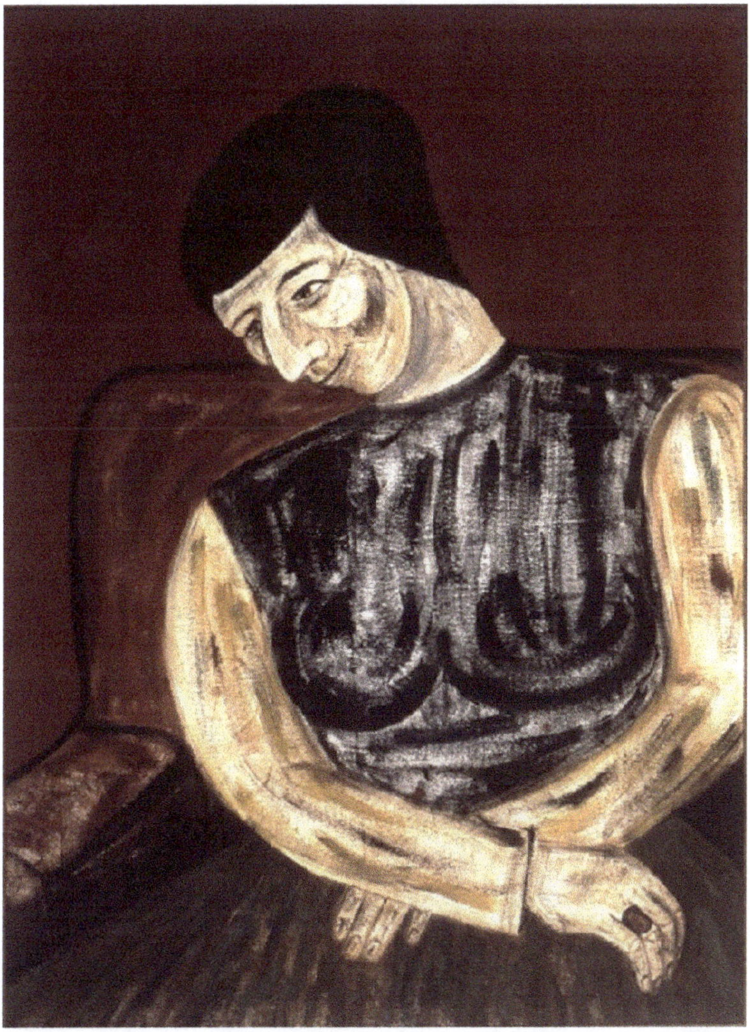

The woman in this image is seated in a brownish-red chair, and the background itself is Indian red. The chair or throne finds its origin as symbol of the all-containing earth mother.[508] There is direct connection between the woman and the chair she is sitting in. It represents her *asana*, her position of authority in the same way that a throne is representative of the royalty of the king and queen.[509] The reddish-brown color suggests Eros-fire in

121

the instinctual nature.[510] The background red links the figure to fire and Eros as well. The ring on her right finger has the word *athanor* inscribed on it, which is the name of the alchemical oven, where the fire of transformation is contained.[511] As a ring symbolizes relatedness, it indicates that the woman is related to the alchemical oven and what it symbolizes.[512] Since it is on her right hand, it suggests a conscious relationship on her part. This is corroborated by the fact that she is looking to her right, the viewer's left. Yet her ringed hand is lying on the right-hand side of the painting, her left. This suggests that movement into the unconscious will lead to more conscious understanding of the meaning of the alchemical furnace.

The mother of alchemy leads one to the secret of the transformative fire. Alchemical literature asserts that it is through fire and by means of many fires that the quintessence of gold or the philosophers stone can be extracted from the prima materia of unconscious life.[513] Heraclitus insists that the cosmos continually transforms itself back into life through fire, as life itself is an "everlasting fire."[514] In northern mythology, the Ragnarök, or twilight of the gods, concludes in a fire that leads to their transformation—that is, to the transformation of the way of apprehending and comprehending life and the instincts.[515]

In the Vedas of India, fire is "Priest of the call" and a "lord of the sacrifice," which as an agent of purification, "away the foes and things that hurt."[516] The Apocalypse of John sees this fire as purifying in addition to being punishment and leading to annihilation.[517] For the pure in heart,however, there is a new heaven and a new earth.[518] Mythologically, there is the fire of hell and the devil, a place of punishment, as well as the healing fire of the Holy Spirit.[519] The Old Testament uses the image of transpersonal fire to represent God's creative and destructive powers.[520] In the Hindu religion, the lord Shiva dances his dance of creation and dissolution in a circle of fire.[521] In one apocryphal saying, Jesus is reported to have said,"He who is near unto me, is near unto the fire"[522] For the alchemists, God is a coincidence of opposites and the mercurial fire, both hell fire and the "fire in which God himself burns in divine love.[523] In part II, *Purgatorio*, of *The Divine Comedy*, Dante must pass through a circle of fire in order to purify his senses so as to be able to enter the earthly paradise.[524]

In this image, the Mother of alchemy is bending down

indicating the need to allow psychic energy to flow downward. In addition to her downward gaze, her earthy appearance suggests where she is to be found. There is a need to descend to a lower center of the psyche, perhaps to the (belly) manipura chakra, the seat of the emotions.[525] Erich Neumann writes that hidden in the womb of the Great Mother is the fire, the dynamic force of life, fire as devouring, destructive, and transformative.[526]

Whenever one is involved in affects or strong emotions, one living in the manipura chakra.[527] Should one identify with the emotions and moods of manipura, one is simply the affect.[528] With a degree of objective consciousness, the fire of passion can be harnessed for spiritual transformation and the gain of wisdom. The mother of alchemy is wisdom,which is to be found, not in the celestial heavens of the intellect, but by conscious and objective experience of lower psychic centers.

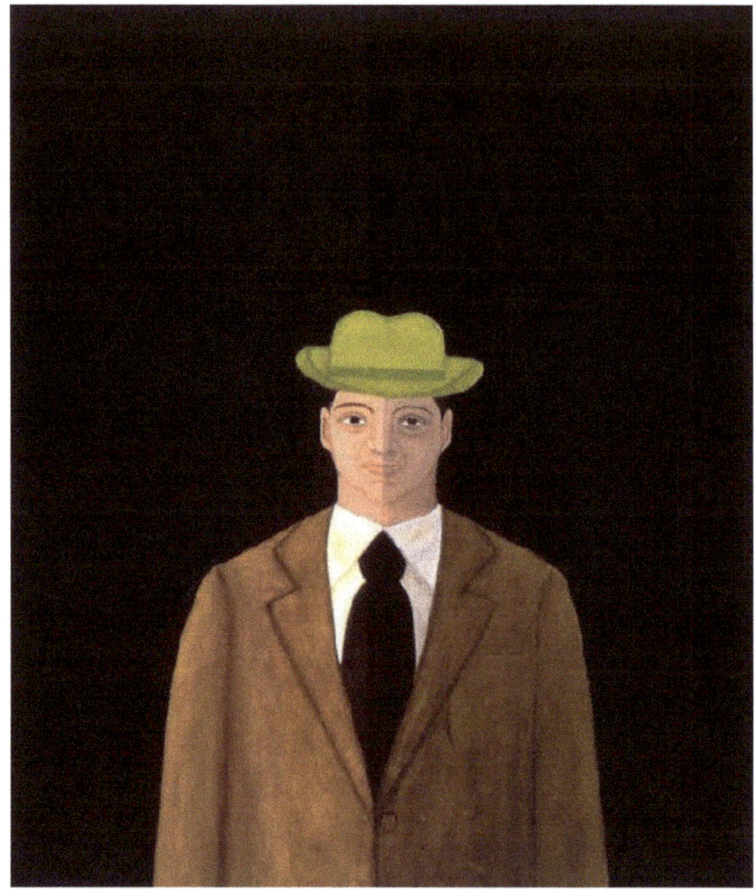

Man Wearing a Green Hat
Integration of Shadow

The two principal colors in this painting are brown and black, with brown dominating the figure and with a black and brown as the background. In addition, one side of the man appears darker than the other. Brown represents the earth and the alchemical <u>coagulatio</u>. This indicates that there is pressure for the psychic contents inherent and the image to be "grounded," that is related to the ego.[529] The dark side of the man indicates that the shadow side is also integrated in this figure. As he is wearing a suit, he seems to represent a business or administrative orientation, the suit being the conventional costume for administrative positions and the business world.

The man is also wearing a green hat. As the hat covers the

head, it signifies what goes on inside it.[530] It is at the summit of the individual and represents a point of view or a way of looking at things and ascribing meaning. Its shape, as well as its color, is significant. The symbolic significance of the color green is spiritual renewal, springtime, regeneration, growth, hope, healing and love.[531] Physiologically, green balances the blood pressure, as well as the distribution and supply of blood, and is helpful against insomnia, fatigue, and weariness.[532] The shape reminds one of the union of the male and female principles of Yoni and Lingam in Hindu philosophy and religion.[533] In a word, then, the green hat represents an attitude and approach that is able to reconcile a grounded shadow and light aspects of the personality, not only in administrative tasks or in the world of business, but in life in general.

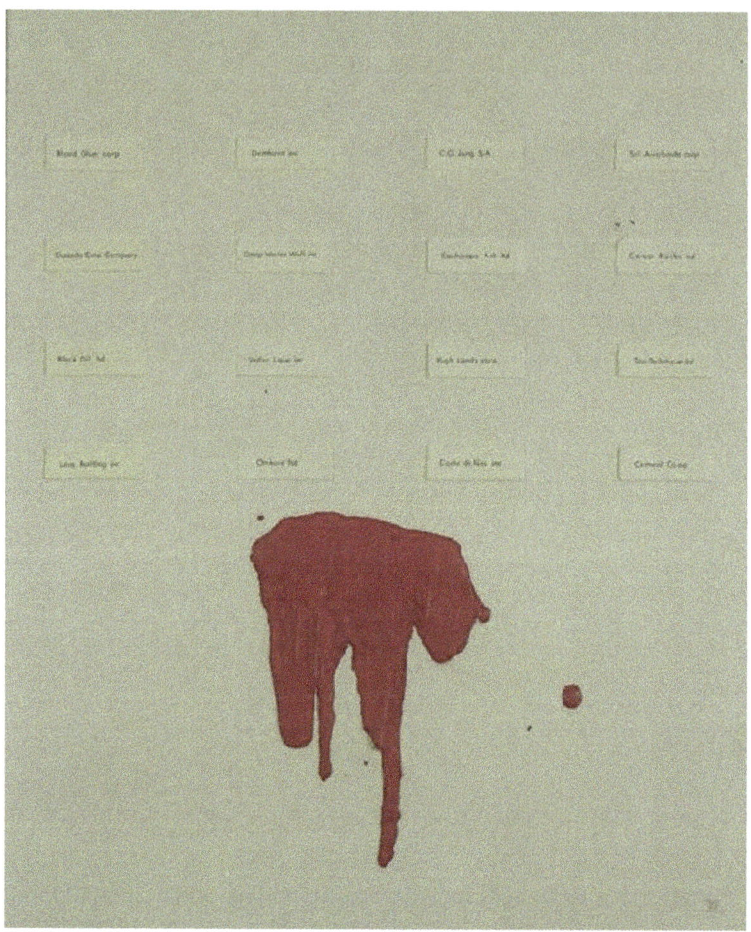

In this image, there are a series of rectangular blocks which are sixteen (16) in number, or four (4) × four (4). Numerologically, this series takes on the power of four (4), a "feminine" number that signifies materialization and karmic limits.[534] It is the power of material creation, giving one the tenacity and stubbornness to perform even onerous tasks. In addition, sixteen (16), reduces to seven (7), the number symbolizing individuation and completion. It represents the periodicity of all life, which unfolds in rhythmic cycles of seven.[535]

All these amplifications suggest the psychological need to bring one's spiritual ideals down to earth, to concretize them so they become a living reality. The concrete three-dimensional nature of the rectangular blocks reinforces this notion. The rectangular shape of the blocks also puts the emphasis on the horizontal nature of the movement.

According to Edinger, blood symbolism is equivalent to both fire and water, both the alchemical *calcinatio* and *solutio.*[536] *Solutio* dissolves ego rigidity and leads to becoming aware of one's dirt while *calcinatio,* a drying-out process psychologically consists of frustration of desire and cupidity.[537] Blood symbolizes living in the instincts, "living in primitive man, living "in nature as it always was."[538] It is the life force, the real seat of life. For this reason, in primitive societies, the male drank the blood of the enemy, particularly a courageous enemy, in order to gain his mana, his soul power.[539]

Living with the blood means living close to the instinctual earth.[540] It means living in Eros, the natural rhythm of life. Accordingly, one no longer feels "master of one's fate" but a helpless part of nature.[541] As the blood flows downward in this image, it suggests the need to descend, perhaps form an overly idealistic viewpoint as indicated by the printing on the blocks, to a more realistic one. Eros keeps one in touch with reality and does not permit fanciful or unrealistic notions, however sublime. But, says Jung, "If you surrender to the terror of the blood, you will discover it leads to development."[542] As blood flows upward as well as downward, living in the blood, meaning in the instincts eventually leads to an upward movement of the psyche that is instinctually related.[543]

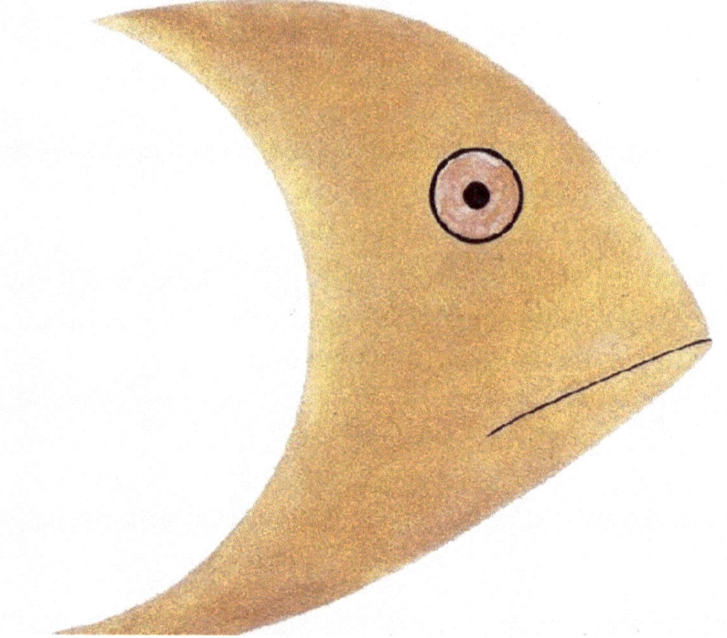

There are several dimensions to be taken into consideration in amplifying this simple-looking image. They are the golden color, the fish's eye, and the (right-directed) lunar shape. The fact that the image only consists of a fish head is also significant.

The fish has been a sacred symbol since time immemorial. Stone sculptures of fish goddesses have been found in both sea and farming areas inland, in old Europe, dating back to the early 6th millennium BCE.[544] Fish was eaten on Fridays at the feast of the mother goddesses as ritual worship of all moon goddesses of the waters and gods of the underworld.[545] In China, Kwai Yin, the Queen of Heaven, has a fish as an emblem.[546] In Judaism, the fish is considered to be the faithful in its true element, the waters of the Torah, and the old Jewish Passover takes place in the fish month of Adar.[547] The fish is the coena pura, the food of the blessed in paradise and symbolizes the heavenly banquet.[548] For this reason, the Jewish "chalice of benediction" is sometimes decorated with fish.[549]

For the ancient Celts, there is a "salmon of wisdom" and other fish believed to be immortal.[550] Beginning somewhere near Alexandria about 200 CE, Christ has been symbolized by a fish.[551]

He is called Ichthys, which *has* been taken to represent Iesous Christos, Theos Huios Soter, Jesus Christ, Son of God, Savior.[552] *Ichthys* is, in fact, Greek for *fish*.[553] Therefore, according to Jung, the fish is a symbol for the archetype of the redeemer.[554] Christ is both "fisher of men" par excellence, and the fish that is eaten during the sacrament of the Holy Eucharist.[555] Moreover, Christ appointed his disciples, beginning with Simon, Andrew, James, and John, to be fishers of men.[556] In Babylonia, Dannes, who legend depicts as having taught the art of writing, the sciences and crafts, the construction of cities, the observation of the stars, and the sowing and harvesting of grains and plants, was a fish-god.[557] In India, Manu (the Indian Noah) caught a small fish that later grew and foretold the future and helped to save him.[558] This fish is Vishnu in his fish avatar who, according to myth, dove into the flood and recaptured the Vedas, the original revealed scriptures and books of knowledge and wisdom, for the Indian Hindu, from the demons who stole them."[559] The god Varuna, lord of the waters, is also depicted as a golden fish.[560]

In some Jewish traditions the "great fish" is considered to be both the creation and the opposite of the highest God, which gradually split into Leviathan and Behemoth.[561] In Christianity, there is a splitting of the fish symbolism into the Christ and the antichrist.[562] This is depicted in the actual shape of the constellation of Pisces, where one fish is shown moving vertically, the other horizontally.[563]

Fish symbolism is therefore very rich, dating back to the Mother Goddess. Essentially it is a symbol of wisdom and knowledge. Psychologically, the fish—that is, wisdom or knowledge—is drawn from the deep waters or the depths of the unconscious and represents an "autonomous content." It is, says Jung, "a symbol of renewal and rebirth."[564] Like the eye of God, its eyes appear to never close as they are, in fact, covered by a transparent film. The alchemists speak of fishes' eyes and scintillae, soul sparks, which often appear as golden or silver.[565] They represent the intelligence of nature, consciousness in nature, the lumen naturae, the light of nature.[566] This light illuminates the darkness of the unconscious, with the answers one seeks that the rational ego does not possess.

The crescent moon shape relates this fish to the moon and such goddesses as Ishtar, Hecate, Demeter, Persephone, and others, representing either the light or dark sides of the moon.[567] Mary is often identified as the moon of the church.[568] As the moon reflects the light of the sun, it symbolizes the "higher" mind or Buddhi in Hindu thought. The receptive, spiritual mind reflects the sun of truth.

In this image, the color of the lunar fish-head is gold, the sun of the earth. Several goddesses have gold as one of their attributes, especially Aphrodite.[569] The moon shape, along with the color gold, therefore,suggests imagination, intuition, intelligence, wisdom, and Eros. The image represents the lumen naturae, the light of nature found in the depths of one's being, that is, in the instinctive entanglements and experiences of life.

According to the early alchemists, the golden head originally refers to the head of Osiris in Egypt, the divine son lover of Isis.[570] The ancient Greek alchemists considered themselves to be "Children of the Golden Head."[571] The alchemists considered the head to be the seat of thought and understanding, and the brain the seat of the spirit, with proximity to the rational soul possessing simplicitas, the ability to let things happen, action through nonaction.[572]

As the image consists of a fish's head, however, these meanings are still not conscious. As the fish is facing toward the right, psychologically, it is swimming into consciousness. It is a right-directed crescent moon, which is the symbol of the new moon, indicating new birth. These amplifications suggest that there is the possibility of a new and wiser way of understanding and reflecting on life and its myriad experiences.

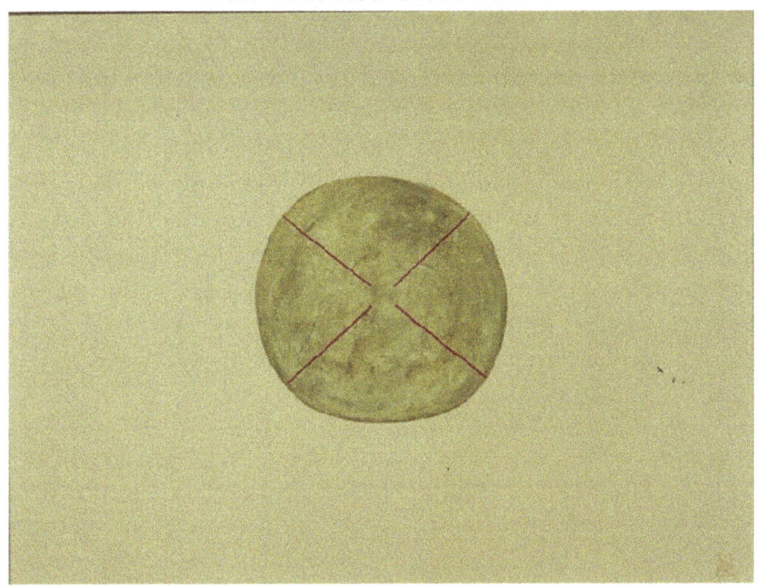

This image reminds one of a hot cross bun as well as the Christian host. The hot cross bun was originally associated with the goddess Eostre and the pre-Christian pagan Easter festival.[573] She was the goddess of the dawn for Anglo-Saxons, Germans, and Franks.[574] The Christian host has a similar significance in that it symbolizes the flesh of Christ, the light of the world. Eating the host is meant to be a ritual enactment of Christ's sacrificial act,which has many pagan precedents.[575] In Mithraism, the religious practitioner absorbed the "medicine of immortality," also a piece of bread imprinted with a cross.[576] By eating the host, one becomes impregnated with the "light of the sun," allowing for birth of the divine child within.[577]

The bun, with its circular shape and division into four (4) parts, is essentially a feminine symbol.[578] In keeping with the feminine nature of the image, in the dream in which I saw it, the painting was done by the well-known American artist, Georgia O'Keeffe. She symbolizes something like the anima representing the spiritualization of Eros and mediatrix to the creative word, the late classical classification of the third level of eroticism,where the fourth level refers to wisdom.[579]

The cross which divides the bun into four (4) parts takes in the significance of the number four (4). This number has the symbolic meaning of materialization, wholeness and living according to inner truth.[580] The brown background and color of the bun itself indicates a relationship of the bun to the earth, a result of the process of alchemical coagulatio, indicating that the meaning behind the symbol can be related to consciousness.[581] The cross saltire, which is the nature of the cross depicted on this image, means "tumbling cross" and indicates the release of creative energy.[582] The color of the cross, red, relates to the alchemical rubedo or "redness of life,", and indicates an animated psyche and Eros-related integration into consciousness.[583] In summary, this simple image symbolizes ego-sacrifice and spiritualized Eros-related creative energy, which can potentially be connected to the ego and integrated into consciousness.

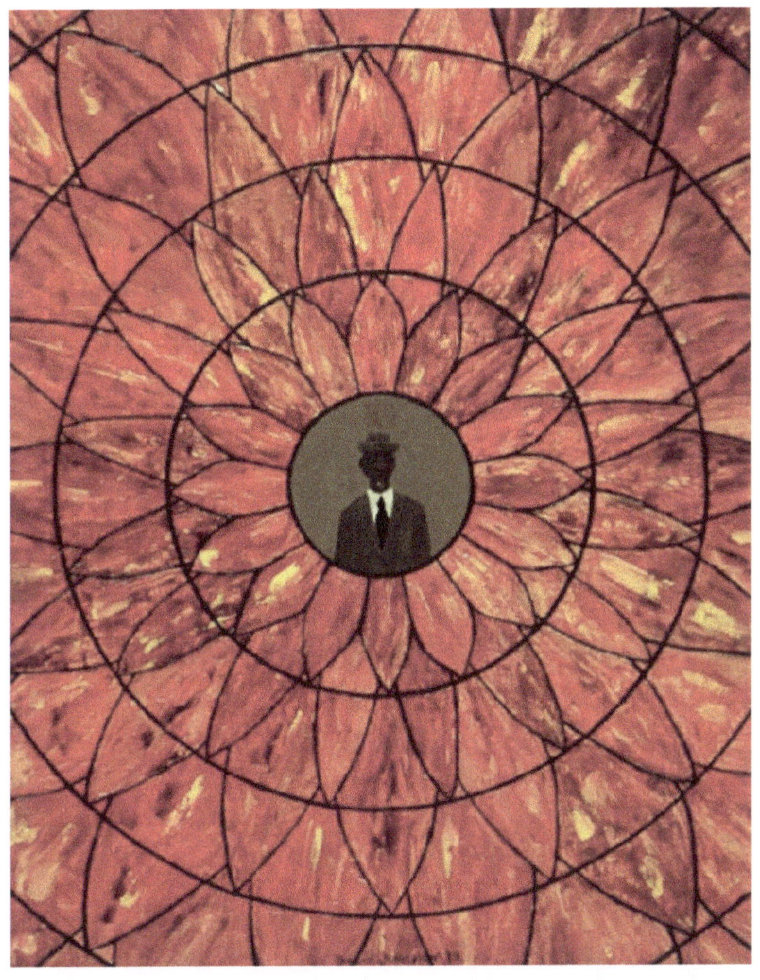

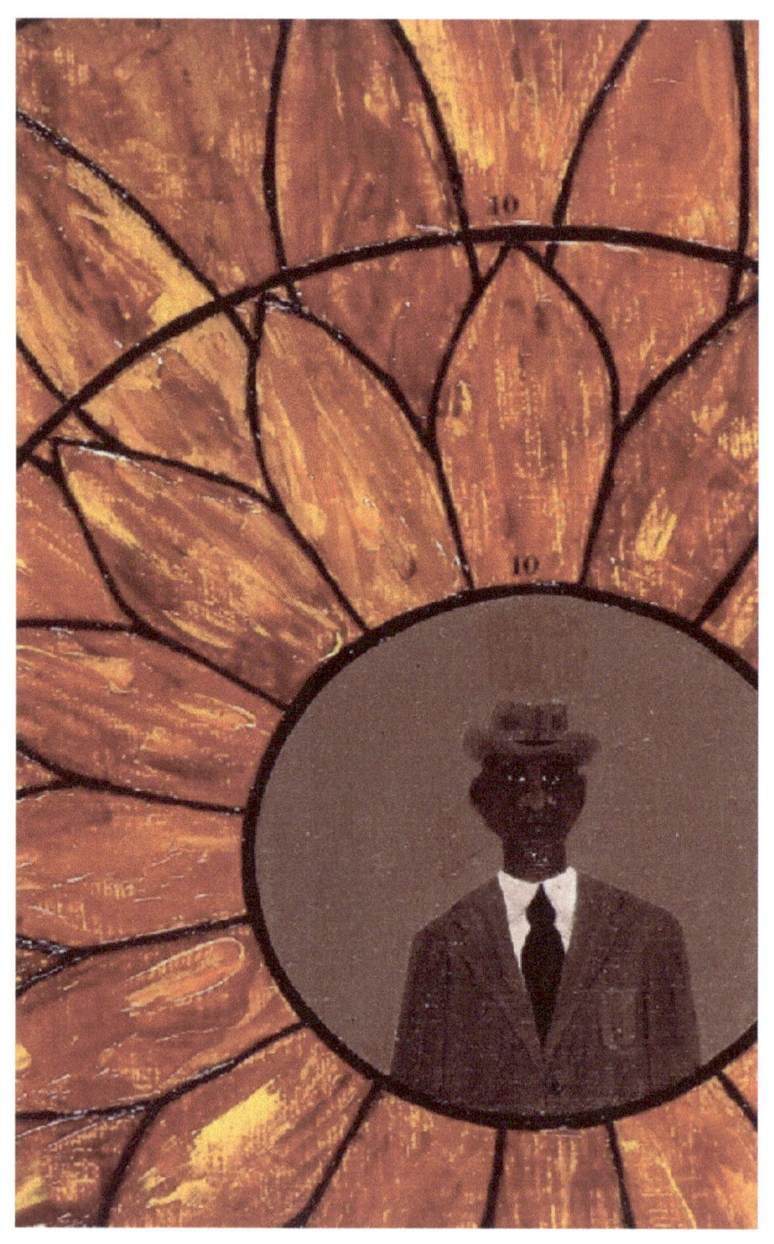

There are several points to be noted about this mandala depicted here. To begin with, the word *mandala* means "circle," although what are referred to as mandalas today take other forms as well as the circle.[584] Second, there is a brown man wearing brown clothes in a brown center. Third, the mandala is, in fact, a flower, reddish brown in color, with a yellow base or background. Finally, the number ten (10) is attributed to each of the circles that *appear* to expand in a wave-like fashion.

A genuine self-generated mandala establishes order during periods of chaos that initially comes with it. It is a symbol of the Self, of unity and wholeness and of eternal recreation.[585] With its flower-like pattern and expanding series of circles, this mandala is reminiscent of many images from the Indian Tantric tradition.[586] The different chakras and centers of consciousness of Kundalini or Tantric Yoga are depicted as flowers with different numbers of petals depending upon the chakra symbolized.[587] The ever-expanding circles suggest the ancient image of universal creation through the vibrational pattern of sound waves.[588] It is "the word" emanating from the center and, as such, means directly influencing life. The number ten (10) is esoterically the perfect number, and according to St. Martin, it is the number of divinity.[589] It represents totality, completeness, and God in manifestation.[590]

The center of the mandala in the occidental world has traditionally been reserved for Christ and sometimes Mary.[591] Mandalas produced in other cultures generally have a center with some spiritual significance, be it a symbol, or empty.[592] The mandala itself represents "a psychic center of the personality not to be identified with the ego."[593] The innermost point represents the center.

The brown man wears a brown hat shaped somewhat like the Yoni-Lingam symbol found in the center of Hindu temples.[594] This symbol indicates universal creation through the union of the male and female principles.[595] The hat is the crown or summit of one's being and signifies what goes on inside it, which is suggested by both its color and its shape.[596] The brown man in the brown center wearing a brown hat is the color of the earth, the physical body, and the instincts.

The reddish-brown petals of the flower over a yellow base point to Eros and instinct. Jung attributes red to the instinctual pole of the archetype.[597] The yellow ground suggests illumination and intelligence behind and supporting the instincts.[598]

The transparent container-like frame suggests four things: the first being spiritualization. On the back of the container, the numbers from zero (0) to ten (10) are inscribed. Esoterically numbers are considered to symbolize the ten (10) supreme principles behind the *created* universe.[599] According to Jung and Marie-Louise von Franz, natural numbers are the most fundamental symbol of the archetype.[600] Zero (0) to ten (10) represent all the basic numbers, as going beyond ten (10), one begins another series of numbers according to the law of the osophic reduction.[601] Theodor Abt reasons they have similar meanings to numbers in the first series of numbers, with elevated or more differentiated significance.[602] The fact that these numbers are inscribed on the back and not the front suggests that their significance is still unconscious to the ego. The second idea that is suggested is that the plexiglass container creates a distancing from the ego, without which this intuitive experience could have been too overwhelming. A third related concept is that of detachment, which allows for some assimilation. And, fourthly, as there is a container, there is the possibility of containing something of this intuitive experience in consciousness.

Turquoise Waves: Transformation

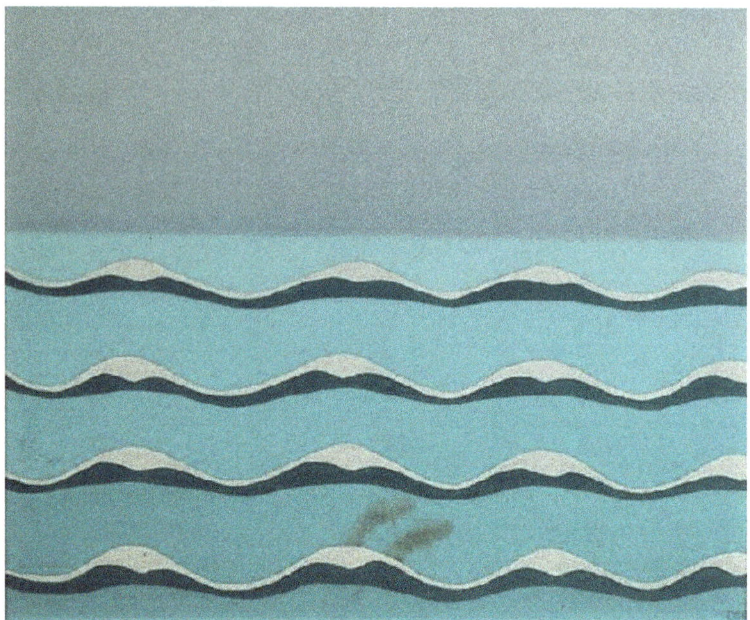

This image simply consists of white capped turquoise waves that rhythmically advance toward the viewer, along with two gray fish. This rhythmic movement suggests a universal force that does not belong to the ego but comes from the collective unconscious. It also implies that the nature of the psyche is rhythmic, with periods of systole and periods of diastole, contraction and expansion. Sexuality, for instance, has a natural rhythm. Whether one lives sexually out or not, one ought to become aware of this rhythm. This means neither repressing sexual feelings nor expressing them in a manic fashion. Only when one becomes aware of this rhythm can one detach from sexuality.

Water represents the unconscious as the mother of consciousness, the origins of new consciousness and new life. The color turquoise gives one an inkling of what that influence might be. It is sacred to the love goddess, she who incites desire not only between humans, but everywhere, including at the cosmic level between heaven and earth.[603]

The two fish symbolize intelligent new content from the unconscious. Two allows for differentiation and refers to the fact that this content is just now becoming conscious. The new content is related to the turquoise water and its rhythmic nature.

One version of the story of the birth of the love goddess, Aphrodite, has her being born from the seafoam.[604] The sperm of the castrated sky god, Ouranos inseminates the water or becomes the sea foam that bears Aphrodite. As the legend has it, she is born of the sea-tossed genitals of Ouranos, around which gather the sea foam.[605] In this image, the white caps could represent the inseminating spirit.

For the ancient Egyptians, turquoise was held to be sacred to Isis and her son lover, Osiris.[606] Many native north Americans consider turquoise to be sacred, representing the marriage of Earth and heaven.[607] In a Navaho myth, this union results in the formation of a small turquoise figure.[608] Another native Indian legend attributes the color of the blue sky to the reflection of a turquoise mountain off a golden spirit eagle.[609] Turquoise consists of the blue (spirit) and green (life of the earth), each of which is transformed in the sacred union, giving birth to turquoise. The desire for love and sex or of spirit for life, in the broadest sense, opens life to a transformative influence.

This transformative influence comes from the collective unconscious and not the ego. This does not mean that the ego has no role to play, but with conscious participation in the individuation process, it becomes relativized to the Self. The ego's primary role increasingly becomes one of assimilating the influences from the Self which results in its transformation. In as much as the psyche is recalcitrant, the ego seems to have an educational role as well.

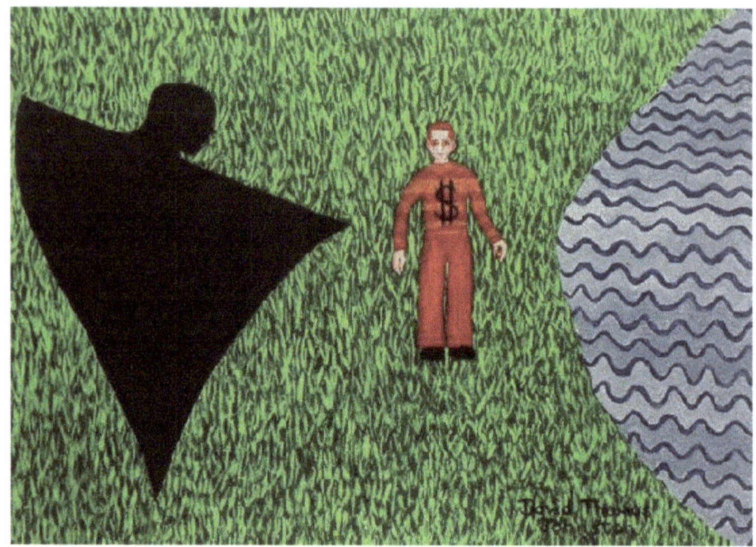

"Money," writes Sri Aurobindo, "is the visible sign of a universal force"and "is indispensable to the fullness of the outer life."[610] "Money," observes Norman Brown, "is the soul of the world."[611] It allows for the possibility of realizing the imagination in life. However, as Hillman notes, money, as archetype, has been used and interpreted in opposing spiritual and materialistic ways.[612] Common observation suggests that along with sex and power, nothing corrupts and drives the ego like money. Sri Aurobindo observes that it is presently normally used for egotistic and asuric purposes,although, as a power of the Divine, it should be placed at the service of the Divine Mother.[613] Similarly, Lockhart argues that money is a talisman of the Self, and ought to be used to achieve its aims—that is, to help fulfill higher lines of destiny in life.[614]

The word *money* has feminine roots.[615] The mid-English *monoie* derives from old French *monie*, which is feminine, and the Latin *moneta*, which is also feminine.[616] Moneta derives from an older word *moneo*, which means,among other things, "to recollect" and "to instruct."[617] The inference is that there is a need to remember the origins of money and the relationship of imagination to money.[618] In the Roman Empire, it was minted in the temple of Juno, Queen mother of heaven, indicating both its divine source as well as its feminine nature.[619]

Money was traditionally considered to be sacred. The word *capital* originally referred to cattle counted by the head.[620] The Greek word for *coin, obolos,* is derived from the spit and spitted portion of the flesh of a bull consumed by the sacrificial fire.[621] Among the ancient Greeks, a portion called the surplus was left on the spit to be consumed by the fire as an offering to the heroic ancestors, now considered to be residing with and having the character of the gods.[622]

A wide split has developed in our realization of the money archetype, suggested by our separating the world and money from the spiritual life. This has led many people interested in spirituality to withdraw ascetically and to deny money, in as much as it goes beyond providing the necessities of life. Sri Aurobindo regards this to be an error, as it leaves money in the hands of what he calls "hostile forces."[623] Hillman observes that "the cut between Caesar and God in terms of money deprives the soul of the world, and the world of soul."[624] The individual is, consequently, deflected onto a spiritual path of denial, and the world is driven by *avarice* and greed.

The spell that money casts over people is graphically demonstrated in that well-being, even "wholeness," is today often equated with wealth, or at the least includes being wealthy. This is an illusory rationalization. But the parsimonious nature does not escape the taint of ego either. Freud sees money as feces and relegates it to the anal region.[625] He observes that neurotic anal fixation includes parsimoniousness and the hoarding of money.

Money, not sex or power, is the principal area of repression in modern psychotherapy. Money matters are still held close to the chest, the ultimate taboo, whereas we talk relatively loosely today of sexual and other formerly forbidden topics. Our attitudes about money, which is based on an archetype, are laden with ego, justifying one to speak of a money complex.[626] This complex can be expressed in many forms, including fear of money, hunger for money, feeling of guilt about money, denying what money can buy, and so on. Indeed, even love relationships are contaminated with the money complex. Many people learn about love or relate to love based on giving and receiving money or objects bought with money.

In this image, the individual is crying. This means an

"abaissement de niveau mental," by way of what the alchemists called solutio, a lowering of conscious awareness to allow for new attitudes to emerge from the unconscious.[627] The horizontal red and orange stripes suggest the image has to do with instinctual Eros (red) and exuberance and abundance (orange).[628] Facing the individual is an inversed black triangle with a head. The downward-pointing triangle reinforces the need for a lowering of consciousness. The figure represents the unknown aspect of the money complex while the head suggests meaning and understanding can be found there.

The individual has some identification with the black figure, as indicated by the black dollar sign on his chest. The dollar sign in the heart center points to the fact that going into the money complex is a matter of heart.

The flowing motion of the waves may indicate the need to let money flow. As the water is blue, spiritual detachment and devotion to the Self comes with the plunge into this realm of the psyche.[629] The more one is conscious of the fact that the money complex is rooted in the archetype, the more one is obliged to let it flow, not for ego cupidity but for the Self and its realization in space and time.

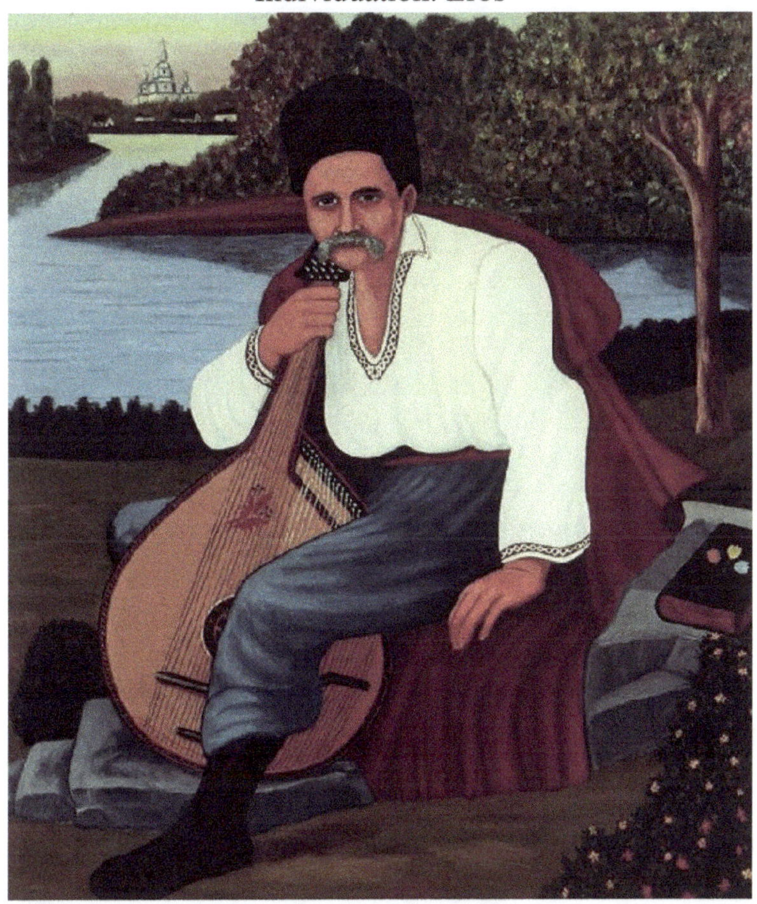

This image, which depicts the Ukrainian artist, poet and hero, Taras Shevchenko, is based on a reproduction. Symbolically, for me, here presents the individuated person with highly differentiated feeling, who is connected to the Self and Eros. The church in the background symbolizes the Self, while the red cape refers to Eros. The river represents the stream of life, and the many-stringed musical instrument, the bandura, suggests the finely tuned feeling function. The book symbolizes knowledge, while the pink, yellow, and blue flowers indicate the subject matter. Esoteric tradition speaks of love (pink), wisdom (yellow), and power (blue) that can be found behind the heart-center.[630]

Carlos Castaneda's spiritual guide, the Yaqui Indian Don Juan, insists that there is only one way, the way of the heart. It is worthwhile to contemplate his following inspirational message:

> For me there is only the traveling on paths that
> have heart, on any path that may have heart.
> There I travel, and the only worthwhile challenge
> is to traverse its full length and there I travel
> looking, looking, breathlessly.[631]

Likewise, C. G. Jung also places great importance on this path, given his stress on Eros and feeling values.[632] His most significant disciple, Marie-Louise von Franz's, last lecture was entitled "C. G. Jung's Rehabilitation of the Feeling Function in Our Civilization."[633] Sri Aurobindo says the psychic being or incarnated Self is found behind the heart-center, and he encourages his disciples to follow its lead.[634] This image, then, refers to knowledge and meaning to be found in living consciously according to Eros and feeling values and the dictates of the psychic being, the Self behind the heart.

Square Grey Man

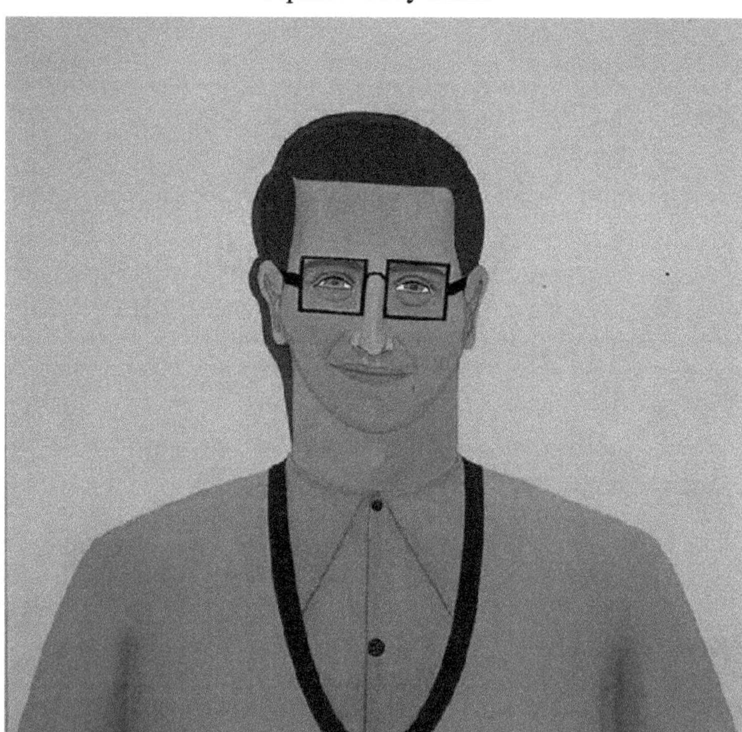

There are three significant aspects to this image: They include (1) the predominantly gray color, (2) the red penumbra surrounding the man's head and neck, and (3) the fact that everything is square, from the iris and pupils of the eyes to the eyeglasses, the hairline, the figure itself and the dimensions of the canvas and frame. Not only are the iris and pupils square, but they are turning toward the rights—that is, there is a movement toward insight. The V-neck sweater suggests a descent of psychic energies is taking place for this realization to become more conscious to the ego.

The goddess Athena is depicted as having gray eyes and as being the Grey Woman.[635] She is the goddess of far-sighted wisdom and practical counsel.[636] She advises on strategy during war and is the champion of heroes.[637] She is the patroness of artisans and weavers as well and teaches the crafts and other useful arts to humankind.[638] As gray is the color of concrete, it can be said to represent concrete reality. What emerges from this image, then, is a sense of wisdom and knowledge in the practical affairs of life. Red symbolizes Eros, libido, life and is a color related to the god Mars.[639]

The red penumbra surrounding the man's head and neck suggests that there is active energy and considerable life force behind consciousness of this movement into more awareness impractical reality.[640] The square means completeness and materialization, and therefore corresponds to the meaning of the color gray.[641] Sri Aurobindo observes that the square, in its essence, symbolizes what he calls the Supermind and Truth-consciousness, which includes the power of effective realization.[642] The suggestion here is that without the dimension depicted in this image, intuition and spiritual insight remains unfulfilled, and the spirit is unrealized in the expression of daily life.

Some alchemist knew that living the alchemical process was ultimately a matter of *res simplex*, simplicity, that is, living in accordance with the archetypal imperative, the will of the Self and "letting things happen," action in non-action.[643] In our complex outer-directed society, to arrive at the point of simplicity is the most difficult thing. I recall the Mother of the Sri Aurobindo Ashram once remarking that the primitive villager in India lives far closer to God than all the intellectuals in Europe.

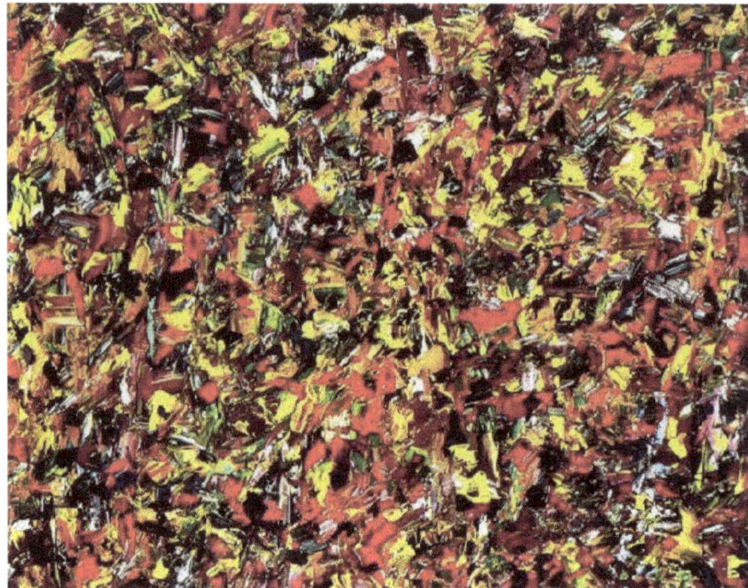

Regarding this image, what comes to mind is that judging from much primitive art, the soul loves bright colors. The painting is, in fact, the result of an active meditation on music by Alex Jones called "Kali's Dream."Unlike the expressionistic mode, it is an introverted experience, where I contemplated the inner sensations caused by the music, and using feeling evaluation, applied color to the canvas. Introverted sensation and feeling dominate in the execution of this painting. The choice and play of colors are meant to, in some way, correspond to the sensations aroused by the music and my feeling response to both the sensations themselves and to the evolving color patterns.

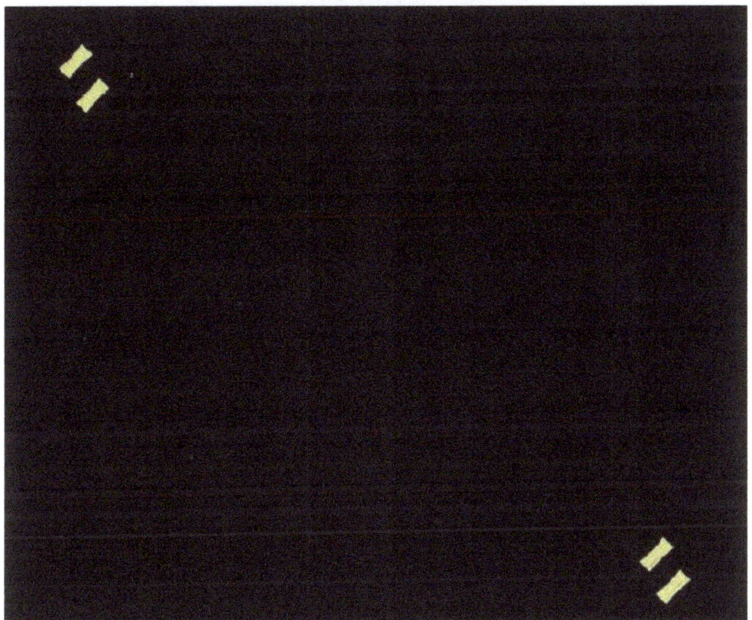

This image includes four bolts of light that are in circulation against a dark background, the outer bolts moving toward the right, the inner toward the left. By the process of circumumbulatio, the alchemists were expressing the notion of circulation in order to "mark off of the sacred precinct," by means of fixation and concentration of energy-force.[644] In Jung's discussion on the Secret of the Golden Flower, he writes that, "Heating is necessary; that is, there must be an intensification of consciousness in order that light may be kindled in the dwelling place of the true Self."[645] Jung observes that not only should consciousness be intensified, by such a process, but life as well.[646] The result is conscious life.

The light lies at the bottom of the dark sea of the unconscious. Darkness gives birth to light, allowing for what has been unconscious to become conscious. The bolts of light moving in opposite directions indicate a lighting up of the unconscious. The new contents from the unconscious are now becoming assessable to consciousness. Askesis or tapas sets "the sun wheel turning," and "the Tao begins to work and takes the lead."[647] Life becomes subjected to the commands from the Self.

The four bolts of light support the idea of the lead being taken by the Self, four (4) being the symbol number of wholeness and materialization.[648] The painting itself is square which has the same numerical significance.[649] Materialization here means insistence on the realization of the new contents of consciousness in the here and now of the external physical world.

Logo for the Business World

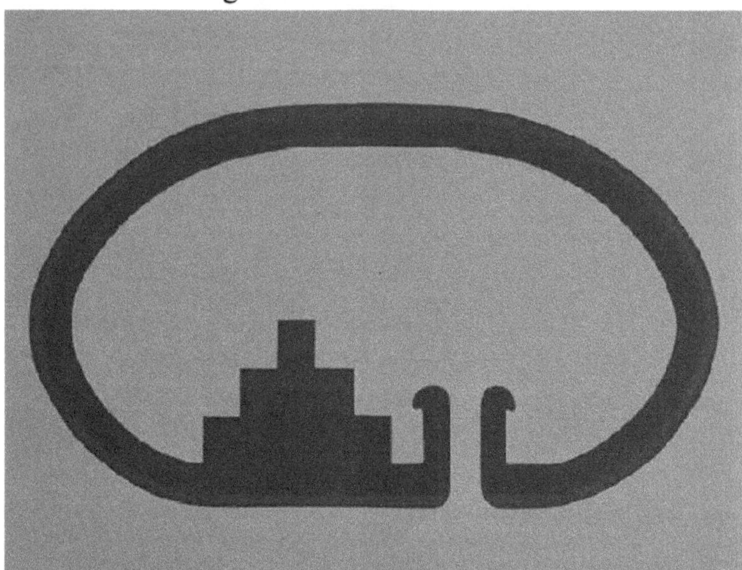

A logo is meant to be a sign or signature that attempts to express in shorthand an image that an institution or company wishes to portray to the public and its employees. Ideally, there is a sincere attempt to discover and express the true meaning or essential purpose of the institution in question. Often, however, it is merely an aspect of the company's persona and represents a sort of camouflage with a manipulative purpose.

This logo symbolizes the business world itself. I will begin my study by discussing the colors used. The figure is made up of blue and a bluish gray, while the background is a light blue-gray. Blue is psychologically related to the spirit or the higher mind as well as qualities of devotion and will.[650] The ancient Romans associated Jupiter and the Greeks, Zeus, with heavenly blue.[651] In Africa, the god of the Ewe is blue and white, and his priests are dressed in these colors.[652] In the Puranas of India, Krishna is depicted with a blue body.[653] The Virgin Mary is often depicted in a celestial blue dress.[654] And finally, many contemporary spiritual leaders describe their "light" as being blue.[655] Physiologically, blue normalizes the flow of blood and reduces inflammation.[656] It is a cool color that induces both sleep and meditation.

The contemporary marketing-oriented company is not interested in cooling people down but "heating" them up. Contrary to the logo portrayed here, much of consumer-oriented business consciously and purposely uses music, color, image, and words to excite desire. In addition, companies are constantly seeking ways to motivate employees to increase their production, again often "heating up" the situation. In a world facing ecological disaster and a world that is psychologically and spiritually bankrupt, what is necessary is a decided "cooling down" and not "heating up."

In this image, gray has been mixed with blue and white, especially for the background, but also for the figure. There is little amplificatory material on the color gray. However, gray eyes have been attributed to the Greek goddess Athena, who was born from the head of Zeus fully armed and fully clothed.[657] Mythology has it that, among other things, Athena is goddess of handicrafts, agriculture and the useful arts.[658] Her traits include far-sighted wisdom, reason, and practical counsel, which are useful qualities for contemporary business.[659] Her warlike attributes, her ability to give guiding counsel and fight on behalf of the winning team, as she did for the Achaeans (Greeks) during the Trojan wars, also suit her to be a guiding figure for modern business, whose strategic and tactical planning resemble war in more ways than one.[660] Finally, the color gray is the color of concrete, giving one the sense of practical, hard reality, with which business is involved.

The shape of the logo is reminiscent of the shape of the Egyptian goddess of creation, Nut, whose two legs and two arms represent pillars upon which the sky rests.[661] According to von Franz, the fact that the Egyptians had a female deity as Sky Goddess-Creatrix and a male Earth-God as mate indicates the concrete nature of their ideas and spirituality.[662] The logo also reminds one of a womb or a cave, which is a feminine symbol of birth and creation.

As indicated by the above amplifications, the meaning behind this symbol, then, is that business is divinely ordained and creative. Industry is in the business of creating technology and material goods. Moreover, practitioners are instruments of the Divine Mother, however unaware they are of this and however much they utilize practices that are antithetical to her ultimate purpose.

At the bottom, there is an opening, suggesting that industry could be open to influences outside its main field of interest. General Systems theory see this as an open system.[663] Ideally, this opening not only includes forces that business is aware of and interested in for practical reasons (e.g., consumers' opinions and social trends) but also forces from the unconscious. Such messages include those that are in diametrical disagreement with some contemporary business practices, especially of large companies, and indeed even the materialistic perception that puts the business world and economics at the center of our lives.

The buildings within this womb-like mandala mount upward in a triangular shape, indicating an aspiration to a higher source. In this view, business and industry would aspire to become a more conscious instrument of the Self, with the role of serving both *God* and man. This aspiration is a far cry from the contemporary view.

Since Adam Smith, the very foundation of our economic system has been based on the selfish pursuit of individual profit.[664] Keynesian economics has built into it the need to stimulate demand based on the appetites.[665] Keynes's lack of psychological sophistication blinded him to the fact that the human appetites come from a bottomless pit and are insatiable. The contemporary materialistic worldview itself is not wrong but exceptionally one-sided and unsympathetic to natural life.

Business has become a behemoth that has swallowed almost all aspects of life. Culture, sport, politics, and even religion and psychology seem to be at the service of business or a reductive business mentality. Business does not care to make a distinction between needs and desires or wants. It sees no harm in its constant stimulation of the consumer's appetites in order to make a profit. Yet this attitude flatly contradicts a religious or ethical attitude and any wise understanding of psychology. Advertisements use art, the science of sound, music, and the creation of images in order to "motivate" the consumer to buy. This is done purposely and deliberately, with the assistance of sophisticated psychological techniques. Our present approach to business justly deserves the epithet of economic barbarism.

Erich Fromm has described a prevalent form of modern-day neurosis as the "marketing character," people who become so impressed by marketing messages and the marketing orientation of our society that they lose their identity and integrity.[666] He suggests that this marketing orientation of business is a major "socially patterned defect"[667] By this, he means that it is considered legitimate by society for business to indulge in these marketing and other questionable practices, which are in fact antihuman and destructive.[668]

Another manner business misuses psychology in a way considered legitimate is in its constant drive to motivate employees to greater productivity. In some sense, this has in fact encouraged a more humane style of management. Yet here, the study of psychology is at the service of productivity and is ultimately harmful. Businessperson and textbooks alike fail to make the obvious connection, at least consciously, between this and the increasing stress and burnout at work.

As these socially patterned defects are considered normal, it makes it more difficult for business leaders to understand that their orientations and practices really affect employees, consumers, and society in decidedly negative ways. One can indeed sympathize with individuals in this present aggressively competitive business world where companies can easily go under without up-to-date marketing practices and the latest and most sophisticated technology and stress on productivity. Moreover, companies that go bankrupt contribute to unemployment.

Yet the present crisis is deeper and more far-reaching than these concerns, and, in truth, it represents a crisis of civilization itself. Industry is essential, by all means; however, what is necessary is industry transformed and in service to the Self, to the Mother and one's fellow human being. Only the individual can initiate the creative changes that are today essential. It begins with a change in consciousness.

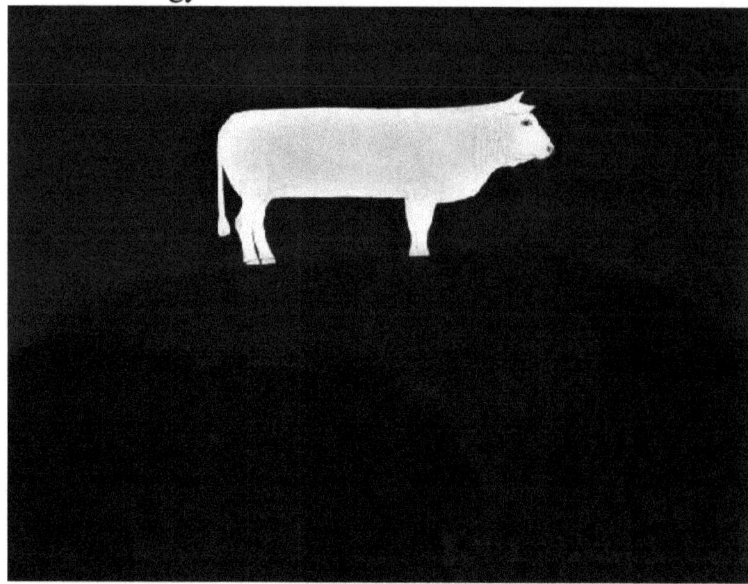

Androgynous Calf on Back of World Buffalo

Astrologically, Taurus the bull is a sign of power and earthly fertility.[669] The buffalo (bison) is analogous to the bull, both representing powerful instincts and passions and the primordial sacrifice. First Nation's people consider the white buffalo to be a sacred messenger and the spirit that gives totally from its essential being.[670] It used to provide everything necessary for the life and survival of the people, including milk, meat, fuel, clothing, and shelter as well as transportation by way of tents and canoes. Hence, in this regard, it is a maternal animal.

Dionysus, the ancient Greek woman's god, was sometimes depicted as a bull.[671] The Mithraic bull, as the great world bull, bull of the beginning, issued forth vine and wheat upon being sacrificed.[672] In Egypt, the Apis bull was has been referred to as Apis, the herald of (the earth-god) Ptah, who carries the truth upward to him of the lovely face (Ptah).[673] Generally, the Apis was considered to be the incarnation of the god Osiris, who was commonly known as "bull of the west."[674]

The bull represents the instinctual attitude or principle, which was repressed with Christianity. The myths of the mythological heroes Hercules and Mithras show the need to sacrifice the bull instinct.[675] This means that there is the need to suppress desires and passions for the sake of a higher self. Buddhism, as depicted in the famous Ten Ox Herding Pictures, on the other hand, shows how an individual must learn to tame the recalcitrant bull.[676] The Buddhist formula suggests full acceptance of the bull, allowing one's ego to be transformed spiritually along with bull-like passions, which is more appropriate for the contemporary individuation process.

In the Mithraic cult, the religion of the Roman Legionnaires during the early centuries of the Christian era, initiates were divided into seven (7) separate classes, including some as animals.[677] In India, the sacred cow is considered to be Vac, the feminine aspect of Brahma or God.[678] As Jung suggests, one must "become a cow" in order to receive the divine power of the instincts in the form of a bull.[679] For the ancient Chinese, cow-like docility is the way of Tao, the "conscious way."[680]

The astrological sign, Taurus, is ruled by Venus.[681] In Greek mythology, a primary association with the cow is Hera, "the cow-eyed," and previous to her, Io, the moon, depicted as a white cow-goddess.[682] In ancient Egypt, her counterpart was Hathor, the cow-headed goddess, the mother of all the gods.[683] The Greeks later identified her as Aphrodite.[684] They represent passion fertility, procreation, the power of nature and bringing forth.[685] In addition, both Hathor and Aphrodite foster music, dancing, love, culture, and beauty as well as numinous sexuality, suggesting ways to assimilate these bull-like drives.[686] In this image, there is an androgynous calf (cow-bull) standing on the world buffalo. The androgynous calf (cow-bull) is itself a symbol of the Self. The white color suggests innocence, purity, and receptivity as well as passivity.[687] One goal of the individuation process is to be able to stand behind one's passions and desires in order to arrive at the principle behind them through detachment. The first step is to accept primitive passions and emotions and not repress them. However, expressing the fire of emotions in an unconscious way can be terribly destructive. The further goal is to stand behind them for the sake of awareness, to allow them to be transformed by the Self.

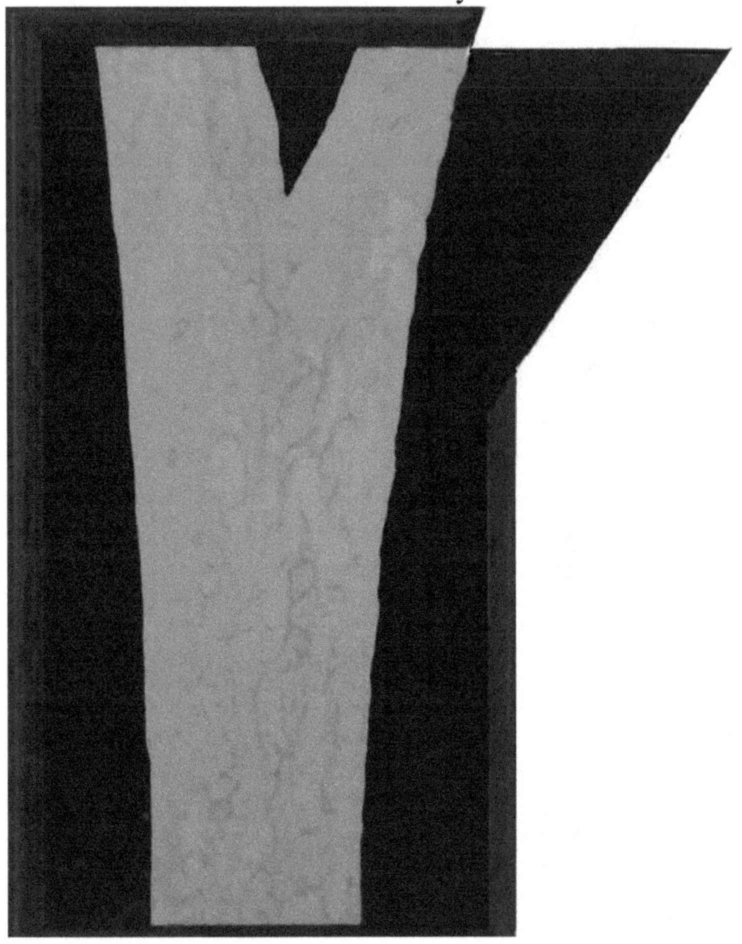

This image consists of two streams of downpouring concrete that coalesce to form one stream, against a black background. The fact that there are initially only two streams may indicate that this process is just becoming conscious. It may, however, indicate the primordial need to separate and divide in order to become more aware, but then to unite and synthesize into a whole. The black background suggests creation ex nihilo, not from the ego, but from the mysterious background of the psyche, the Self. The gray concrete represents the daily concrete hard reality of life. The descending stream reflects the downward direction of psychic energy, which in terms of the chakras, or centers of consciousness refers to something like the muladhara, the physical chakra. Life in the physical world is grounded in the muladhara chakra, which, in Jung's interpretation, consists of such daily routines as paying the bus ticket, preparing a meal, and doing clerical work.[688] It is normally unconscious, a world of participation mystique. But for individuation to occur, it is essential to have a firm hold in physical reality.

Along with the downward thrust of the concrete flow, there is also a movement in the shape of a right-angle triangle toward the right that goes beyond the limits of the frame. According to ancient Egyptian wisdom, all right-angle triangles have the same essential meaning as the sacred triangle, indicating a movement directed by the Self.[689] In India, triangles represent the Mother of form considered to be the channel through which unity becomes manifest in the world of multiplicity.[690] In this case, it means going beyond the normal (horizontal) restraints of life, with the frame indicating the defined limits. This implies that one can only break through limits if one first has a solid base and well-disciplined and defined limits in life which to break. Otherwise, there is simply enantiodromia or change into the opposite, a revolutionary movement where the formerly repressed now becomes dominant. But creative resolution requires, first, being conscious of limits that the Self may eventually break, directing one to go beyond them, while creating new form. It is noteworthy that it is not the ego but the Self that is the barrier breaker.

Golden Fish II

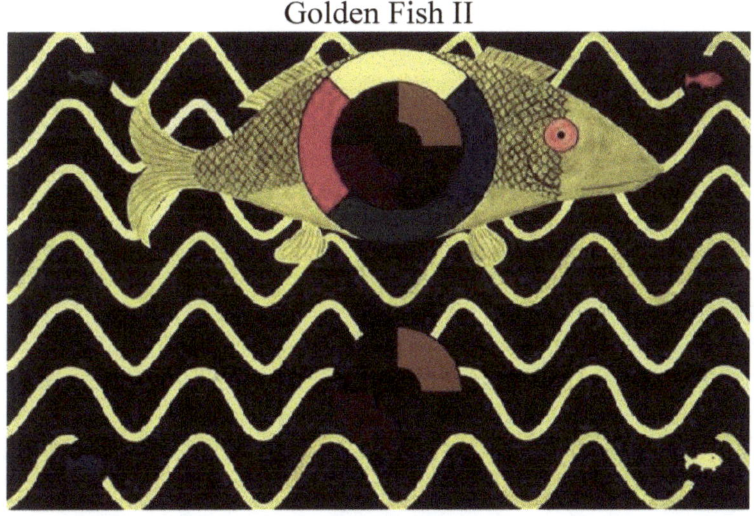

This image of a painting is not simply an aesthetic variation on Golden Fish I. Done a few years later, there are some noteworthy changes between the two images. It represents further psychological development over what is depicted in the first image.

Firstly, there is nothing but a black circle at the center of the mandala. Unlike most western mandalas, there is no figure at the center, only a symbolic representation of the Nothing that is the All, out of which comes creation ex nihilo, a mystery. This indicates that the ego is further relativized and more conscious of its relationship and dependence on the Self, or the Divine Mother. Since the axis has been further shifted toward the Self, the ego sees itself less as the doer and initiator and more as the instrument and assimilator of the demands from the unconscious. The fourcolor circle has now rotated to the left, so yellow is on the top, green the bottom, blue the right, and red the left, perhaps symbolizing the functions of intuition, thinking, feeling, and sensation in that order.[691] Although the (green) sensation function is at the bottom, and still inferior, there is no sense or need to bring order into it as in the previous golden fish painting. It is as if the need to go through the inferior function to the collective unconscious is potentially replaced by a more direct contact through one's (still relative) "wholeness" to the unconscious, the black center. This is made possible by a better, more accepting relationship between the ego and the *anima*, the mediatrix to the unconscious.

Secondly, the brown circle is now inside the four functions, suggesting that the earth and one's instinct are more central, with each of the four functions being rooted in the instincts.[692] The earth is related to the alchemical process of coagulatio, the psychological ground for the conscious expression of each of the functions.[693] That there are two brown mandalas suggests the coming to consciousness and a separating out of the instincts from their contamination with any of the functions. Figures that come in pairs usually have this significance.

Thirdly, the four small fish are no longer contained inside the container mandala and mother fish, but they are presently out in the "cosmic sea," each fish being supported by the black void. All this indicates that one potentially operates with each function in more direct contact with the unconscious—that is, one operates through relative "wholeness," one lives with greater detachment and a different attitude to life, now directed more by the Self. As the image consists of fishes, this new attitude and expression is still relatively unconscious.

Finally, the waves now have an added vertical dimension to them. This suggests more spiritual aspiration as background. Nonetheless, the general thrust of the image continues to be horizontal—that is, the emphasis is still on the process of life.

Eros on the Outside, Logos Inside

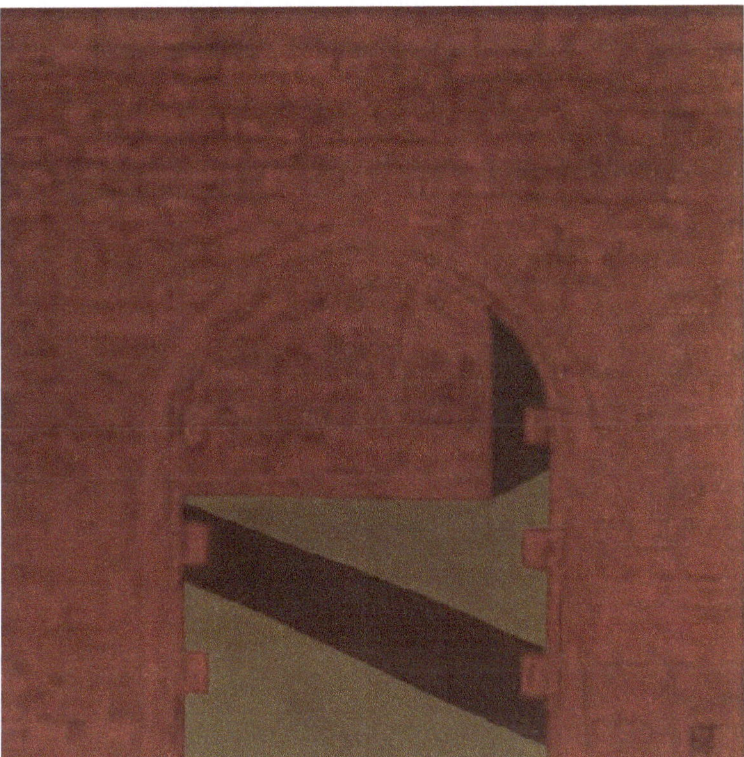

This is an impressionistic image of a red brick enclosure, with yellow (ochre) earth and a shadow falling across the inner *court*. In this image, Eros (red) and Logos (yellow) interrelate, with the inside being Logos and the outside being Eros. This suggests that one finds meaning through Eros.

Jung loosely defines the intuitive concept of Eros as representing relatedness and Logos as representing discernment, understanding, and meaning.[694] Red indicates Eros.[695] The exterior is depicted by the red bricks of Eros, painted impressionistically, which imparts an ambience and a certain vagueness that may aptly express this concept. Eros is also suggested by the curved nature of the archway. The yellow (ochre) interior indicates Logos.[696] The entrance has teeth-like protrusions, perhaps suggesting a mouth. Among other things, the mouth is the point of convergence between the external and internal worlds.[697] One speaks of the mouth of a cave. The mouth can indicate devouring, as well as the power of speech and the creative word.[698] There is an Egyptian hieroglyph that shows a mouth with a solar disk inside of it, suggesting the afore- mentioned idea of the power of the *creative* word. Guénon contends that in the Mandukya Upanishad, the mouth represents integral consciousness.[699]

As there are seven (7) "teeth," this number takes on symbolic significance. The number seven (7) is the symbol number of the individuation process. It represents both the natural rhythm of life and nature and creative formative power.[700] Teeth, according to Sri Aurobindo, represent habits.[701] Allendy identifies teeth as representing an active primordial weapon of attack.[702] Jung interprets teeth to mean the ability "to put your teeth into something," having a good grip on life.[703] It can include such widely different meanings as gripping a concept or idea or attacking aggressively.[704] In Gnostic literature, teeth represent the wall that fortifies the inner person.[705]

The contemporary person is precariously cut off from instincts and Eros. Relevant meaning in life can be found by descending and entering the cave of Eros in order to be consciously related to one's instinctual nature. The goal of Chinese alchemy is to come to the yellow earth, so "the tangible earth" can "become real."[706] This indicates the need to become conscious of the instinctual pole of the archetype—that is, of the insistence of the dynamic aspect of the psyche to express itself. A shadow lies across the inner yellow earth, adding a further dimension of complexity to the image. This suggests that there is a shadow darkness that comes with the light of Logos.

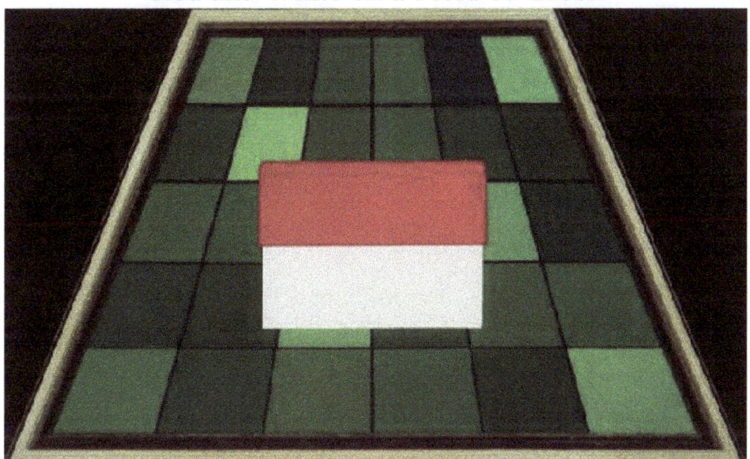

The first thing that strikes the eye with this image is its unusual shape and the grid-like pattern, which creates a kind of visual paradox. One's line of vision runs simultaneously both vertically and into the background depths. The brown grid work suggests interconnectedness, instinctual Eros.

In Indian thought, Brahman is said to create the world through his *ShaktiMaya*, or consciousness-power, which is not only "conceptually creative" but "dynamically executive," requiring definitions, limits, and order.[707] Similarly in Greek thought, it is *Moira*, the original creative power who weaves the web of destiny.[708] It suggests being bound, which in this painting is in three dimensions: vertically, horizontally, and inwardly at an angle. Perhaps the vertical thrust relates to one's aspirations, the horizontal relates to life movement, and the inward direction suggests depth. The grid patterns are made up of "rectangles," indicating a concurrent materialization.[709] The horizontal "limits" to the rectangular shape also suggests realization in time and space.

Green suggests natural vegetative growth, renewal, springtime, and healing.[710] It represents life and hopeful expectancy. In this painting, one does not have a feeling of wild nature, the wildness of Artemis or Diana, for instance, but civilized nature, perhaps the nature of Aphrodite.[711] With the grid work comes the feeling of order in the way a farmer's field has order.

The central image appears to be a slightly rectangular red-and-white structure, like a barn. For the alchemists, the red-white union represents the *coniunctio* of opposites, of *Sol* and *Luna*, the red sun and the white moon, the union of soul and spirit.[712] Red, in this case, is active, hot, creative, vigorous, and masculine.[713] White represents purity and innocence; it is cool, receptive, reflective, and feminine.[714] Red and white are king and queen, and, in the *Rosarium*, the "ruddy-limbed husband" united with the "white skinned lady" refers to the royal marriage of *Sol* and *Luna*.[715] In Egypt, the *coniunctio* was represented by the union of the (red) goddess of the north (*Uatchet*) and the (white) goddess of the south (*Nekhebet*), and by the union of the red and white crowns.[716] In *Kundalini yoga*, there are reported to be three currents: the central *susumṇā*, the white *iḍā* (moon, feminine, water) on the left, and the red *pinqalā* (sun, masculine, fire) on the right, the goal being the unification of the *iḍā* and the pinqalā.[717] For the alchemists, through *askesis*, the *albedo* (whitening) gives way to *rubedo* (reddening) and a transformed reality.[718] The white state of innocence awaits the red groom, for the cool white to be activated by the hot reddening.

In summary, the painting depicts orderly sensuous nature, bound vertically, horizontally, and inwardly. It is not a suppressed nature but a civilized nature. This is the background for the *coniunctio* of red and white, the active and the receptive, reflective nature. In practical terms, this indicates that the imagination and reflective mind which comes from the whitening is there prior to activity. This means first imagination and reflection, then action or activity grounded in the imagination rather than activity as reaction or un-reflected activity.

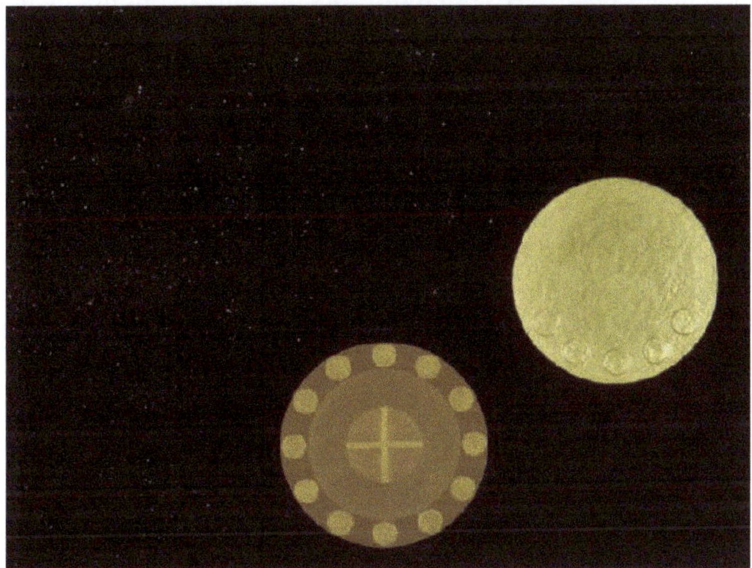

Hear, oh man!
Out of chaos
Comes the dancing star.
It paves the way.

Awake, oh man!
Descend and find
The dancing star,
The Self.

Look! The chaos, night
That symbol star,
The earth transformed
The golden light

In *Thus Spoke Zarathustra*, Nietzsche has Zarathustra utter: "I tell you, one must still have chaos in one to give birth to a dancing star. I tell you: You still have chaos in you."[719] In this painting, the night sky represents the chaos of the unknown, now illuminated by the scintillae and the star of the Self. This image also reminds me of the following Mithraic saying: "I am a star which goes with thee and shines out of the depths."[720] The star symbolizes eternal uniqueness, individual identity.[721] In *Seven Sermons to the Dead*, Jung writes that the star is what man ought to pray to in order to increase its light.[722] In Egyptian mythology, the ba was at times depicted as a star.[723] The ba, which is a coincidence of opposites, represents individuality, the quintessence of the natural man.[724] According to folklore, among all the thousand stars in the sky, there is one that is "our star." That implies that there is one star that represents individual destiny, and the consummation of totality. The several stars in the heavens are the scintillae, or little soul sparks and sparks of light, referred to by the alchemists and Meister Eckhart; they are the lumen naturae of Paracelsus.[725] They are centers of consciousness and incipient images of the archetypes which come laden with meaning.[726]

The star in this image of my painting is a golden concrete circle, containing five (5) small golden circles, which taken together form a crescent moon. The Self is both one and many. In relating an inner experience, a dying man reports, "I felt like I was a round-ball and almost like I might have been a little sphere like a BB on the inside of this round ball."[727] In commenting on this dream, von Franz says, "It seems to describe the 'correct' relation of the ego to the Self, that is, the ego is a part of the whole and at the same time one with the whole."[728] This example illustrates the paradoxical relationship between the purified ego and the Self.

The five (5) golden circles within the larger circle could possibly have a somewhat similar significance. Numerologically, the number five (5) symbolizes the Godin man, the quintessence, mercury, the ego as "captain of its ship, master of its destiny"—that is, the purified ego, transparent to the Self.[729] The higher buddhi or spiritual mind is often symbolized by the moon, which reflects the radiant light of the sun. In Western tradition, this notion is represented by Sophia, the goddess of wisdom who revels as "the inwardness" of God's creation.[730] Numerologically, the number six (6) (the five [5] small circles plus the one larger circle) symbolizes the union of male and female in the act of creative generation.[731] It is attributed to Venus, the goddess of attraction and desire, and also signifies the interrelationship of the Divine and the human.[732]

The golden color and concrete nature of this symbol is significant. Gold is a heavy metal and can only be discovered at the lowest point, which suggests that the highest psychological and spiritual value can only be found in accepting the material world—that is, one's earth and instinctual nature. The concreteness of the image reinforces this perspective. Moreover, as Jung informs us, "We are living in what the Greeks called the kairos—for a 'metamorphosis of the gods', of the fundamental principles and symbols"—that includes transformation of the instincts.[264] Some of the alchemists sought to produce a transformation and regeneration of the subtle body. Various sources that describe the transfigured body add further intuitive amplifications to these images. Alchemical texts suggest that this body becomes as much spiritual as corporeal, as much psyche as body.[733]

In Egyptian mythology and in the Mithraic cult, transfiguration is described as acquiring a garment of light, which also signifies the fulfillment of individual destiny.[734] After commenting on one of her own dreams, von Franz indicates that completes wholeness is only attained with the union of the ego, and the *resurrected* body (the subtle inner body).[735]

Finally, Plotinus observes that in its pure state the soul is ethereal.[736] It receives a sun-like body as it descends from the original Logos to the imaginative state. Descending further, it takes on a moon-like shape and becomes more bound to forms. And in *Liber de lunaticis Theophrasti*, Paracelsus contends that the individual has two bodies, one made of the elements, the other of the stars, which, according to von Franz, when united give the unus mundus.[737]

These comments lead to the second mandala, which is golden brown. Brown is the color of the earth and the instincts. There is indication of a spiritualizing influence suggested by the golden hue, and the paradoxical fact that the image is less concrete than the other mandala. In alchemical literature, the earth represents the process of coagulatio, which implies that the experience can be related to the ego.[738]

As a mandala, it is also a symbol of the Self.[739] This center takes the form of a cross, in itself a symbol of the union of the opposites, above and below, left and right.[740] The four arms of the cross imply the square or number four (4), which numerologically is a feminine number symbolizing materialization, the principle of creation.[741] It also represents truthconsciousness and implies integrating of the four functions of consciousness and wholeness.[742] It is noteworthy that the cross stands on its own and that there is no figure crucified on it. Such a union of opposites, however, can only come through enduring often intense emotional conflicts between the instincts which are released in the fully committed battle of life. Only then can one discover the spiritual meaning behind the emotions.

There are twelve outer circles, which numerologically signify a regenerated life consecrated to the Self.[743] The number thirteen

(13) (12 peripheral circles plus the center) symbolizes death and regeneration—that is, the death of ego and consecration to the Self.[744] The thirteenth *card* in the Tarot deck is Death, typically referring to death of ego value or attitude.[745] The twelfth card is the hanging man, which indicates the necessary suspension of the ego and reversal of the world order.[746] Christ's first disciples numbered twelve, as did the inner circle of Sri Ramakrishna.

With these amplifications, perhaps one can visualize the number twelve (12) as the symbol of the Universal Mother of life in eternal embrace with the Supreme. One can also relate to the Self as being both the one and the many. In the Indian Tantric tradition, the anahata and heart chakra is depicted having twelve petals, where the psychic being at the heart center represents the soul involved in historical life. Indian philosophy delineates the Purusha, or Jivatman as the one, and its manifold expressions in nature as Prakriti.[747]

The metallic gold, the abstract symbols, and the cosmic nature of the painting point to its faraway origin, distant from the ego. Yet the influence is potentially there, and the role of the ego is to open itself to this transformative process in the routine of everyday life. Life, then, becomes directed onto the path of a more spiritual destiny.

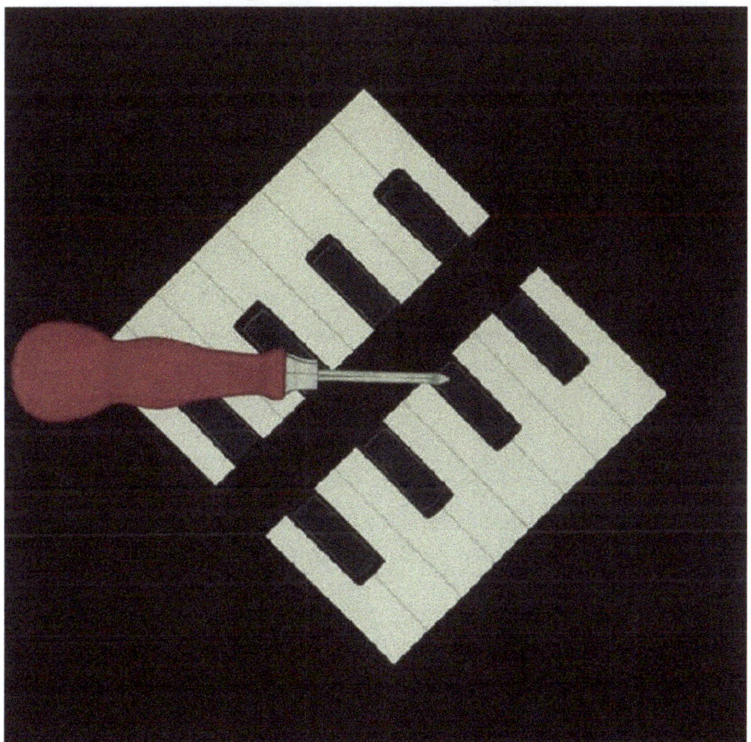

In this image, which consists of a square music box and screwdriver against a dark brown background, one finds an interesting interplay of the masculine and feminine principles. The background color symbolizes the earth and instincts and provides a ground for the images in the foreground. The painting itself is square, which, along with the brown color, suggests grounding experience in physical reality.[748]

The handle and container for the screwdriver is shaped with curved lines, suggesting the feminine principle. Jung attributes red to the instinctual end of the archetype.[749] Red is also the color attributed to Mars and, as such, represents active creativity and vigor.[750] The metal screwdriver head is made of straight lines and is masculine. The suggestion here is that the masculine Logos is rooted in a feminine container as a son to his mother. The handle container is itself instinctually related to active creative masculine energies. At this point, it may be interesting to note that the first hexagram of the *I Ching*, the Chinese Book of wisdom, is the Creative, the masculine principle.[751]

The screwdriver is a useful and necessary tool used for tightening or loosening screws in the process of repair or building. The masons, who claim to date back to the temple builders in ancient Egypt and include the architects for the temple of Solomon as well as for the beautiful gothic churches constructed during the middle ages, understand that the symbol tools of their craft are to be used for construction of an inner temple.[752] In this light, the screwdriver signifies the ability to tighten up one's discipline in order to construct a firm edifice of spiritual values for the inner temple.

The music box is square, and there are four black keys on each half. The square and the number four (4), which is feminine number, have the same symbolic value, which is truth-consciousness and materialization.[753] The keys form an image similar to the second hexagram of the *I Ching*, the Receptive, the feminine principle.[754]

The music box is tilted to the right and forms a diagonal for an imaginary right-angle triangle of a square. In ancient Egypt, all right-angle triangles had the same essential meaning as the sacred triangle, which was sometimes depicted with a pharaoh as the diagonal.[755] The pharaoh was the incarnation of a deity, for instance the sun god Ra or of Horus.[756] The diagonal is reconciliation of the vertical forces of aspiration and the horizontal energies of life. Geometric growth, according to the principles of sacred geometry, is depicted as the image of the square with its diagonal which forms the side of a second square.[757] This relationship between proportion and progression represents a key to sacred geometry, which is that all nature belongs to the ever-flowering progression of constant charge.[758] Finally, as a music box, it signifies not only Eros but the feeling function.

In summary, the image depicts the active creative principle symbolized by the screwdriver and the passive receptive principle of the music box. Active use of the screwdriver leads to instinctually related discipline and results in discernment in life. The music box suggests there is an inner receptivity to this discipline and Logos, which will lead to discernment in Eros and feeling, realized in the course of the daily flow of life The horizontal screwdriver also shows receptivity to feminine energy, as well as that the required discipline takes place in the adventure and battle of life through which one gains conscious discernment.

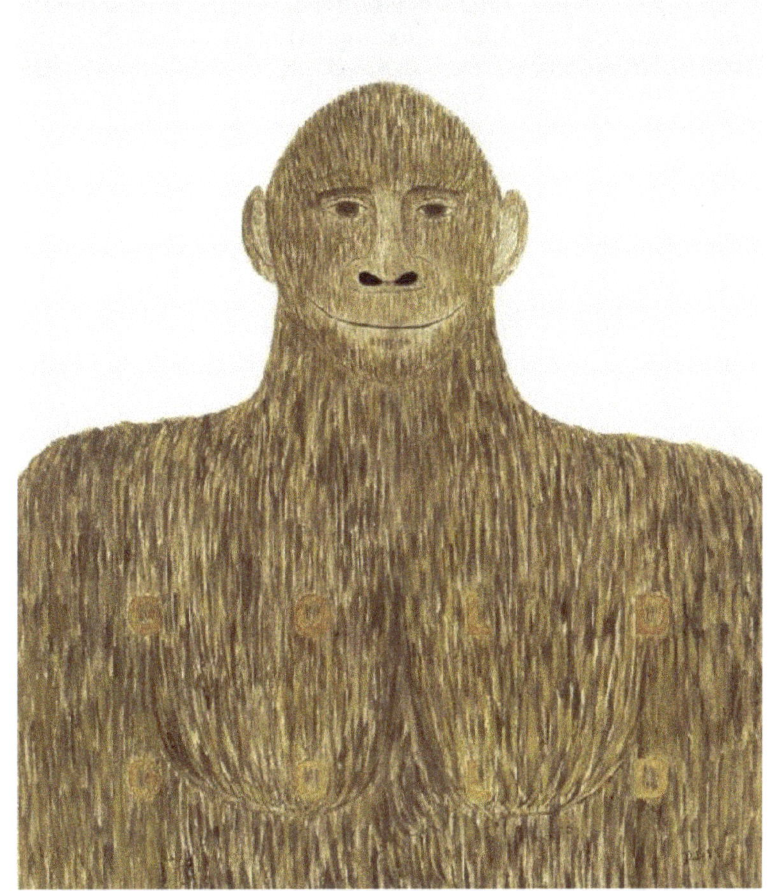

Western tradition considers the monkey or ape to represent humankind's baser instincts, especially sensuality, and it has generally been depicted symbolically as spiritually dangerous.[759] Monkeys are portrayed as having the vitality and strength of the devil. Western Christianity sees the devil as *Simia Dei*, the Ape of God and God's shadow and the monkey as an idolater.[760]

In Eastern traditions, on the other hand, the monkey symbolizes, among other things, a messenger, and wisdom and devotion.[761] In fact, one can observe monkeys at the dawn of day sitting and looking at the sun, apparently in a state of worship. The monkey god, Hanuman, is worshiped in India as the god of devotion and is renowned for his physical strength, vitality, and chastity.[762] Legend has it that no one equals him in learning and understanding of the Sastras (Scriptures). In China, the monkey Hou Tsu is said to eat and drink, yet becomes a fully enlightened Buddha.[763] In the Chinese horoscope, Sagittarius, is depicted as a monkey.[764] He is, in addition, seen as the father of music and dance. In ancient Egypt, the ape was venerated as one of the forms of Thoth, the Egyptian Hermes, from whom comes the words *wisdom* and *poetry*.[765] The sacred ape symbolizes wisdom hailing the light. Jung once remarked that his Wise Old Man was a monkey.[766] Taken together, Eastern and Western traditions point to the fact that the monkey or ape is a trickster-like god in his animal form, representing both shadow and wisdom.

Among other things, the monkey is known for its mimicry. This is an aspect of the mind that feels compelled to mechanically read any message placed in front of it, an advertisement for instance, even should one desire to avoid it. Moreover, monkeys, "the dancing animal," chatter and prance around restlessly, suggesting that they represent the restless aspect of the life mind as well.

This is an image, then, of the mechanical physical mind (mimicry) and the lower life mind (prancing about, chattering). The physical mind deals with concreteness, while the lower life mind indicates sensuous desire, and restlessness. In this painting, the ape does not appear to be destructive, but benign, a transformed ape. Not only is the image benign, but "Gold-Gold" is inscribed on the ape's chest—literally inscribed, be it noted. The Gold Institute, in fact, has several advertisements with very sensual images and similar literal inscriptions. The repetitive and literal nature of the message has a hypnotic effect, engaging the physical mind. Primitive peoples and the primitive in all of us repeat prayers and supplications to the gods due to this hypnotic power. Likewise, Roman Catholic devotees are enjoined to repeat "Hail Marys," eastern orthodox monks repeat the Jesus prayer, or prayer of the heart, and the mantra is meant to be continuously repeated.

Gold is considered by the alchemists to be the noblest metal and signifies great value, light, or wisdom in nature that reconciles opposites.[767] It is the alchemical treasure. As the heaviest metal, it is found at the lowest point in the psyche.[768] In fact, there is reputed to be an extraordinary amount of gold at the earth's core. Chemically, gold is identified as the element Au, which is derived from the Latin, aurum, meaning "glowing dawn." It is "concretization" of the sun, the sun of the earth. Gold has mana. As it does not rust, gold represents immortality as well as the medium that links the natural and the supernatural, the earth and the heavens.

The message depicted here, then, is that a natural wisdom can be found by accepting the lower vital and physical minds—that is, both the restless energetic, sensuous life force, and the mimicking, literal, repetitive physical mind that sees the world as it is. Acceptance leads to the transformation of these instincts and awareness of natural wisdom.

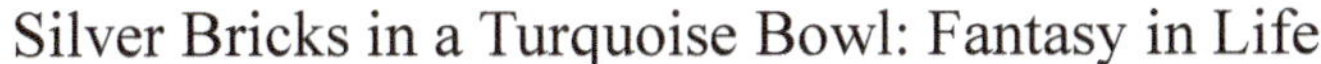

Silver Bricks in a Turquoise Bowl: Fantasy in Life

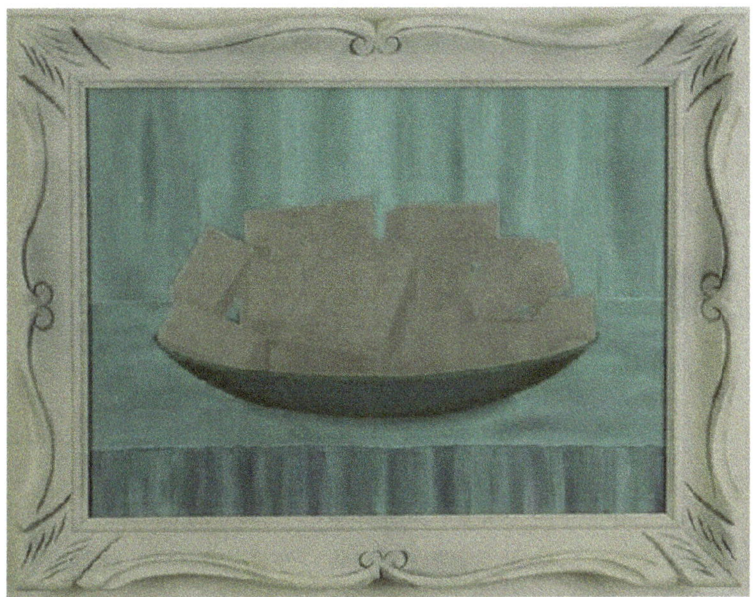

There are two principal colors in this image: turquoise and silver. Both the background and the containing bowl are turquoise, the dominant color. Turquoise was sacred to Isis and Osiris in Ancient Egypt, as it was to the love goddess Venus.[769] Turquoise consists mainly of phosphate of aluminum and copper, the metal of Venus.[770] Turquoise is a marriage of blue and green, the blue sky and the green growth of life on the earth. In a Navaho myth, the ancestors of the hero see the sky father descending, and the earth mother rising to meet him. Where they unite on top of the mountain, the ancestors find a little figure made of turquoise.[771] In another version, they give birth to a woman who rejuvenates and transforms herself.[772] In a similar vein, Aeschylus, in the *Danaides*, writes:

> The great and amorous sky curved over the earth and
> lay upon her as a pure lover. The rain, the humid flux
> descending from heaven for both man and animal, for

both thick and strong germinated the wheat, swelled
the furrows with fecund mud and brought forth the
buds in the orchards. And it is I who empowered these
moist espousals, I the great Aphrodite. [773]

The bowl is an expression of the feminine principle, a womb that contains or gives birth. It is the psyche as container or receptacle for contents from the Self. The goal of individuation is shifting of the axis from the ego to the Self. Inner work helps to form containers—that is, attitudes and values that allow for contents from the Self to be realized and expressed.

Such a psyche can contain silver bricks. Silver is the moonbeams of the earth, as gold is the Sun of the earth. It represents the spiritualized feminine principle suggesting receptivity and reflection.[774] As the moon reflects all planetary influences, silver embodies all metals.[775] In fact, silver has the following properties: it is a conductor, it is heavy and hard, and it is useful.[776] It has aesthetic qualities allowing one to make refined silver and jewelry.

Psychologically, it represents imagination, but imagination that is concrete and solid in realization, not abstract imagination alien to the life of the earth and life.[777] Moreover, due to its affinity with sulfur, symbolizing burning passion, imagination is not only passive fantasy, but also creative and active, potentially effective.[778] In alchemy, silver precedes gold, allowing the gold of truth to be lived concretely and not remain as some abstract ideal.[779]

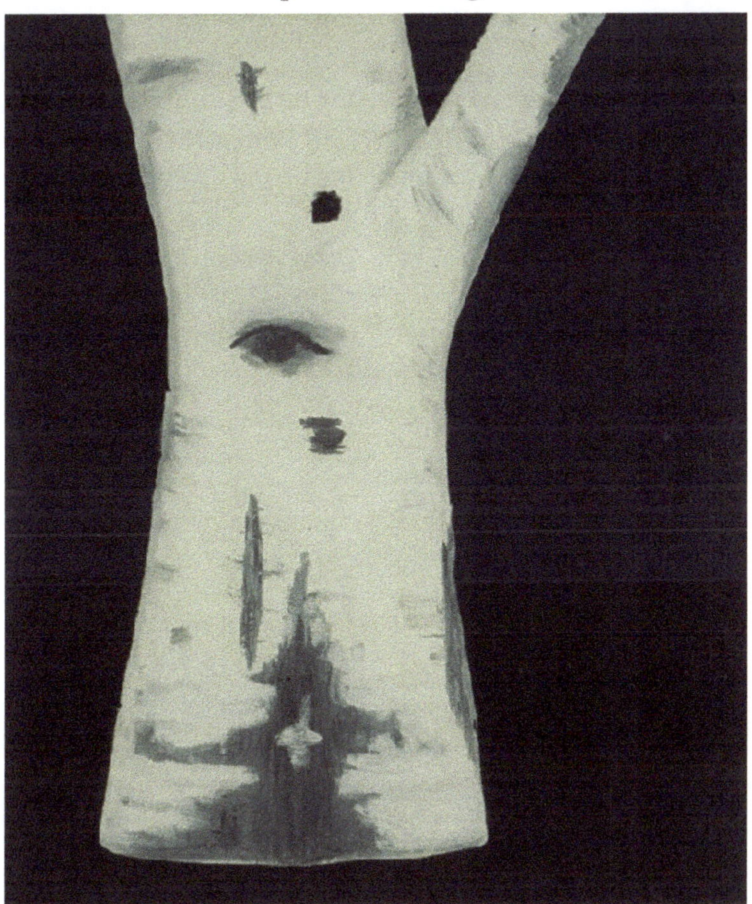

The tree represents a process of psychic growth that develops under different laws than those of the ego-will and, for that matter, instinctual aspects of the psyche that are symbolized by animals of different sorts. The tree grows in a long process from seed to maturity in a spiral fashion and represents a similar movement in the psyche. The tree indicates the way of the spirit, the growth of a natural relationship between the conscious and the unconscious.[780]

In this painting, there is a white tree against a dark background. In the Chinese symbol of the Tai Chi, a white dot or masculine yang is to be found in the dark feminine yin.[781] This refers to the psychological fact that after descending into the dark depths of the psyche, one discovers a spontaneous process that, on its own, lifts one into a more conscious state.[782] There is enantiodromia into the opposite.

The tree has variously symbolized knowledge and life and death.[783] It is known by the alchemists as the philosophical tree, implying that the process symbolized by the tree essentially represents knowledge and wisdom.[784] In this case, the tree appears to be aspiring upward, given the "expanded chest" and branch and arms extended upward, as if seeking understanding and light. A natural instinctively rooted process in the psyche spontaneously aspires upward for knowledge.

The black spot at the "chest level" of the tree, corresponds to the heart *chakra*. Since it is black, the aspiration and its goal concerned with are not yet known. Generally, however, the heart center is concerned with matters of human will, knowledge, and love in relation to life.[785]

One of the difficulties of many people who first start seeking inwardly, especially from the western world, is pulling too much from the ego. This amounts to spiritual ambition, and it leads to inflation. Although the ego can help at the outset, one can apply far too much ego-will in one's seeking and aspirations. This can cause psychological and even at times physical problems. It is well to remember that there is a natural movement in the psyche that aspires for light and consciousness.

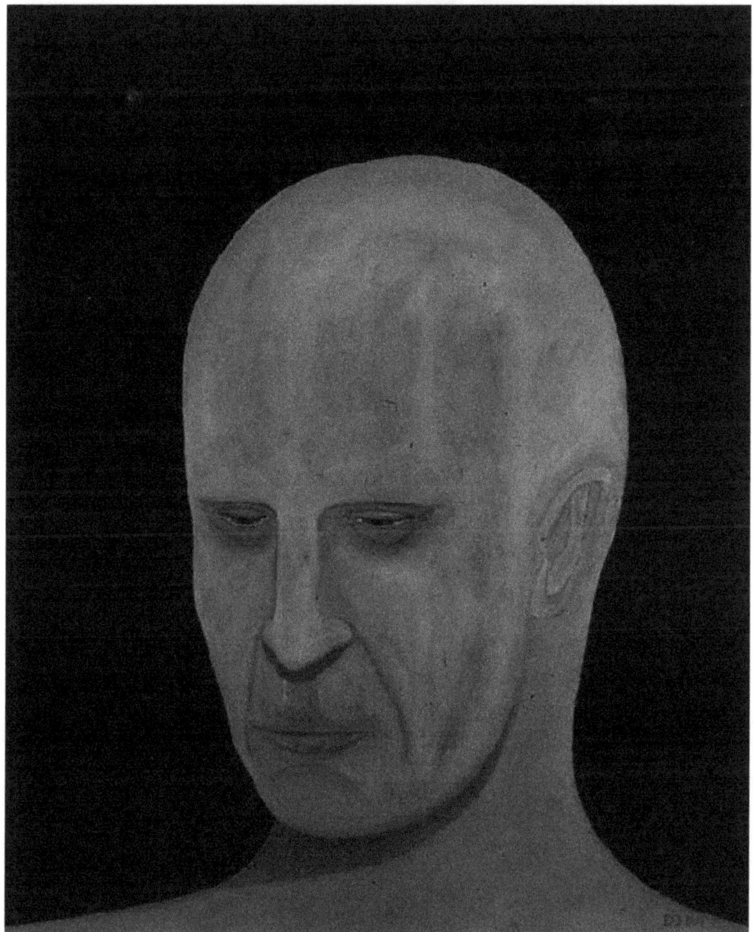

The black background indicates potential for creation *ex nihilo*, creation from the mysterious background of the psyche. The head symbolizes meaning and understanding and represents the seat of consciousness.[786] In ancient Egypt, the head symbolized the temple in the individual, the organizing center of awareness.[787] According to the later alchemists, it is the place of the "divine part," the omega element and a synonym for the transformative substance.[788] Hair suggests mental activity, thoughts, while complete hairlessness indicates receptivity to thoughts other than those of the discursive mind.[789]

Many meditation practices involve watching thoughts. Jung's inner guru, Philemon, told him that thoughts are like "animals in the forest, or people in a room, or birds in the air," giving Jung insight into the objectivity of the psyche.[790] Since ancient times, monks of many religions and creeds have their hair shaven to signify spiritual initiation and symbolic renunciation of worldly life in order to concentrate on their religious vocation.[791] The intense expression and introverted eyes indicate meditation, consciousness directed inward and away from superficial concerns. It is an image of *askesis* or *tapas*, "the concentration of energy-force."

The blue and red hue of the head, and blue and red eyes indicate the nature of the meditation—concentration on the duality of Eros (red), and spirit (blue). The phallic-shaped head suggest an active penetrating attitude in search of the "transcendent function" beyond the duality. The conflict of opposites, it should be noted, is based on life demands and experience, not same abstraction, as might be the case for one who has withdrawn from the world.

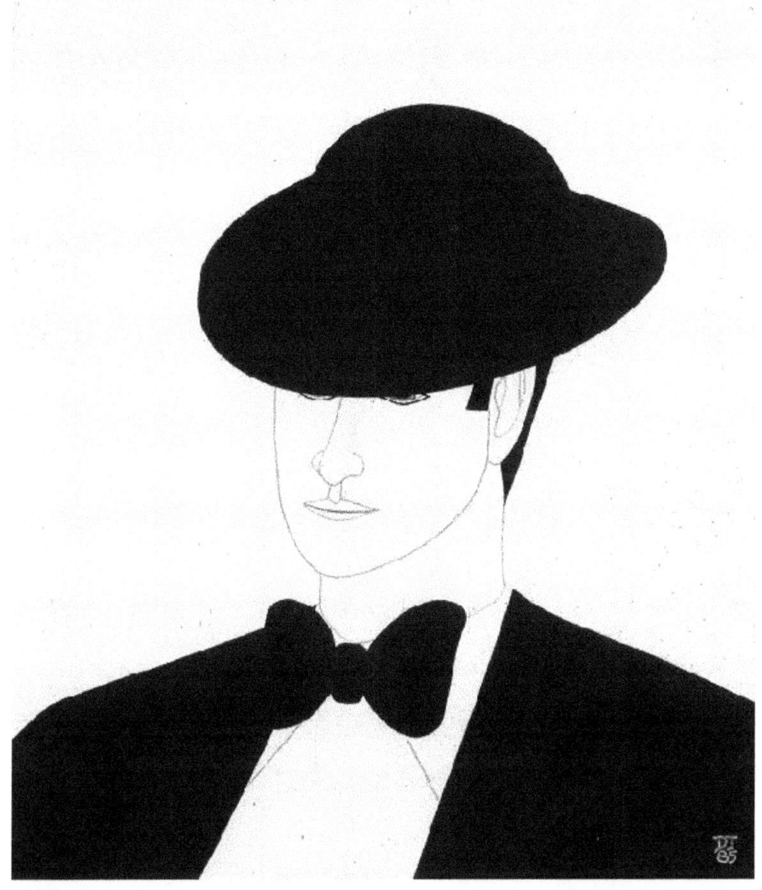

The figure of the teacher, along with the background, is a study in black and white—the two fundamental opposites, the black *yin* and the white *yang*, the feminine and the masculine. All colors units in the white and disappear in the black. The cocky tilt of the hat and the individual's confident demeanor suggests a masculinity rooted in the instincts. His black coat, hat, bow tie, and eyes link him to the feminine, the Great Mother, and the unknown.[792] The whiteness of the face and background suggests the fundamental masculine ground. It is as if this male figure is a masculine representative of the Mother. As Sri Aurobindo observes, the goal of the integral yoga is to experience that one is "truly a child and eternal portion of her consciousness and force," male and female alike.[793]

The teacher is an educator and guide. Jung gives the example of a man that dreamt that the white magician was dressed in black and that the black magician had found the lost keys to paradise although he did not know what to do with them.[794] For self-knowledge, one needs to go into the unknown aspects of the psyche in order to light up the darkness. The figure depicted in this image reminds one of the white magician of this dream, or perhaps even a synthesis of the white and black magicians. His black coat and hat indicate the unknown where, as teacher and guide, he is the master. His black eyes indicate his soul-relatedness with the unknown, the realm of the mothers.

The black bow tie suggests a butterfly, which in turn is related to the *labrys*, the two-headed axe.[795] It has been a symbol of the goddess of regeneration and transformation dating back some five (5) thousand years.[796] The butterfly is also the symbol for the psyche and the breath of life.[797]

Indeed, the Greek word *psyche* means both "soul" and "butterfly."[798] As the bow tie encircles the neck and throat, the significance of the center of consciousness, known as the *vishuddha chakra* in Indian *Tantric* yoga, is relevant. The throat *chakra* is symbolized by a white elephant, which implies that the strength of an elephant is given to psychic realities through creative speech.[799] Words have power, clothing as they do the psychic reality behind them. This suggests the need for discernment in verbal expression, but also the potential for expressing the creative Logos. At a deeper level, the *vishuddha chakra* represents the reality of psychic factors as experienced through the symbol—that is, the experience of the unitary nature of the world.[800]

It is significant that this figure is instinctually masculine in attitude and appearance, although there is also an openness and delicacy in his facial expression. This corresponds to the psychological truth that even though one of the tasks of individuation is to integrate values of the opposite sex into consciousness, one still retains one's essential gender identity.

This image, then, points to accepting the unknown dark side of the psyche. This leads to psychological transformation and regeneration. The bow tie around the throat *chakra* essentially suggests an orientation to the world where the world is experienced as a psychic reality by way of the symbol.

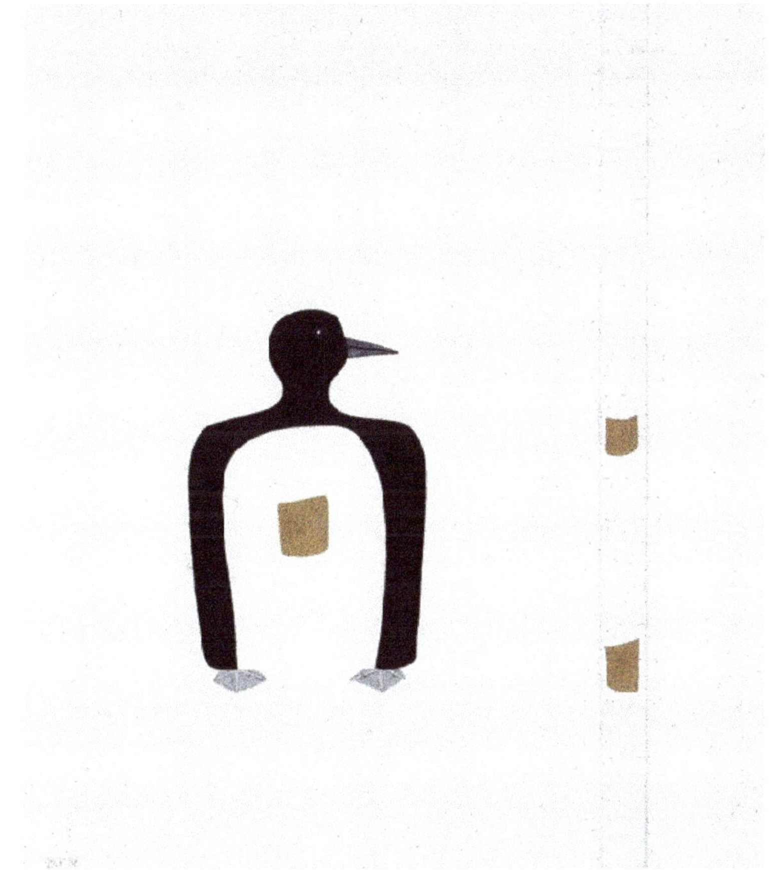

Although this is an image of a more of a mythological penguin than a depiction of a real penguin, some idea of the penguin's habits may prove interesting amplification.[801] The penguin lives up north and is at home on both land and in water. Due to an extra layer of blubber, it is protected against the cold. Its food is fish. It mates on the land, and when feeding its young, the parent and infant identify each other through sound.

Looked at symbolically, perhaps one can say that the penguin represents a natural link between the conscious (land) and the unconscious (water). Relating to each other through sound implies a relatively highly developed sense of hearing and the ability to hear the "word" especially differentiated as expressed in relationship and life. As the penguin is at home in the north, it represents an instinct with the widest dualities—for instance, god and the devil.[802] Its black-and-white coat has a similar significance.[803]

In the painting, there is a black-and-white rectangular-shaped animal-bird with a gold patch in the center, on a white background. The black and white colors suggest wide-ranging dualities, whereas gold is related to the sun and contains the highest value.[804] According to the alchemist Michael Meir, in its daily round, the sun has spun threads of gold all around the earth.[805] Yet gold, the heaviest metal, is found at "the lowest point" and mined at great depths.[806]

The vertical rectangular shape indicates that the emphasis is to be placed on height and depth. The white background indicates the alchemical state of *albedo*, the end product of the process of *calcinatio*.[807] It is what the alchemists refer to as the "white foliated earth," a state of innocence and purity.[808] This prepares the ground for the next two operations, *separation* and the *coniunctio*. *Separatio* is a process of discernment of the opposites, which are brought together by the "purified sun" or "gold" principle and reconciled through the coniunctio.[809] The alchemical recipe requires the adept to "sow your gold in white earth."[810]

The bird looks toward the white tree that is straight and perfectly vertical, linking height to depth. Thus, there appears to be a relationship between the bird and the tree, which is supported by the fact that the tree has gold patches like the penguin. The whiteness of the tree suggests a receptive attitude to influxes from the heights as well as the vegetative instincts in the psyche.

Duality exists not only in thought but at all levels of the psyche, including the instinctual. A descent in the psyche leads one to becoming more aware of its dualistic instinctual qualities, here reconciled by the gold. One finds truth, not in some rarefied air, but in being grounded in the earthly instincts.

This leads to a discussion of the white tree, which is connected to the heights as well as being rooted in the earth. This implies a natural vegetative instinct that seeks the heights, that is receptive, and need not strain for spiritual aspiration. The psyche itself, from an instinctual base, naturally seeks a vertical ascension. The fact that there are two gold patches on the tree may indicate that this process is just beginning to become conscious.

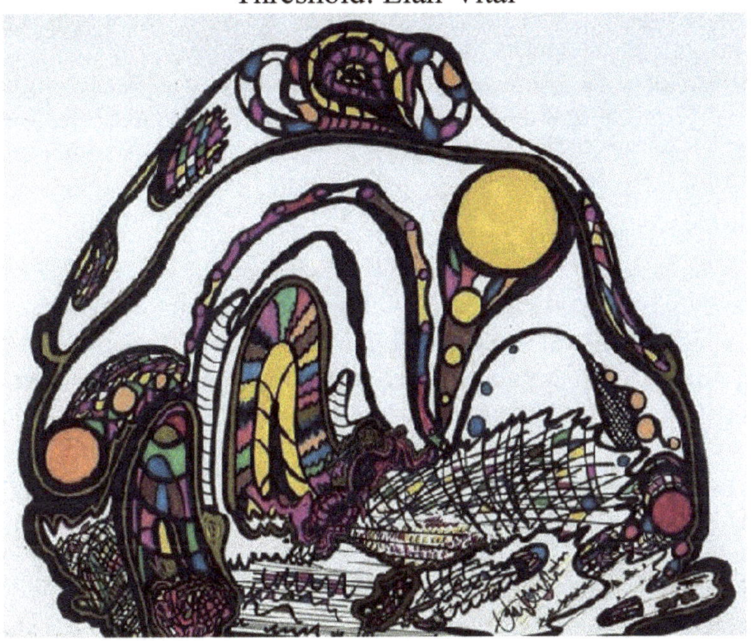

In the painting for this image, I did not work from any preconceived notion or inner image as in my other ones. The painting is rather a free flow of line and color, intuitively perceived and then evaluated. On contemplating the finished drawing, I concluded that what I had painted here was energy, exuberant energy as indicated by the élan *created* by the bright colors and the nature of the forms. The phallic shapes suggest directed energy, while the many colors signify the multiple expression of the libido or psychic energy in life.

This image is an expression of the spirit *Mercurius*, which in alchemical literature is said to wear *omnescolores*, or all colors.[811] Bergson's élan vital comes to mind. There is also a sense of motion particularly in the movement from left toward the right.[812] This movement toward the right implies the coming to consciousness of the complex symbolized here, perhaps something like the energy archetype.

There is also a suggestion that this vital energy is contained, particularly due to the outer line, making this into a kind of *mandala*. Jung makes two interesting observations that are relevant to this discussion. Firstly, he suggests that mass in motion would characterize the psyche insofar as it appears in space.[813] Secondly, he observes that one might assume that the psyche gradually rises from minute extensity to infinite intensity at death.[814] In other words, there is at that time no more extensity of the psyche in time and space, but only intensity. Jung concludes that psyche (per se) is highest intensity in the smallest space.[815] The feeling of containment in this image suggests intensity rather than extensity—that is, it indicates interiorization of psychic energy. However, the sense of man in motion indicates that it is a primordial image of the psyche itself as it is experienced in space and time.

After completing the painting, I came across some writing and pictures by an artist-scientist by the name of L. Alcopley. In discussing his work, he gives further amplificatory material that, I believe, is applicable to this painting. He argues that people in the Western civilization perceive space as containing all entities or objects, while for the Oriental, space is an invisible pleroma that contains energy that permeates everything as an active agent.[816] One of the intriguing aspects of this painting is the use of the white space as an integral and necessary part of the image. In this way, the Western worldview that space contains entities is depicted.

Jung's insistence that Western man must find his own path and not rigidly apply dogma or a discipline from the east seems to be relevant here. Even Native Indians from North America indicate that their path is the opposite of the Tibetan Buddhists. This difference between the east and the west seems to be fundamental, and something every seeker ought to consider, even though the end goal may be similar.

However, Alcopley also integrates the Eastern view in his perception of reality. He says that in his study of the life processes, he is constantly aware of a world where everything is in motion.[817] He studies giant molecules of polymer, which he sees as a flow or motion of elementary spatial processes, where the distribution of space plays a significant role. He observes that the conception of space in his pictures is filled with elementary processes, like those of an apparently "inanimate" origin. There is no suggestion that the images objectively portray molecules, or any such thing—but that the feeling is similar. Although my painting does not resemble Alcopey's paintings, it strikes me as having a similar feeling to the one described here.

For further amplification, I will now turn to the scientific worldview, both ancient and contemporary. According to F. M. Cornford, the primitive worldview is that anything capable of moving itself or something else is alive.[818] The only moving force in the world is life or soul substance—that is, psychic energy. Motion is eternal, and since *physis*, the world soul is alive, this motion is probably not distinguishable from growth, the characteristic movement of life according to Anaximander. This view resembles the Eastern view.

Around 500 BC in the Occident, there was the development of a worldview that, up until only recently, dominated the scientific community.[819] The atomists proposed that matter consists of tiny particles they called atoms, that are constantly in motion, however moving mechanically in the void. In their view, there is nothing but empty space between the atoms, devoid of soul substance. Motion became mechanical and was communicated by colliding particles of matter which were no longer associated with growth and life.

Today, many physicists tend to view the material universe as a "cosmic dance of energy."[820] David Bohm sees the background of existence as an infinite vast sea of energy, an implicate "non-manifest" order.[821] He posits the existence of "unbroken wholeness" between the implicate order and the manifest explicate order of the observable world. Fritjof Capra views particles as consisting of "bundles of energy."[822] He says that subatomic particles have a space aspect and a time aspect. The space aspect allows them to appear as objects with a certain mass, the time aspect as process involving the equivalent energy. Capra compares the material universe to the dance of Shiva.

The movement and vibrant colors in this painting impart the sense of dance, growth, and, certainly, life. As indicated earlier, there is also an integral sense of space, with mass filling the space. There is even a sense of time and process as one's eyes are drawn from left to right across the painting.

The painting began with the black figure outlined in red toward the bottom third of the painting. Von Franz reports a dream of an individual about to die, of a square black box with flashes of red light.[823] The radiating red light suggests energy. Finally, the painting is replete with net-like or lattice-like configurations. In "death" experiences, people sometimes report coming to a net or a grid, a curtain of threads, or a lattice, which psychologically represent thresholds.[824] Von Franz observes that there are numerous energic processes where relatively sudden changes take place, for example, at the freezing point and at the boiling point when a liquid evaporates.[825] Death itself, and the alchemical *mortificatio*, is such a threshold.[826]

In summary, this image seems to represent a threshold experience of life and death of ego, that is which allows for a deepening of the experience of psyche. It also suggests an internalization of psychic energy, energy which is the primal stuff of life and the world. Dying to ego brings more intense life, a closer relationship to the élan vital.

The Symbolic Three (3) and Four (4)

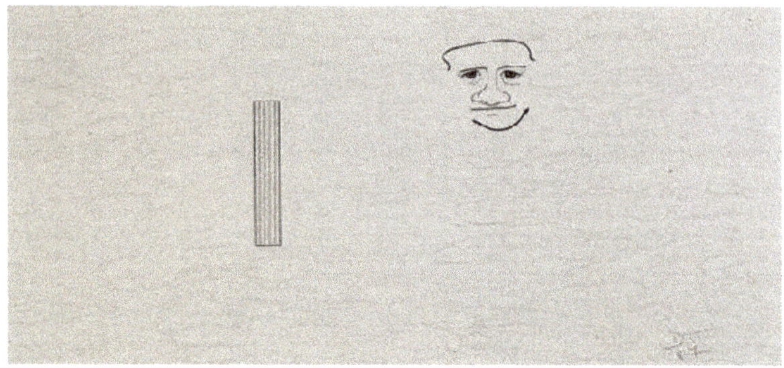

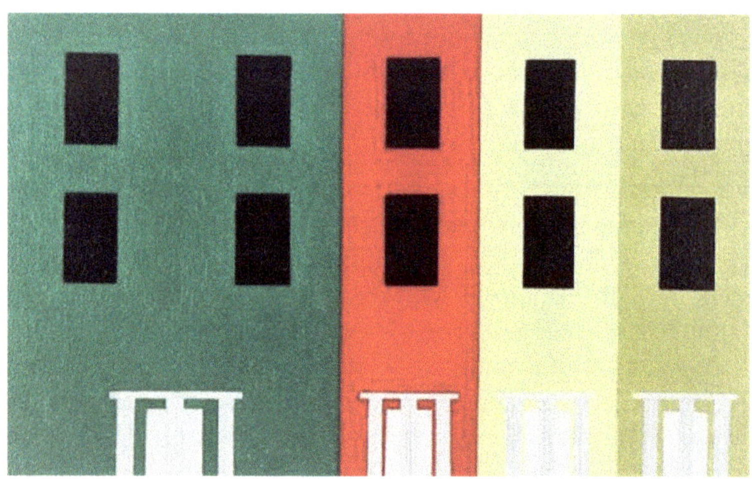

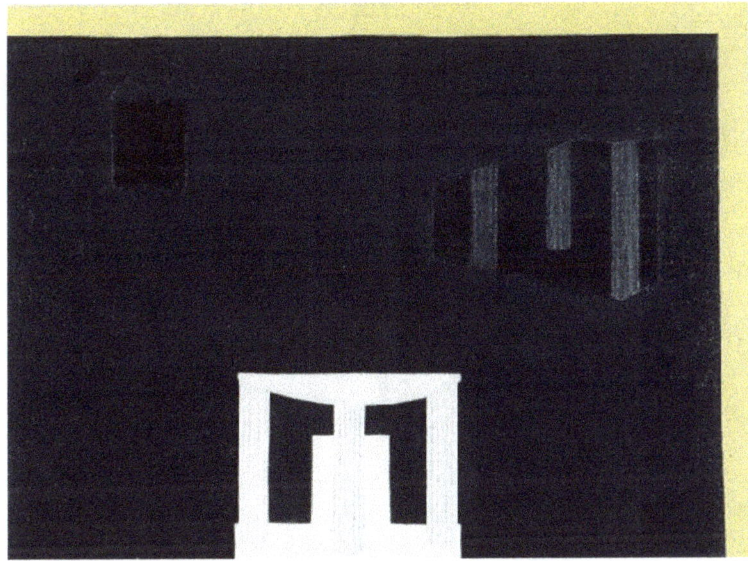

There are three images here that belong together. At a psychological level, the number three (3) symbolizes process, movement, dynamic actualization, and insight in service to wholeness and oneness.[827] Its spontaneous appearance indicates that such a process is taking place in the psyche.

The *first* image which represents the beginning of the process is a lead drawing. In alchemical literature, lead is an agent of *coagulatio*, considered to be a poisonous metal and the cause of troubles and depression.[828] Likewise, in astrology the planet Saturn, whose metal is lead, is said to cause depression.[829] But Saturn is the god of individuation and represents limits, boundaries, even prison, all of which help in the differentiation of one's psychic reality.[830]

In alchemy, lead is related to the *prima materia* as is chaos.[831] In the picture, the scribbly lines in the background also suggest chaos and the potential reality of the wave function in quantum physics. The head in the picture, however, symbolizes meaning, understanding. The implications are that out of the chaos (scribbly lines) and depression (lead) comes meaning, order, Logos, and the actual reality of quantum physics.[832] Like the "world tree," the upright pillar suggests root support, stability, and being centered.[833] It represents the spinal column, which ideally stands erect. In Egyptian mythology, the Tet, a pillar was reputed to contain the body of the god Osiris.[834] The "setting up of the Tet" symbolized the reconstitution of his dismembered body and was accompanied by these words from the Book of the Dead:

Rise up thou, O Osiris!" Thou hast thy backbone. O still-Heart!

Place thou thy self upon thy base.[835]

Thus, the feeling of "slouching" and being beaten and depressed is being replaced with that of standing erect and being centered. Life once again takes on meaning and significance.

In the second picture, there are strong solid colors which emit a sense of life, vibrancy, and power. As in the drawing, the rectangular shape emphasizes the horizontal rather than the vertical. However, the upright columns, pillars, doors, windows, houses, etc., indicate a vertical movement as well. The sense of power comes from the colors, but also from the tension between the vertical and horizontal movement depicted in the painting as well as the painting's compactness. While the horizontal movement suggests life, the vertical movement implies a connection with spirit and consciousness. There is not only life, but consciousness-life. This gives power, as one moves with the life-force without impeding it.

In this painting, there is also the tension between the symbolic three (3) and the symbolic four (4). There are three (3) pillars in each house and four (4) houses that make up the whole. Moreover, the rectangular shape partakes of the symbolic significance of the number four (4). Thus, there is a tension between the dynamic process and the fixed, the concrete, the static. Creative realization unrolls in temporal succession as it is fixed in space.[836]

The pillars and doors are white, the color of receptivity and reflectiveness.[837] *The* three (3) upright columns indicate process.[838] Thus, one passes over the threshold represented by the doors and enters the "houses of color." In other words, the dynamic process involves being open and receptive to the influence of the vibrations of these "symbolic" colors in one's life.

Just what are these influences? Red is the color of Eros, of relatedness and feeling. It means being related to oneself, the inner impulses as well as to people outside. This is Eros. Feeling allows one to make value judgments in relationships and generally in questions of ethics and aesthetics. For the alchemists, redness was referred to as the *rubedo*, and related to the philosopher's stone and the redeeming blood of Christ.[839] Yellow is the color of light, illumination, insight.[840] It relates to clarity in thoughts or for intuitions in life and helps one to go with the flow. Blue is the color of spiritual will, intuitions, and the higher mind.[841] Green is the color of life and the sensation or reality function. It allows one to see and sense things as they are, without distortion.

As the green "house" is double the size of the other houses, it implies that compensatory pressure is stronger there. The reality function encourages one to be actively involved, yet to stay with the humbleness of day-to-day life as it is instead of flying off with impulses and intuitive insights that have no grip on reality.[842] The fact that there are four (4) windows in the "house" of the sensation function puts the emphasis on the fixed, the concrete and wholeness.[843] In the other "houses," there are only two (2) windows, indicating an emphasis on polarity in life.[844]

The sensation function is the closest to the earth and helps ground ideas, insights, and intuitions. Brown suggests the earth and represents the alchemical *coagulatio*.[845] It, too, implies grounding and being with the earth, but also that the whole process coagulates firmly around a central ego.[846]

The ten (10) black windows look like the horizontally organized second hexagram of the *I Ching*. This hexagram represents the receptive, the feminine.[847] Once again there is the notion of being receptive to the vibrations represented by the "houses of colors" in one's life, to yield to their influences. A masculine will, suggested by the upright pillars, on its own is too willful and seeks too much clarity. It does not like darkness or black (the color of the windows), the world of the "feminine."

The ten black windows or five (5) broken lines suggests the influence of the symbolic number five (5). (In the *I Ching*, the hexagrams are actually made up of six (6) lines.)[848] Five (5) is the number of the "inner master," the person with inner control.[849] It suggests two things: being aware of and supporting unfolding destiny, and suffering.[850] One goes with life and does not defend against it or escape. Although there is inevitably suffering in such an approach, it is meaningful. Such a life is both intense and at times joyful.

The situation depicted in this image gives way to the one shown in the following painting. It is noteworthy that this picture has been painted on paper canvas, a relatively inexpensive material. It is also more squarish than the previous painting although still slightly rectangular. There are three (3) white pillars and a white door. The house is black with a black window and three (3) black pillars inside the house shown in cross section. There is a yellow light around and behind the image.

The three pillars suggest process and receptivity as well as being upright and centered in the masculine will. One enters the white door with a reflective, receptive attitude to find the dark feminine yin. As the house is squarish, it is a relatively static inner space, a space of inner brooding. The three (3) upright black pillars, however, suggests process and centeredness. Through this inner meditative state comes light of consciousness, indicated by the yellow light surrounding and behind the black.

But why is this image painted on relatively inferior quality material? Perhaps because this inner meditative brooding, the dark yin-like state is normally held cheaply. It is the dark "feminine" that is rejected. It is this state mind, however, that brings illumination and awareness. It is consciousness in nature that the masculine mind represses, twists, and tries to dominate.

The Living Bread

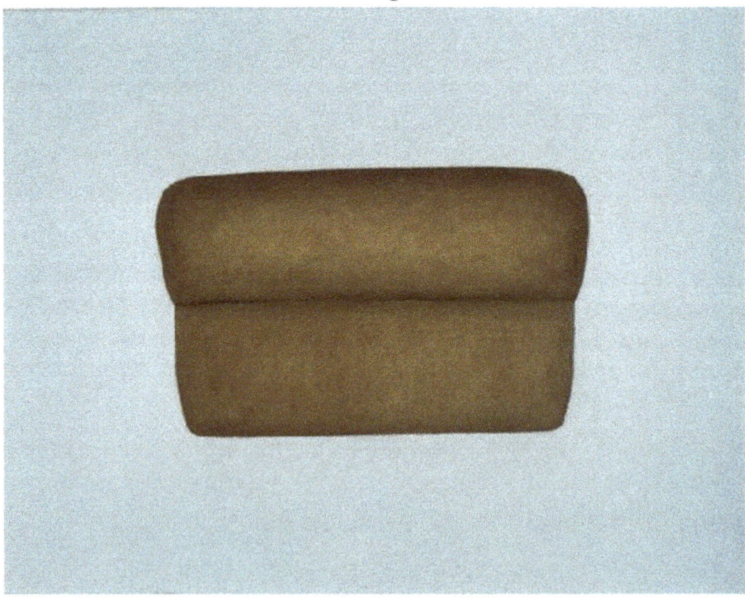

It is interesting to compare the meaning of this image with that of the "Bun with Red Cross Saltire" image and amplification. Bread or buns are essentially feminine in nature, gifts from the grain mother.[851] Yet in the former cases, the image in the dream was painted by the acclaimed artist Georgia O'Keeffe, while, in this case, in the dream, it was painted by an unassuming man.

The sky-blue background indicates the alchemical operation, sublimatio, that is a process of spiritualization. Sublimation in this sense should not be confused with Freud's notion of sublimation, which is reductive and a reaction to repression. This is not the case with spiritual sublimation, which is an abstracting process sui generis and comes with understanding and meaning.

The image is related to the masculine principle of Logos. Amplification for such an image can be found in Jesus Christ as "food of eternal life, the Logos."[852] He is, he proclaims, the true manna, the "bread of God is that which comes down from heaven and gives life to the world"[853] The image also points to essential unity in diversity. In the words of St. Paul, "Because there is one loaf, we who are many are one body, for we all partake of the same loaf."[854]

In Catholic Christianity, the doctrine of transubstantiation has it that the host or bread is literally transformed into the flesh of Christ during the Eucharist.[855] When understood as the flesh of a mystical body of Christ or glorified body, or archetype of the Logos, this doctrine is understandable.[856] As such, eating the bread during the Eucharist is a sacrificial act.[857] Thomas Merton observes that the general meaning of sacrifice is that one "express outwardly in a significant act, (one's) intense submission to and dependence on a "numinous' power."[858] One can extend the meaning of sacrifice in observing that the final goal of life is to make all one's actions sacred, or seeing the sacred in all one's activities. Jung warns that "man has forgotten that life is sacrificial."[859]

The paradox of the bread being a gift from the so-called masculine principle of Logos can be understood by the fact that all creation comes through the Mother. In Christian theological speculation, God creates the world through *Sapientia Dei*, "the sum of the archetypal images in the mind of God."[860] In the Hindu religion, he creates through Shakti-Maya.[861] *Om* is the Word, the mother of all sound and the original source of creation.[862] In this sense, this image relates to the fourth stage of the late classical classification of Eros, that is the full spiritualization of Eros, or wisdom.[863]

In the dream where I see this image, I am with my father at the airport, where we meet an unassuming man, wearing brown sports jacket and slacks, who has just arrived. My father wants to tell him something, but it is of little or no interest to the man. Later, we are outside, and a group of people crowd around him. He eventually emerges from the crowd with this painting that, to my surprise, he has just done.

The humble man is a "male" representative of the mother. My father represents collective values and attitudes which are of little interest to the man who is related to the Logos, "the word made flesh." The essential meaning of the image, then, is the need to express more eternal verities in life rather than traditional collective attitudes and values. Although the ego needs to come to terms with actively expressing such truths in the world as it is presently ordered, life itself will came to its aid, through wisdom.

Conclusion

In *I Am the Way*, I begin with several essays on art and the individuation process as described by C. G. Jung. This gives the reader a background on the value of art to deepen the life process and its significance. I then have a section of images, where I show the image of selected paintings, and then amplify the image in question. In this way, I demonstrate how to use art as a meditative process to increase consciousness of the opposites of the psyche. I follow what I understand to be Jung's method of consciously participating in the individuation process, while bringing in ethical deliberations based on the significance of the image in question and life circumstances. In fact, using art as a medium is only one way of following Jung, but it is the way that, over the years, has suited me best. Other art forms, including dance, music, poetry, or simply dialoguing with the unconscious could be used just as fruitfully, depending upon individuals and their disposition. Otherwise, the importance of becoming conscious of one's dreams and trying to understand their message is of prime importance to consciously individuating. The way as described by Jung is not meant only for the elite, as in past historical times, but is potentially open to everybody destined to consciously live the individuation process.

About the Author

David T. Johnston has been a practicing psychologist in Victoria, British Columbia, Canada, for the past twenty-four years. He is an ardent student of C. G. Jung's path of individuation as well as Sri Aurobindo and the Mother's Integral Yoga. In both paths, knowing through experience is essential. Dr. Johnston received his PhD in clinical psychology from the Pacifica Graduate Institute in Carpinteria, California, in 1996. Following Jung's method, he has been using art as an active meditative approach to self-understanding for the past forty-five years. His art is a meditative means for him to enhance a living dialogue between consciousness and the unconscious.

Bibliography

Abt, Theodor. 2005. *Introduction to Picture Orientation: According to C. G. Jung.* Edited by Fritz Luton. Zurich: Living Human Heritage Publications. pp. 152–165 passim.

Alcopley, L. 1968. "Drawings as Structures and Non-Structures." *Leonardo: International Journal of the Contemporary Artist.* Vol. 1. Number 1. January 1968. New York: Pergamon Press, ltd. pp. 3–15 passim.

Ames. Winthrop, ed. 1974. *What Shall We Name the Baby?* Assisted by Florence A. Doody. A Kangaroo Book. New York: Pocket Books. A Division of Simon & Schuster, Inc. p. 182.

Aquinas, Thomas. 1966. Aurora Consurgens. A Document Attributed to Thomas Aquinas on the Problem of Opposites in Alchemy. *A Companion Work to* C. G. Jung's Mysterium Coniunctionis. Edited with a Commentary by Marie-Louise von Franz. Translated by R. F. C. Hull and A. S. B. Glover. London: Routledge & Kegan Paul. pp. 155, 156, 370.

Argüelles, Miriam & José. 1977. *The Feminine: Spacious as the Sky.* Boulder Colorado: Shambhala Publications, Inc. pp. 41, 43–45 passim. 45, 58, 138–139.

Argüelles, José. 1975. *The Transformative Vision: Reflections on the Nature and History of Human Expression.* Boulder Colorado: Shambhala Publications, Inc. p. 145, 145–147 passim, 145–149 passim, 148–149 passim.

Aurobindo, Sri. 1971. Sri Aurobindo Birth Centenary Library. Popular Ed. 30 vols. Vol. 11. *Hymns to the Mystic Fire.* Mandala 8. Pondicherry: Sri Aurobindo Ashram Press. p. 338, 339, 343, 346.

Aurobindo, Sri. 1977. Sri Aurobindo Birth Centenary Library. Popular ed. 30 vols. Vol. 17. *The Supramental Manifestation.* 8 parts, part V, Heraclities. Pondicherry: Sri Aurobindo Ashram Press. pp. 337.

Aurobindo, Sri. 1972. Sri Aurobindo Birth Centenary Library. Popular ed. 30 vols. Vol. 17. *The Hour of God.* XI parts, part III, *On Yoga: The Web of Yoga.* Pondicherry: Sri Aurobindo Ashram Press. p. 48.

Aurobindo, Sri. 1970. Sri Aurobindo Birth Centenary Library. Popular ed. 30 vols. Vol. 18. *The Life Divine*. Two books, book 2, part 1. Pondicherry: Sri Aurobindo Ashram Press. pp. 325–326 passim, 346–347 passim.

Aurobindo, Sri. 1972. Sri Aurobindo Birth Centenary Library. Popular ed. 30 vols. Vol. 12. *The Upanishads*. 2 parts, part II, *The Upanishads: Katha Upanishad: Second Cycle. First Chapter Verse 12*. Pondicherry: Sri Aurobindo Ashram Press. p. 256.

Aurobindo, Sri. 1972. Sri Aurobindo Birth Centenary Library. Popular ed.30 vols. Vol. 25. *The Mother: With Letters on the Mother and Translation of Prayers and Meditations*. Three Parts, Part I *The Mother*. Pondicherry: Sri Aurobindo Ashram Press. pp. 11, 12,11–14 passim.15–18 passim, 17, 19, 30.

Aurobindo, Sri. 1970. Sri Aurobindo Birth Centenary Library. Popular ed. 30 vols. Vol. 28. *Savitri*, Three Parts, Part 1, book 2, Canto 10, *The Kingdoms and godheads of the Little Mind*. Pondicherry: Sri Aurobindo Ashram Press. p. 245.

Bates, Brian. 1983. *The Way of Wird: Tales of an Anglo-Saxon Sorcerer*. London: Arrow Books Limited. pp. 172–176.

Bauval, Robert, and Ahmed Osman. 2015. *The Soul of Ancient Egypt.: Restoring the Spiritual Engine of the World*. Toronto: Bear & Company. p. 19.

Bear, Sun, Wakun. 1980. *The Medicine Wheel, Earth Astrology*. Illustrated by Mimimosha and Thunderbird Woman. Englewood Cliffs: Prentice Hall, Inc. pp. 32–33 passim. 32–33, 134–135 passim.

Bolen, Jean Shinoda, MD. 1984, *Goddess in Every Woman: A New Psychology of Women*. Forward by Gloria Steinman. San Francisco: Harper & Row Publishers, pp. 75, 78–81 passim. 76, 78, 81, 79–81 passim. 91–92 passim.

Branston, Brian. 1980. *Gods of the North*. London: Thames and Hudson. pp. 286–294 passim.

Brunner, Cornelia. 1963. *Anima as Fate*. Preface by C. G. Jung. Translated by Julius Heuscher. Edited by David Scott May. Dallas: Spring Publications, Inc. pp. xi–xv passim, 73, 126–127 passim.

Budge, E. A. Wallis. 1974. The Egyptian *Heaven & Hell*. Lasalle Illinois: open Court Publishing Company, p. 20.

Budge, E. A. Wallis. 1969. *The Gods of the Egyptians: Studies in Egyptian Mythology.* Two Vols. Vol. 1. New York: Dover Publications, Inc. pp.53– 54 passim, 437–444 passim. 473, 501–502, 510–511, 506–507 passim, 517, 521.

Budge, E. A. Wallis. 1969. *The Gods of the Egyptians: Studies in Egyptian Mythology.* Two vols. Vol. 2. New York: Dover Publications, Inc. p. 104. 196–197 passim.

Budge, E. A. Wallis. 1971. *Egyptian Magic.* With 20 illustrations. New York: Dover Publications, Inc. pp. 44, 47, 55– 56 passim.

Burton, Maurice and Robert. 1976. *Encyclopedia of the Animal Kingdom.* London: Octopus Books. pp. 330–331 passim. 428–430 passim.

Campbell, Joseph. 1970. *The Masks of God: Primitive Mythology.* Viking Compass Book. New York: The Viking Press Inc. pp. 271, 272 passim.

Campbell, Joseph. 1974. *The Masks of God: Occidental Mythology.* Viking Compass Book. New York: The Viking Press Inc. pp. 20, 165

Campbell, Joseph. 1962. *The Masks of God: Oriental Mythology.* Viking Compass Book. New York: The Viking Press Inc. p. 165

Campbell, Joseph. 1974. *The Mythic Image.* Bollingen Series C. Princeton: Princeton University Press. pp. 296–298 passim.

Capra, Fritjof. 1982. *The Turning Point: Science, Society and the Rising Culture.* New York: Bantam Books, Inc. pp. 53–54 passim, 78–79 passim.

Carson, Lionel. 1965. *Great Ages of Man: Ancient Egypt.* Time Life. New York: Time Life Books. pp. 54–55.

Casson, Leonel, ed. 1983. *Great Ages of Man: Ancient Egypt.* Time Life Books. pp. 90–91 passim.

Castaneda, Carlos. 1968. *The Teachings of Don Juan: A Yaqui Way of Knowledge.* New York: Washington Square Press Publication of Pocketbooks. p. 11.

Chetwynd, Tom. 1982. *A Dictionary of Symbols.* A Paladin Book London: Granada Publishing, Limited. pp. 130, 149, 185, 186, 303, 317–318, 365.

Chetwynd, Tom. 1986. *The Dictionary of Sacred Myth: The Language of Your Soul*. Mandala Books. London: Union Paperbacks. pp. 9, 100–103 passim, 121, 122, 123–124 passim, 166, 167.

Chetwynd, Tom. 1987. *A Dictionary for Dreamers*. London: Paladin Grafton Books, a division of the Collins Publishing Group. pp. 53, 68–71, 67–68 passim. 68–69 passim, 68–71 passim. 69–71 passim. 93, 124–127 passim, 182. 166–167 passim.

Ching, I. The Richard Wilhelm Translation. Rendered into English by Cary F. Baynes. Foreword by C. G. Jung. Preface to the Third Edition by Helmut Wilhelm. Bollingen Series XIX. Princeton NJ: Princeton University Press.

Cirlot, J. E. 1976. *A Dictionary of Symbols*. Translated from the Spanish by Jack Sage. Second Ed. New York: Philosophical Library, Inc. pp. 19, 56– 60 passim, 56, 57, 65–66 passim. 82, 137, 138, 141 144–145 passim. 173–175 passim, 221, 254, 272, 287, 289, 309–310 passim, 313–315 passim, 316–318 passim, 331–332 passim, 332, 346–350 passim, 349– 350 passim.

Cooper J. C. 1985. *Symbolism: The Universal Language*. Wellingborough North Hamptonshire. The Aquarian Press. pp. 48–50 passim, 72, 73–74 passim, 74.

1 Corinthians 10:4. *The Holy Bible*. Revised Standard Version. The New Testament. p.903.

1 Corinthians 10:17. *The Holy Bible*. Revised Standard Version. The New Testament. p. 904.

Cornford, F. M. 1957. *From Religion to Philosophy: A Study in the origins of Western Speculation*. Harper Torchbooks: The Cloister Library. New York: Harper & Row, Publishers. pp. 7–11 passim, 14, 155–158 passim.

Cumont, Franz. 1956. *The Mysteries of Mithra*. Translated from the second revised French ed, by Thomas J. McCormick. New York: Dover Publications, Inc. p. 39.

Dante. 1973. *The Divine Comedy: Canto I: Hell*. Translated by Dorothy L. Sayers. Middlesex: Penguin Books, Inc. p. 71.

deLubicz, R. A. Schwaller. 1977. *The Temple in Man*. Translated by Robert and Deborah Lawlor. Illustrated by Lucie Lamy. New York: Inner Traditions International. pp. 48–49 passim, 49.

deLubicz, R. A. Schwaller. 1985. *The Egyptian Miracle: An Introduction to the Wisdom of the Temple*. Inner traditions

Rochester Vermont: Bear & Company. pp. 96, 102, 216.

de Vries, Ad. 1974. *Dictionary of Symbols and Imagery*. London: NorthHolland Publishing Company. P. 47. 57, 101, 141, 161, 163,187, 188, 219–220 passim.231, 240, 243, 247, 288, 335, 340, 343, 366, 382–384 passim, 386–387 passim.438–439, 442–445 passim 463, 477.

Downing, Christine. 1981. *The Goddess: Mythological Images of the Feminine*. New York:The Continuum Publishing Company. pp. 38, 79, 135, 149, 150, 193, 233.

Duncan, Malcolm E.1976. *Duncan's Ritual of Free Masonry*. New York: David Mckay Company, Inc. pp. 70, 150, 158, 150–153 passim, 158–160 passim.

Edinger, Edward F. 1991. *Anatomy of the Psyche: Alchemical Symbolism in Psychotherapy*. Chicago Illinois: Open Court Publishing Company. pp. 12–13, 19, 38, 40, 43, 47–48 passim, 47–50 passim, 58–59 passim. 66, 72–74 passim, 80, 83–84, passim. 85–86, 93–95 passim, 84–85 passim, 117, 118, 142–144 passim, 143–144 passim., 147–151 passim, 152, 161, 209, 215.

Edinger, Edward F. 1987. *The Christian Archetype: A Jungian Commentary on the Life of Christ*. Toronto: Inner City Books. p. 137.

Editor, 1967. *Encyclopedia Britannica*, Inc. 24 Vol. Vol. 10. Gold. Toronto: William Benton Publisher, pp. 536, 536a, 536b, 537.

Editor, 1967. *Encyclopedia Britannica*, Inc. 24 Vols. Vol. 22. Toronto: William Benton Publisher. p. 415.

Editor. 1969. *A Glossary of Sanskrit Terms in the Synthesis of Yoga*. Pondicherry: Sri Aurobindo Ashram. pp. 27–28, 39, 45–46, 48– 49, 56– 57.

Eliade, Mircea. 1974. *The Myth of the eternal Return or, Cosmos and History*. Translation from the French by Willard R. Trask. Bollingen Series XLVI. Princeton NJ: Princeton University Pres, pp. 17–18 passim.

Eliade, Mircea. 1978. *A History of Religious Ideas. Two Vols. Vol. One. From the Stone Age to the Eleusinan Mysteries*. Translated by Willard R. Trask. Chicago: The University of Chicago Press. pp. 130–131.

Flegel, Peter. *Does Western Philosophy have Egyptian Roots?* In

Philosophy Now: A Magazine of Ideas. Issue 128. (2018). London. pp. 1– 6 passim.

Frankfort, Henri. 1961. *Ancient Egyptian Religion: An Interpretation.* New York: Harper and Row, Publishers. pp. 10, 51–53 passim, 52.

Friedrich, Paul. 1978. *The Meaning of Aphrodite.* Chicago: The University of Chicago Press. p. 26.

Fromm, Erich. 1982. *To Have or To Be. With a Note on World Perspectives —What This Series Means by Ruth Nanda Anshen.* A Bantam New Age Book. New York: Harper & Row, Publishers, Inc. pp. 129–132 passim. 132–139 passim.

Genesis 28:22. *The Holy Bible.* Revised Standard Version. The Old Testament.

1 Genesis 1–5. *The Holy Bible.* Revised Standard Version. The Old Testament. p.1.

Genesis 3:5. The Jerusalem Bible. The Old Testament. p. 17.

Gilbert, Katherine Stoddert, Joan K. Holt, and Sara Hudson (eds.). 1976. *The Treasures of Tutamkamun.* New York: Ballantine Books, Ltd. p. 105.

Gimbutas, Maria. 1982. *The Goddesses and Gods of Old Europe. 6500– 3500 BC: Myths and Cult Images.* Berkley and Los Angeles: University of California Press. Harper San Francisco: A Division of Harper Collins Publishers. pp. 108, 186, 186–190 passim. Ibid. p. 187.

Gimbutas, Maria. 1991. *The Language of the Goddess.* San Francisco: Harper San Francisco: A Division of Harper Collins Publishers. Pp. 270– 275 passim.

Goethe. 1973. *Faust.* Two parts. Part One. Translated by Philip Wayne. Penguin Classics. Harmondworth England: Penguin Books, Inc. pp. 39– 42 passim, 70–99 passim.

Graves, Robert. 1978. *The White Goddess.* New York: Farrar, Strauss and Giroux. pp. 51–52 passim, 58, 358.

Grimal, Pierre, ed. 1973. Larousse World Mythology. New York Toronto: The Hamlyn Publishing Group, Ltd. p. 237.

Greene, Liz, 1984. *The Astrology of Fate.* York Beach, Maine: Samuel Weiser, Inc. pp.28–29 passim. 260.

Haggard, H. Rider. 1978. *She.* Sevenoaks Kent: Hodder and Stoughton

Paperbacks. A division of Hodder and Stoughton, ltd. p. 141.

Halevi, Z'ev Ben Shimon. 1975. *An Introduction to the Cabala*. New York: Samuel Weiser, Inc., p. 12.

Hall, Nor. 1980. *The Moon and the Virgin: Reflections on the Archetypal Feminine*. Illustrations by Ellen Kennedy New York: Harper and Row, Publishers. pp. 8–10, 20–22 passim, 118–124 passim.170, 170–171 passim.183–184 passim, 187, 188.

Hamilton, Edith. 1953. *Mythology: Timeless Tales of Gods and Heroes*. A Mentor Book. Illustration by Steele Savage. New York: New American Library Literature. pp. 29, 30, 29–30 passim. 144, 151, 151–152 passim. 188–192 passim.

Hannah, Barbara. 1981. *Encounters with the Soul: Active Imagination as Developed by C. G. Jung*. Santa Monica, Cal: Sigo Press. p. 22.

Hannah, Barbara. 2018. *The Animus: The Spirit of Inner Truth in Women*. Vol. 2. Edited by David David Eldred and Kennedy-Xypolitas. Willmette Illinois: Chiron Publications. p. 243.

Heline, Corinne. 1977. *Sacred Science of Numbers*. Los Angeles: New Age Press, Inc. pp. 1–2, 26–28 passim, 35, 38, 39–41, 44, 46–48, 46–48 passim, 53, 58–59 passim.60, 84, 83, 86, 90, 103, 104–105–107 passim.

Heline, Corinne. 1983. *Healing and Regeneration Through Color*. Camarillo CA: Devorss & Company. pp. 61, 60–61 passim.

Heline, Corinne. 1971. *The Bible and the Stars*. La Canada, CA: New Age Press, Inc. pp. 39–41 passim. 40.

Hillman, James. 1979. *The Dream and the Underworld*. New York: Harper & Row, Publishers. pp. 55, 145, 54, 56.

Hillman, James. 2007. *Anima: An Anatomy of a Personified Notion*. Dallas: Spring Publications, Inc. p. 20, 28.

Hillman, James. 1982. "A Contribution to Soul and Money." In *Soul and Money*. 6 parts, part two. Dallas: Spring Publications, Inc. pp. 35–36 passim. 37, 39.

Hillman, James. 1980. "Silver and the White Earth—Part One." *Dallas: Spring: An Annual of Archetypal Psychology*. pp. 24–29 passim, 29–30.

Hillman, James. 1981. "Silver and the White Earth—Part Two." *Dallas: Spring: An Annual of Archetypal Psychology*. pp. 21–22 passim. 21–26 passim, 22, 23, 37–38 passim 60–61 passim.

Hoeller, Stephan. 1982. *The Gnostic Jung and the Seven Sermons to the Dead*. A Quest Book. Wheaton Illinois. The Theosophical Publishing House. pp. 140–145 passim. 157–158 passim.

Homer. 1961. *The Odyssey*. Translated by Robert Fitzgerald. Drawings by Hans Erni. Book 10. The Grace of the Witch. Garden City, New York. Doubleday & Company, Inc. pp. 177–194. passim.

Hosea 11:1. The Jerusalem Bible. The Old Testament. p. 1464.

Jaffé, Aniela. 1979. C. G. *Jung: Word and Image*. Translation by Krishnan Winston. Bollingen Series XCVII: 2 Princeton N.J.: Princeton University Press. p. 77–79 passim.

Jaffe, Aniela. 1979. C. G. *Jung: Word and Image*. Translation by Krishnan Winston. Bollingen Series XCVII: 2 Princeton N.J.: Princeton University Press. p. 77. 78–79 passim.

1 John 1:5. *The Holy Bible*. Revised Standard Version. The New Testament. p. 835.

John 14:12. *The Jerusalem Bible*. Alexander Jones, general ed. The New Testament. p. 177, 851.

John 6:33. *The Jerusalem Bible*. Alexander Jones, general ed. The New Testament. pp. 158.

The Revelation of John. 8:9. *The Holy Bible*. Revised Standard Version. The New Testament. pp. 972–973 passim.

The Revelation of John. 21–22. *The Holy Bible*. Revised Standard Version. The New Testament. pp. 979–981 passim.

The First Letter of John 5:7–8. *The Jerusalem Bible*. Alexander Jones, general ed. The New Testament. p. 419.

Jonas, Hans. 1963. *The Gnostic Religion: The message of the Alien God and the Beginnings of Christianity*. Second Ed. Revised. Boston: Beacon Press. pp. 62–65 passim, 15–15 passim, 165–169 passim.

Jones, Alex. 1983. *Seven Mansions of Color*. Camarillo CA; Devorss & Company.pp. 6–13 passim. 20–22 passim.42–43 passim, 49–50 passim. 37–39 passim.106–107, passim.) 106–109 passim. 119.112–114 passim. 114. 114–115 passim.

Jung, C. G. *Memories, Dreams, Reflections*. 1965. Recorded and edited by Aniela J. Jaffé, Translated from the German by Winston and Clara Winston, New York: Vantage Books, A division of Random House, pp. 183, 389.

Jung, C. G. 1959. *Modern Psychology: Vols. 3 and 4.* "The Process of Individuation." Vol. 3. Eastern Texts. Notes on Lectures Given at the Eidgenössiche Technische Hochschule. October 1938–March 1940. Zurich. Taken by Barbara Hannah. Zurich: C. G. Jung Institute. p. 767.

Jung, C. G. 1974. The Collected Works. 19 vols. Vol. 5. *Symbols of Transformation.* 2 parts. Part 2 The Dual Mother. Second ed. Second printing. Bollingen Series XX. Princeton NJ: Princeton University Press. p. 382.

Jung, C. G. 1975. The Collected Works. 19 vols. Vol. 10. *Civilization in Transition.* 7 parts. Part IV, The Undiscovered Self. Second ed.. Bollingen Series XX. Princeton NJ: Princeton University Press. p. 304.

Jung, C. G. 1975. The Collected Works. 19 vols. Vol. 11. *Psychology and Religion: West and East.* 9 parts. Part III, Section III: 3, Parallels to the Transformation Mystery.* Second ed. Third printing. Bollingen Series XX. Princeton NJ: Princeton University Press. pp. 240–241.

Jung, C. G. 1975. The Collected Works. 19 vols. Vol. 11. *Psychology and Religion: West and East.*9 parts, Part III. *Transformation Symbolism in the Mass.* Second ed. Third printing. Bollingen Series XX. Princeton NJ: Princeton University Press. pp. 228, 229, 240– 241 passim, 437.

Jung, C. G. 1975. The Collected Works. 19 vols. Vol. 11. *Psychology and Religion: West and East.* 9 parts. Part VI. *Answer to Job.* Second ed. Third printing. Bollingen Series XX. Princeton NJ: Princeton University Press. p. 437.

Jung, C. G. 1977. The Collected Works. 19 vols. Vol. 12. *Psychology and Alchemy.* 3 parts. Part III, *Religious Ideas in Alchemy.* Second ed. Fourth printing. Bollingen Series XX. Princeton NJ: Princeton University Press. pp. 236–237 passim. 438, 464.

Jung, C. G. 1977. The Collected Works. 19 vols. Vol. 12. *Psychology and Alchemy.* 3 parts. Part II. *Individual Dream Symbolism in Relation to Alchemy.* Second ed. Fourth printing. Bollingen Series XX. Princeton NJ: Princeton University Press. pp. 47, 87, 120, 196.95–101 passim. 99.

Jung, C. G. 1977. The Collected Works. 19 vols. Vol. 12. *Psychology and Alchemy.* 3 parts: Part III, chapter 6. *Alchemical Symbolism in the History of Religion.* Second ed. Fourth printing. Bollingen Series XX. Princeton NJ: Princeton University Press. p. 453.

Jung, C. G. 1977. The Collected Works. 19 vols. Vol. 13. *Alchemical Studies.* 6 parts. Part II. Second printing. Bollingen Series XX. Princeton NJ: Princeton University Press. pp. 438, 464.

Jung, C. G. 1977. The Collected Works. 19 vols. Vol. 13. *Alchemical Studies.* 5 books. Book V. *The Philosophical Tree.* Second printing. Bollingen Series XX. Princeton NJ: Princeton University Press. pp. 251– 349 passim, 278–283 passim, 291n. 295–296 passim, 333.

Jung, C. G. 1977. The Collected Works. 19 vols. Vol. 13. *Alchemical Studies.* V Books. Book II. *The Visions of Zosimos.* Second printing. Bollingen Series XX. Princeton NJ: Princeton University Press. pp. 72, 76–77. 81,92–93 passim, 95, 98–99 passim. 98.

Jung, C. G. 1977. The Collected Works. 19 vols. Vol. 13. *Alchemical Studies.* 5 books. Book III. *Paracelsus as a Spiritual Phenomenon.* Second printing. Bollingen Series XX. Princeton NJ: Princeton University Press. pp.116, 134, 148, 152–153 passim.160, 160–163 passim.

Jung, C. G. 1977. The Collected Works. 19 vols. Vol. 13. *Alchemical Studies.* 5 books. Book IV. *The Spirit Mercurius.* Second printing. Bollingen Series XX. Princeton NJ: Princeton University Press. p. 210, 226, 227.

Jung, C. G. 1977. The Collected Works. 19 vols. Vol. 13. *Alchemical Studies.* 5 books. Book I. *Commentary on the Secret of the Golden Flower.* Second printing. Bollingen Series XX. Princeton NJ: Princeton University Press. pp. 16, 21–22 , 25 281–283 passim.

Jung, C. G. 1977. The Collected Works. 19 vols. Vol. 12. *Psychology and Alchemy.* 3 Parts. Part III. *The Work.* Fourth printing. Bollingen Series XX. Princeton NJ: Princeton University Press. p. 293.

Jung, C. G. 1975. The Collected Works. 19 vols. Vol. 8. *The Structure and Dynamics of the Psyche.* 7 books. Book III. *On the Nature of the Psyche.* Second ed. Third printing, with corrections. Bollingen Series XX. Princeton NJ: Princeton University Press. pp. 211, 211–212 passim, 211– 213 passim.

Jung, C. G. 1975. The Collected Works. 19 vols. Vol. 9.1. *The Archetypes and the Collective Unconscious*. 6 parts. Part IV. *The Psychological Aspects of the Kore*. Second ed. Fourth printing. Bollingen Series XX. Princeton NJ: Princeton University Press. pp. 184n,185.

Jung, C. G. 1975. The Collected Works. 19 vols. Vol. 9.1. *The Archetypes and the Collective Unconscious.*6 parts. Part I. *Archetypes of the Collective Unconscious*. Bollingen Series XX. Princeton NJ: Princeton University Press. pp. 33–37 passim.

Jung, C. G. 1974. The Collected Works. 19 vols. Vol. 14. *Mysterium Coniunctionis*. Second ed. Second printing. Bollingen Series XX. Princeton NJ: Princeton University Press. pp. 48, 304n., 491.

Jung, C. G. 1974. The Collected Works. 19 vols. Vol. 14. *Mysterium Coniunctionis*. 6 parts. Part IV. *Rex and Regina*. Second ed. Second printing. Bollingen Series XX. Princeton NJ: Princeton University Press. pp. 288–289 passim.

Jung, C. G. 1974. The Collected Works. 19 vols. Vol. 14. *Mysterium Coniunctionis*. 6 parts. Part II. *The Paradoxa*. Second ed. Second printing. Bollingen Series XX. Princeton NJ: Princeton University Press. pp. 48–52 passim. 51, 53, 64, 255, 288–289 passim.

Jung, C. G. 1974. The Collected Works. 19 vols. Vol. 14. *Mysterium Coniunctionis*. 6 parts. Part V. *Adam and Eve*. Second ed. Second printing. Bollingen Series XX. Princeton NJ: Princeton University Press. p. 395, 434–436 passim.

Jung, C. G. 1975. The Collected Works. 19 vols. Vol. 9,1. *The Archetypes and the Collective Unconscious*. 6parts. Part IV. *The Psychological Aspects of the Kore*. Second ed. Fourth printing. Bollingen Series XX. Princeton NJ: Princeton University Press. p. 185.

Jung, C. G. 1975. The Collected Works. 19 vols. Vol. 9,I. *The Archetypes and the Collective Unconscious*. 6parts. Part VI. *Concerning Mandala Symbolism*. Second ed. Fourth printing. Bollingen Series XX. Princeton NJ: Princeton University Press.

Jung, C. G. 1975. The Collected Works. 19 vols. Vol. 9,II. *Aion: Researches into the Phenomenology of the Self.* 15 parts. Part VI. The Sign of the Fishes. Second ed. Fourth printing. Bollingen Series XX. Princeton NJ: Princeton University Press. p. 73, 89, 115, 118–119 passim. 183.

Jung, C. G. 1977. The Collected Works. 19 vols. Vol. 12. *The Structure and Dynamics of the Psyche. 7 parts. Part III, On the Nature of the Psyche.* Second ed. Third printing with corrections. Bollingen Series XX. Princeton NJ: Princeton University Press. p. 211–212.

Jung, C. G. 1971. The Collected Works. 19 vols. Vol. 13.*MysteriumConiunctionis.* 6 parts, Part VI. *The Conjunction.* Second edition. Second printing. Bollingen Series XX. Princeton NJ: Princeton University Press. p. 513.

Jung, C. G. 1970. The Collected Works. 19 vols. Vol. 16. *The Practice of Psychotherapy: Essays on the Psychology of the Transference and Other Essays.* 2 parts, Part II. *Specific Problems of Psychotherapy: An Account of the Transference Phenomena (Based on the Illustrations to the "Rosarium Philosophorum.")* Second ed. Second printing. Bollingen Series XX. Princeton NJ: Princeton University Press. pp. 174, 247–248 passim. 284, 299, 287, 300–301 passim. 314.

Jung, C. G. "Psychological Commentary on Kundalini Yoga: lectures One and Two." *New York. Spring: An Annual of Archetypal Psychology and Jungian Thought.* 1975. pp. 8–9 passim, 9, 10, 15, 15–18 passim. 16, 17, 21.

Jung, C. G. "Psychological Commentary on Kundalini Yoga: lectures Three and Four." *New York. Spring: An Annual of Archetypal Psychology and Jungian Thought.* 1976. pp. 14–16 passim. 25–27 passim. 27–30 passim.

Jung, C. G. 1976. *The Visions Seminars.* Two Books. Book 1. From the Complete Notes of Mary Foote. Postscript by Henry A. Murray. Zurich: Spring Publications, Inc. pp. 100, 101, 172,168–170 passim. 170, 214– 215 passim. 244, 244–246 passim.

Jung, C. G. 1976. *The Visions Seminars.* Two Books. Book 2. Part 13. From the Complete Notes of Mary Foote. Postscript by Henry A. Murray. Zurich: Spring Publications, Inc. pp. 90, 93, 94, 96, 95–96 passim 96–98 passim. 204–205 passim, 205,259, 260, 341, 406, 406–407 passim. 513.

Henderson, Hazel. 1981. *The Politics of the Solar Age: Alternatives to Economics.* Garden City, NY: Anchor Press/Doubleday. pp. 190–194 passim. 221–222 passim.

Kerenyi, Karl. 1979. *Goddess of Sun and Moon.* Translated from German by Murray Stein. 4 parts, Part III. *The Golden One-*

Aphrodite. Irving, Texas: Spring Publications, Inc. p. 41–60 passim.

Kerenyi, Karl. 1978. *Athene, Virgin and Mother in Greek Religion*. Translated from German by Murray Stein. With Translator's Afterthoughts. Zurich: Spring Publications. pp. 22. 22–23 passim.

Krajenke, Robert W. 1976. *The Psychic Side of the American Dream: Revitalizing the American Spirit*. Virginia Beach: A.R.E. press. pp. 40–44 passim.

Kul, Djwal. 1976. *Intermediate Studies of the Human Aura*. Dictated by the messenger, Elizabeth Clare Prophet. Los Angeles: Summit University Press. pp. 77–82 passim, 78–79 passim. 79–80 passim. 91–88 passim Plate 6, plate 7, plate 8plates 2, 9, pp. 28–29 passim.

Lawlor, Robert. 1982. *Sacred Geometry: Philosophy and Practice*. New York: Crossword Publishing Company. pp.12,26, 27, 72–73 passim.

Layard, John. 1988. *The Lady of the Hare: a Study in the Healing Power of Dreams*. Forward by Robert Johnson. Boston: Shambala Publications, Inc. pp. 178–179 passim.

Lenardon, Robert J., and Mark P. O. Norford. 1977. *Classical Mythology*. pp. 101–103 passim. 2nd ed. New York: Longman, Inc. pp. 101–103 passim, 101–102 passim.

Lockhart, Russell A. "Coins and Psychological Change." In *Soul and Money*. 6 parts, part 1. Dallas: Dallas Institute of Humanities. Pp. 14–18 passim. 18–19 passim, 19. 19–20 passim.

Luke 21:19. *The Holy Bible*. Revised Standard Version. The New Testament. p. 829.

Luke, Helen. 1975. *Dark Wood to White Rose: A Study of Meaning in Dante's Divine Comedy*. Pecos, New Mexico: Dove Publications, pp. 71– 76 passim.

Mattoon, Mary Ann. 1984. *Understanding Dreams*. Dallas: Spring Publications, Inc. pp. 69–71passim.

Matthew 2:14–15, 19–20. *The Jerusalem Bible*. The New Testament. p. 17. Matthew 16:18. *The Holy Bible*. Revised Standard Version. The New Testament. pp. 1, 771.

Matthew 22:21. *The Holy Bible*. Revised Standard Version. The New Testament. p. 777.

Mark 1:16. *The Holy Bible.* Revised Standard Version. The New Testament. p.786.

McGuire, William, Hull, R.F.C., eds. 1980. *C. G. Jung Speaking: Interviews and Encounters.* Picador edition. London: Pan Books, ltd. Pp. 108, 109 passim.

Meir, C. A. 1967. *Ancient Incubation and Modern Psychotherapy.* Translated by Monica Curtis. A volume from the studies from the C. G. Jung Institute, Zurich. Forward by C. G. Jung. Evanston: Northwestern University Press. pp. 5–11 passim, 26–27 passim.

Monick, Eugene. 1980. *Phallos: Sacred Image of the Masculine.* Toronto: Inner City Books. pp. 30–31 passim.

Mookerjee, Ajit. 1971/1972. *Tantra Art. Its Philosophy & Physics.* New Delhi: Ravi Kumar. Pp. 77–79 passim. 119

Mookerjee, Ajit. 1982. *Kundalini: The Arousing of the Inner Energy.* New York: Destiny Books. pp. 39–41.

Morford, Mark P. O., Lenardon, 1977, *Classical Mythology.* Second Ed. New York: Longman, Inc., pp. 101, 395.101–102 passim.

Mother, The. 1961. *The Mother on Sri Aurobindo. Pondicherry:* Sri Aurobindo Ashram Press. p. 3.

Merton, Thomas. 1976. *The Living Bread.* London: Burns and Oates, pp. 13, 29, 35, 82.

Miller, David L. 1984. "On Literalism: The Letter and the Monkey." Dallas. *Spring: An annual of Archetypal Psychology and Jungian Thought.* Pp. 152–153.

Nichols, Sally. 1980. *Jung and Tarot.* New York: Samuel Weiser, Inc. pp. 227–247 passim, 214, 215–225 passim.

Neumann, Erich. 1954. *On the Moon and Matriarchal Consciousness.* Translated by Hildegard Nagel. Zurich: Spring Publications. pp. 91–92 passim, 83–99 passim.

Neumann, Erich. 1956. *Amor and Psyche: The Psychic Development of the Feminine: A Commentary on the Tale of Apuleius.* Translated from the German by Ralph Manheim. Bollingen Series LIV. Princeton: Princeton University Press. pp. 3–53, passim.

Neumann, Erich. 1974. *The Great Mother: An Analysis of the Archetype.* Translated from the German by Ralph Manheim. Bollingen Series XLVII. Princeton NJ: Princeton University

Press. pp. 49, 48–49 passim, 65–67 passim, 98–100 passim. 98–99 passim. 150, 152–153 passim, 158, 219, 240–243 passim 242–243 passim, 332.

Nietzsche, Friedrich. 1974. *Thus Spake Zarathustra*. Translated with an Introduction by R. J. Holingdale. Middlesex: Penguin Books, Inc. p. 46.

Norelli-Bachelet, Patrizia (Thea). *The Truth of That which Moves*. Kodaikanal, Tamil Nadu. *The Vishaal Newsletter*. Vol. 0, Number 1. October 1985. p. 6.

Norelli-Bachelet, Patrizia (Thea). *The Supramental Change*. Kodaikanal, Tamil Nadu. *The Vishaal Newsletter*. Vol. 0, Number 3. February 1986. pp. 27–28.

Norelli-Bachelet, Patrizia (Thea). 1975. *The Gnostic Circle: A Synthesis in the Harmonies of the Cosmos*. Panorama City, California: Aeon Books, Corecki Corporation. pp.1–3, 1, 2, 12, 13, 14,67, 69, 109, 110, 209–222 passim,

Norelli-Bachelet, Patrizia (Thea). 1981. *The New Way: A Study in the Rise and Establishment of a Gnostic Society.* Kodai Kanal India: Aeon Books. p. 142.

Norelli-Bachelet, Patrizia. 1974. *Symbols and the Question of Unity.* 3 parts. Part III. Basics of Symbols: The Language of Unity. Wassenaar, Holland: *Servire Publishers* pp. 18, 66, 66–67 passim.67–68 passim. 69, 109, 110.

Ouseley, S. G. J. 1976. *Color Meditations: With Guide to Color Healing*. Romford, Essex: L. N. Fowler & Co., Ltd. pp 22–24 passim. 23–25, 64–68. 73, 98.

Ouseley, S. G. J. 1976. *The Power of the Rays: The Science of Color Healing*. Romford, Essex: L. N. Fowler & Co., Ltd. pp 74–75 passim. 75–76 passim.

Pandit, M. P. Compiler. 1966. *Dictionary of Sri Aurobindo's Yoga.*

Pondicherry: Dipti Publications. pp. 31, 32, 33, 64, 65, 196–197 passim. 252–261 passim. 157, 184, 257–274, 295–296.

Paris, Ginette. 1986. *Pagan Meditations, The Worlds of Aphrodite, Artemis, and Hestia.* Dallas: Spring Publications, 12, pp. 16–19 passim. pp. 27–28 passim.

Peck, Scott. 1985. *People of the Lie: The Hope for Healing Human Evil.* A Touchstone Book. New York: Simon and Schuster, Inc. p.

203. 62, 177, 207, 121.

Portman, Adolf Christopher Rowe, Dominique Zahan, Ernst Benz, Rene Huyghe, and Toshihikom Izutsu. 1977. *Color Symbolism: Eranos Excerpts.* Composed by Susan Haule. Edited by Robert Weining, Translated from German by Lee B. Jennings. Zurich: Spring Publications. p. 142. 1180.

Qualls-Corbett, Nancy. 1988. *The Sacred Prostitute: Eternal Aspect of the Feminine.* Forward by Marion Woodman. Toronto: Inner city Books. p. 138.

Rank, Otto. 1989. *Art and Artist: Creative Urge and Personality Development.* New York: W. W. Norton & Company. pp. 140, 143, 161–168 passim, pp. 144–145 passim, 339–340 passim, 357–358 passim, 361–366 passim, 305–314 passim.

Rest, Freidrich. 1959. *Our Christian symbols.* Illustrated by Harold Minton.

Lebaron Pennsylvania: The Christian Education Press. p. 10, 31.

Rudhyar, Dayne. 1971. *New Mansions for New Men.* Wassenar, The Netherlands: NV Servine. p. 123.

Sardello, Robert J. 1983. "Money and the City." In *Money and the Soul of the World.* Two parts, part I. Dallas: the Dallas Institute of Humanities and Culture. pp. 2, 9. 6–7 passim. 13–14 passim.

Schweizer, Andreas. 2010. *The Sungod's Journey Through the Netherworld: Reading the Egyptian Ancient Amduat.* Ithaca: Cornell University Press. pp. 60, 153. 4–5 passim, pp. 1–209 passim, 122–123, passim.

Severnson, Randolph. 1983. "Money and Nature." In *Money and the Soul of the World.* Two parts, part 2. Dallas: the Dallas Institute of Humanities and Culture. p. 31.

Shamdasani, Sonu, ed. 1996. *The Psychology of Kundalini Yoga: Notes of the Seminar Given in 1932 by C. G. Jung.* Bollingen Series XCIX. Princeton NJ: Princeton University Press. pp. pp. xlvii –liv passim, passim.75.

Spiegelman, J. Marvin, PhD, and Mikusen Miyuki, PhD. 2018. *Buddhism and Jungian Psychology.* 3 parts, part 2. *The Zen Oxherding Pictures.* 2nd ed. Temp, AZ: New Falcon Publications. pp. 29–113. 103–113 passim.

Squire, Charles, *Celtic Myth and Legend, Poetry and Romance.* Van

Nuys, California: Newcastle Publishing co., Ltd. p. 416.

Stevens, Anthony. 1982. *Archetypes: A Natural History of the Self.* First Quill Edition. New York: William Morrow and Company, Inc. pp. 274–275 passim.

The I Ching or Book of Changes. 1967. The Richard Wilhelm Translation. Rendered into English by Cary F. Baynes. Preface by Helmut Wilhelm. Forward by C. G. Jung. Bollingen Series XIX. Princeton: Princeton University Press. pp. passim, 3–9 passim, 10.

Thompson, Frances. 1980. *The Hound of Heaven.* With Decorations by Jean Youre. Wilton Connecticut: Morehouse-Barlowe Co., Inc. p. 41.

von Franz, Marie-Louise. 1974. *Number and Time: Reflections Leading toward a Unification of Depth Psychology and Physics.* Translated by Andrea Dykes. Studies in Jungian Thought. James Hillman, general editor. Evanston: Northwestern University Press. pp 9–10 passim, 45, 73–74 passim, 102, 101–111 passim, 101–104 passim, 102, 108,125, 131, 129–131 passim. 131, 163, 211, 215, n.7.

von Franz, Marie-Louise. 1975. *C. G. Jung: His Myth in Our Time.* Translated from the German by William H. Kennedy. New York: The C. G. Jung Foundation for Analytical Psychology, Inc. pp. 105–106.

Von Franz, Marie-Louise. 1975. *Creation Myths.* Second unrevised printing. Zurich: Spring Publications. pp. 50–51 passim. 122–123 passim, 124, 161–164 passim.

von Franz, Marie-Louise. 1980. *The Psychological Meaning of Redemption Motifs in Fairy Tales.* Toronto: Inner City Books. pp. 71, 72.

von Franz, Marie-Louise. 1980. *Alchemy: An Introduction to the Symbolism and the Psychology.* Toronto: Inner City Books. p. 265.

von Franz, Marie-Louise. 1986. *On Dreams and Death: A Jungian Interpretation.* Translated from the German by Emanuel Xipolitis Kennedy and Vernon Brooks. Boston: Shambhala Publication Inc. pp. 40, 72, 83, 97–99 passim, 97, 110, 111, 111–116 passim, 120–123 passim, 124, 125 passim, 138,139, 139–141 passim, 144, 253, 147, 148, 151, 152, 153, 154.

von Franz, Marie-Louise, Jung, Emma. 1972. *The Grail Legend.* Translated by Andrea Dykes. London: Hodder and Stoughton, Ltd. pp. 180. 324.

von Franz. 2008. "C. G. Jung's Rehabilitation of the Feeling Function in Our Civilization." *Jung Journal*, 2:2, 9–20.

Walker, Barbara G. 1988. *The Woman's Dictionary of Symbols and Sacred Objects.* Illustrated by the author) San Francisco: Harper and Row Publishers. pp.4, 49, 61, 61– 62 passim,92, 92–93 passim, 99,151,295, 306, 307,374, 415. 482–483 passim, 482, 483, 507, 525–526 passim.

Ware, Timothy. 1992. *The Orthodox Church.* New York: Penguin Books. pp. 230, 232.

Warner, Marina. 1976. *Alone of All Her Sex: The Myth and the Cult of the Virgin Mary.* Oxford: Oxford University Press. p. 216. 257 266.

Weekly, Ernest. 1967. *An Etymological Dictionary of Modern English.* Two vols. Vol. One. New York: Dover Publications, Inc. p. 760.

Werther, Davis, Schwind, Das, Miner. 1985. *Canadian Personnel Management and Human Resources.* 2nd ed. Toronto: McGraw-Hill Ryerson, Limited. pp. 14–16 passim.

Wescott, Wynn. 1911. *Numbers: Their Occult Power and Mystic Virtues.*

New York: Allied Publications. Pp. 95–96. www.auntyflow.com/palmistry/Jupiter.finger.

Zeller, Max. 1975. *The Dream: The Vision of the Night.* Edited by Janet Dallet. Los Angeles: The Analytical Psychology Club and the C. G. Jung Institute. pp. 170–171 passim.

Zimmer, Heinrich. 1972. *Myths and Symbols in Indian Art and Civilization.* Edited by Joseph Campbell. Bollingen Series VI Princeton: Princeton University Press. pp. 154–155 passim.

1   C. G. Jung (as recorded in Theodor Abt, 2005, p. 15).

2   Ibid, p. 7.

3   Ibid, p. 24.

4   Ibid., p. 16.

5   1986.

6   Campbell, as reported in Gulick, 1990 and Miller, 1990; Henderson, 1984.

7   1990.

8   p. 117.

9   1986.

10 pp. 112–113.

11 1986.

12 1972.

13 p. 122.

14 p. 123.

15 p. 123.

16 P. 131.

17 p. 132.

18 As reported in Campbell, 1986, pp. 137–138 passim.

19 1990.

20 Hillman, 1984.

21 Richard Underwood, 1990, p. 26.

22 1985.

23 p. 203.

24 p. 25.

25 p. 221.

26 As reported in May,1985.

27 p. 238.

28 p. 146.

29 As reported in King, 1990.

30 Schiller, 1981.

31 Snell, As reported in Schiller, 1981.

32 p. 121.

33 Ibid.

34 Sri Aurobindo, as reported in Johnston, 1989.

35 1956.

36 pp. 212, 217.

37 Ibid. p. 217.

38 Ibid. p. 217.

39 Hillman, 1983, pp. 108–109.

40 p. 225.

41 Sri Aurobindo, 1978, p. 343.

42 Hillman, 1984, p. 26.

43 p. 31.

44 As reported in Hillman, 1984, p. 28.

45 p. 33.

46 p. 39.

47 p. 34.

48 p. 34.

49 Plotinus, As reported in Hillman, 1984.

50 1972, p. 58–59.

51 1984.

52 Read, 1962, Neumann, 1983.

53 As reported in Armstrong, 1962.

54 Sri Aurobindo, 1972, p. 333.

55 1974.

56 As reported in Sharp, 1987, p. 21.

57 p. 121.

58 1985.

59 1986.

60 1974, p. 121.

61 1991, p. C-8.

62 Ibid.

63 1974, p. 121.

64 Jung, 1974, p. 28.

65 1972, p. 214.

66 Ibid.

67 As reported in Johnston, 1989.

68 1980.

69 1984.

70 1985.

71 1983, pp. 186–187.

72 1989.

73 1974.

74 Henderson, 1990.

75 1974; 1984, pp. 53–54.

76 Jung, as reported in Sharp, 1987.

77 Jung, as quoted in Adler, 1975, pp. 482–488.

78 1984.

79 Campbell, 1986, p. 122.

80 1967, p. 18.

81 1974.

82 1988, pp. 74–75.

83 Rank, 1989.

84 Armstrong, 1987.

85 Ibid. p. 48.

86 Hillman, 1981.

87 1967, p. 18.

88 1970.

89 1962.

90 1983, pp. 24, 37.

91 1987, p. 22.

92 Ibid. p. 37.

93 1959, 1974.

94 1977.

95 1971.

96 Sri Aurobindo, 1971, p. 131.

97 Sri Aurobindo, 1972, p. 333.

98 1987.

99 1972, p. 333.

100 Sri Aurobindo, 1972, p. 71.

101 As quoted in Adler, 1975, p. 316

102 As quoted in Adler, 1975, pp. 81–83.

103 Ibid. pp. 107–108.

104 1989, p. 470.

105 1987.

106 1987, p. 4.

107 1987, p. 45.

108 1987.

109 Sri Aurobindo, 1972, p. 333.

110 As quoted in Sharp, 1982, p. 21.

111 1980.

112 1970.

113 As quoted in Armstrong, 1987, p. 68

114 Sri Aurobindo, As quoted in Purani, 1962, p. 63.

115 Ibid. p. 75.

116 1974.

117 Ibid. p. 28.

118 1971.

119 Ibid. p. 91.

120 1975.

121 1975.

122 1976, P. 347.

123 As reported in Hannah, 1976.

124 Ibid. p. 128.

125 Oh Shinnah, 1977.

126 1975a, p. 436.

127 1975b, p. 44.

128 1975a.

129 1966.

130 As quoted in Poncé, 1991.

131 1966.

132 1971, p. 460.

133 1968, p. 226.

134 As reported in Jaffe, 1979, p. 78.

135 Ibid., p. 78.

136 Jung, 1969, p. 211–213 passim.

137 Capra, 1983.

138 As reported in Johnston, 1990, p. 213.

139 Ibid. p. 213.

140 As reported in Johnston, 1991.

141 1977, pp. 211–333 passim.

142 The Richard Wilhelm translation of the I Ching, pp. 97–98.

143 von Franz, 1980.

144 Johnston, 1990.

145 Johnston, 1991.

146 1968.

147 1980.

148 As reported in von Franz, 1980.

149 The Richard Wilhelm Translation. Rendered into English by Cary F. Baynes. Foreword by C. G. Jung. Preface to the Third Edition by Helmut Wilhelm.

150 Barbara G. Walker, 1988, p. 415.

151 Erich Neumann, 1956, pp. 3–53 passim.

152 Nor Hall, 1980, pp. 20–22 passim.

153 Mary Ann Matoon, 1984, pp. 69–72 passim.

154 Maria Gimbutas, 1991, pp. 270–275 passim; Maria Gimbutas, 1982, p. 186.

155 Ibid. p. 187.

156 Nor Hall, 1980. p. 9–10.

157 Maria Gimbutas, 1982, p. 186.

158 S. G. J. Ouseley, 1976, pp. 25, 67–68.

159 Ibid. pp. 23–24, 64–65; Halevi, Z'ev Ben Shilom, 1975, p. 12.

160 Wynn Westcott, 1911, pp. 95–96; Corinne Heline, 1977, pp. 1–2.

161 Ibid. pp. 14–15; Marie Louise von Franz, 1974, p. 45.

162 As reported in Patrizia Norelli-Bachelet (Thea), 1985, p. 6.

163 Sri Aurobindo, 1972, p. 48.

164 Miriam and José Arguelles, 1977, pp. 138–139.

165 Patrizia Norelli-Bachelet (Thea), 1986, pp. 27–28.

166 Miriam and José Arguelles, 1977, p. 138.

167 Ibid, p. 138.

168 Ibid. p. 139.

169 Ibid, p. 139–140.

170 Ibid. p. 139.

171 Corinne Heline, 1977, p. 1.

172 Ibid, p. 6.

173 Ibid, p. 11–12.

174 Ibid, pp. 9–10.

175 Patrizia Norelli-Bachelet (Thea), 1975, p, 13; Marie Louise von Franz, 1974, p. 102.

176 As reported in Ibid, p. 102.

177 Patrizia Norelli-Bachelet, 1974, pp. 66–67 passim; Marie Louise von Franz, 1974, p. 129.

178 Marie Louise von Franz, 1974, p. 131.

179 Corinne Heline, 1977, pp. 26–28 passim.

180 M. P. Pandit, 1966, pp. 252–261 passim; Patrizia Norelli-Bachelet (Thea), 1981, p. 142.

181 Marie Louise von Franz, 1974, p. 129–131 passim.

182 Ibid. p. 129–131 passim.

183 Corinne Heline, 1977, p. 39.

184 Ibid, p. 35.

185 Carlos Castaneda, 1968, p. 11.

186 Corinne Heline, 1977, p. 40.

187 Ibid. p. 46.

188 Ibid. p. 46.

189 Ibid. p. 46–48 passim.

190 The Mother, 1961, p. 3.

191 The Mother, 1961, p. 3.

192 Corinne Heline, 1977, pp. 56–57.

193 Ibid. p. 60.

194 Marie Louise von Franz, 1974, p. 128.

195 Corinne Heline, 1977, pp. 68–69.

196 Ibid. p. 70–72 passim.

197 Ibid. p. 66.

198 Ibid. p. 74, 76.

199 Ibid. pp. 82–84 passim.

200 Patrizia Norelli-Bachelet, 1975, pp. 1–3 passim.

201 Ibid. p. 209–225 passim.

202 Corinne Heline, 1977, p. 83.

203 Ibid. pp. 83, 88.

204 Ibid. p. 90

205 Ibid. p. 86.

206 Ibid. p. 90.

207 Robert Bauval, Ahmed Osman, 2015, p. 19.

208 Barbara G. Walker, 1988, p. 367.

209 Andreas Schweizer, 2010, pp. 60, 153.

210 Ibid. pp. 4–5 passim.

211 Ibid, pp. 1–209 passim.

212 Ibid, pp. 4–5 passim.

213 Otto Rank, 1989, pp. 144, 145 passim, 339–340 passim, 357–358 passim, 361–366 passim, 305–

1. 314 passim.

214 Matthew 2:14–15, 19–20,The Jerusalem Bible, The Old Testament. p. 17; Hosea 11:1, The Jerusalem Bible, The Old Testament. p. 1464.

215 Andreas Schweizer, 2010, pp. 122–123, passim.

216 Peter Flegel, 2018, pp. 1–6 passim.

217 Joseph Campbell, 1970, pp. 271–272 passim; Ad de Vries, 1974, p. 101.

218 Barbara G. Walker, 1988, pp. 149–150, 337; Ad de Vries, 1974, p. 141.

219 Ibid. pp. 136–137.

220 Ibid. pp. 101.

221 Miriam and José Arguelles, 1977, p. 58.

222 Lionel Carson, 1965, pp. 54–55.

223 Tom Chetwynd, 1987, pp. 166–167.

224 Ad de Vries, 1974, pp. 438–439; Gilbert, Holt, Hudson, (editors) 1976, p. 105.

225 Ibid. p. 105.

226 Henri Frankfort, 1961, p. 52.

227 Matthew 22:21. The Holy Bible, Revised Standard Version p. 777.

228 Dante, Translated by Dorothy L. Sayers, 1973, p. 71.

229 Marie Louise von Franz, 1975, pp. 105–106.

230 www. auntyflow.com/palmistry/Jupiter.finger.

231 John 1:5, The Holy Bible Revised Standard Version: The New Testament, p. 835.

232 Luke 21:19, The Holy Bible. Revised Standard Version. The New Testament, p. 829.

233 Scott Peck, 1985, p. 203.

234 Ibid. pp. 62, 177, 207; Ibid. p. 121.

235 C. G. Jung, 1977, p. 87.

236 Ad de Vries, 1974, p. 243; C.G. Jung, 1975, pp. 240–242.

237 Ibid. pp. 228–229.

238 Ibid. pp. 229.

239 Ad de Vries, 1974, p. 231.

240 C. G. Jung, 1975, p. 229.

241 Ibid. p. 394.

242 Sri Aurobindo, 1972, p. 256.

243 Barbara Walker, 1988, p. 140.

244 Ad de Vries, 1974. p. 185–186.

245 J. E. Cirlot, 1976, pp. 137–138.

246 Ibid. pp. 19, 137–138, 272.

247 C. G. Jung, 1975, p. 211.

248 Sri Aurobindo, 1970, p. 245.

249 Tom Chetwynd, 1987, p. 70.

250 Pandit, M. P., 1966, p. 31.

251 Ad de Vries, 1974, p. 57.

252 Ibid. p. 57.

253 E. A. Wallis Budge, 1974, p. 20.

254 Ad de Vries, 1974, pp. 161, 163.

255 Ajit Mookerjee, 1982, pp. 39, 41.

256 C. G. Jung, 1975, pp. 9, 15.

257 Ajit Mookerjee, 1982, p. 40.

258 C. G. Jung, 1975, pp. 15–18 passim.

259 Ibid. p. 10.

260 Ibid. p. 9.

261 Ibid. pp. 21–22.

262 Ibid. pp. 12–13, 15; C. G. Jung, 1976, pp. 25–27 passim.

263 Ibid. p. 25–27 passim.

264 Ibid. pp. 28–29.

265 Ad de Vries, 1974, p. 340.

266 Editor, 1969, pp. 56–57.

267 C. G. Jung, 1976, pp. 27–30 passim; C. G. Jung, 1975, pp. 16–17, 21.

268 J. E. Cirlot, 1976, pp. 313–315 passim; Ad de Vries,1974, pp. 442–445 passim.

269 Ibid. p. 444.

270 Edward F. Edinger, 1991, pp. 80, 152.

271 Corinthians 10:14. The Holy Bible, Revised Standard Version. The New Testament, p. 903.

272 Ibid. p. 771.

273 Winthrop Ames, editor, 1974, p. 182.

274 Genesis 28:22. The Holy Bible, Revised Standard Version. The Old Testament, p. 21; J. E. Cirlot, 1976, p. 314.

275 Otto rank, 1989, pp. 140, 143, 161–158 passim.

276 Ibid., pp. 161–168 passim.

277 Patrizia Norelli-Bachelet, 1974, pp. 66–67.

278 C. G. Jung, 1970, pp. 81, 86, 88–89.

279 Maurice and Robert Burton, 1976, pp. 428–430 passim.

280 Ibid., p. 430.

281 Ibid., p. 430.

282 Erich Neumann, 1974, p. 150; Joseph Campbell, 1962, p. 165.

283 Erich Neumann, 1974, pp. 65–67 passim, 152–153 passim.

284 Ibid., p. 152.

285 Ibid., p. 332.

286 Sri Aurobindo, 1972, p. 30.

287 Ibid. pp. 15–18 passim.

288 Marie Louise von Franz, 1974, pp. 101–111 passim.

289 Ibid., pp. 101–111 passim.

290 M.P. Pandit, Compiler, 1966, pp. 157, 184, 295–296 ; Djwal Kul, 1976, pp. 77–82 passim.

291 Marie-Louise von Franz, 1986, pp. 97–99 passim; Sonu Shamdasani, Editor, 1996, pp. xlvii –liv passim.

292 Tom Chetwynd, 1987, pp. 68–71 passim; C. G. Jung, 1975, p. 335.

293 Tom Chetwynd, 1972, p. 70; M. P. Pandit, Compiler, 1966. pp. 31–32 passim.

294 Tom Chetwynd, 1987, p. 69; C. G. Jung, 1975, p. 335.

295 Tom Chetwynd,1972, p. 93.

296 C. G. Jung, 1977, p. 211–212 passim.

297 Djwal Kul 1976, pp. 91–98 passim.

298 C. G. Jung, 1977, pp. 211–212 passim.

299 Ibid. p. 212.

300 Corinne Heline 1977, pp. 35–36 passim.

301 Ibid. p. 38.

302 Ibid. p. 39.

303 Ibid. p. 44.

304 C. G. Jung, 1977, pp. 438, 464.

305 Marie-Louise von Franz, 1986, p. 97.

306 Tom Chetwynd, 1987, p. 68–71 passim.

307 Edward F. Edinger, 1991, pp, 84–85 passim.

308 Ibid. p. 85.

309 M. P. Pandit, Compiler, 1966. p. 31; S. G. J. Ousley, 1976, p. 93.

310 Marina Warner, 1976, p. 216.

311 M. P. Pandit, Compiler, 1966. p. 31.

312 Ibid., p. 31.

313 C. G. Jung, 1977, pp. 76–77 passim.

314 Edward F. Edinger, 1991, pp. 47–50 passim, 72–74 passim.

315 Genesis 1, 1:5. The Holy Bible, Revised Standard Version, Old Testament, p. 1.

316 Ibid. p. 1.

317 S. G. J. Ousley, 1978, p. 66; M. P. Pandit, Compiler, 1966. p. 32.

318 E. A. Wallis Budge,1971, pp. 55–56.

319 C. G. Jung, 1974, p. 51.

320 C. G. Jung, 1977, p. 72.

321 R. A. Schwaller de Lubicz, 1977, pp. 48–49 passim.

322 Ad de Vries, 1974, p. 243.

323 J. E. Cirlot, 1976, p. 141.

324 C. G. Jung, 1975, p. 240.

325 Ibid., p. 240.

326 Ibid., pp. 240–241.

327 J. E. Cirlot, 1976, p. 254.

328 John 1:1–5. The Holy Bible, Revised Standard Version, New testament, p. 835.

329 Tom Chetwynd, 1987, p. 53.

330 C. G. Jung, 1975, p. 437.

331 C. G. Jung, 1977, p. 291.

332 C. G. Jung, 1977, p. 95.

333 Ad de Vries, 1974. p. 389.

334 John 16:18. The Holy Bible, Revised Standard Version, New testament, p. 771.

335 Patrizia Norelli-Bachelet, 1974, pp. 66–67 passim.

336 Ibid., p. 66 67 passim.

337 Marie-Louise von Franz, 1975, pp. 122–123 passim.

338 Ibid., pp. 122–123 passim.

339 Ibid., p. 123.

340 Ibid., p. 123.

341 Ibid. p. 123.

342 Edward F. Edinger, 1991, p. 47.

343 Marie-Louise von Franz, 1975, p. 124.

344 Ibid. p. 124.

345 Patrizia Norelli-Bachelet, 1974, pp. 18, 66–67.

346 Marie-Louise von Franz,1975, pp. 161–164 passim.

347 Barbara S. Walker, 1988, pp. 61, 62 passim.

348 Ibid., p. 61.

349 Ibid. pp. 61–62 passim.

350 M. P. Pandit, p. 31.

351 Edward F. Edinger, 1991, p. 83.

352 Jung, as recorded in William McGuire, R. F. C. Hull, Editors,1980, pp. 108–109 passim.

353 C. G. Jung, 1977, pp. 295–296 passim.

354 Marie-Louise von Franz, Emma Jung, 1972, p. 324.

355 Ibid., p. 324.

356 Sri Aurobindo, 1971, p. 343.

357 The Jerusalem Bible, The New Testament, p. 419.

358 C. G. Jung, as reported in Edward F. Edinger, 1991, p. 147.

359 The Jerusalem Bible, The New Testament, p. 177.

360 Tom Chetwynd, 1982, p. 149.

361 Patrizia Norelli-Bachelet, 1975, p. 14.

362 Marie-Louise von Franz, 1974, pp. 101–104 passim

363 Ibid., p. 102.

364 Ibid., p. 125.

365 Patrizia Norelli-Bachelet, 1975, p. 69.

366 Patrizia Norelli-Bachelet, 1974, pp. 66–67 passim; Marie-Louise von Franz, 1974, p. 131.

367 Tom Chetwynd, 1986, p. 124; Nor Hall, 1980, pp. 183–184.

368 Ernest Weekley, 1967, p. 760; Nor Hall, 1980, p. 187.

369 Barbara G. Walker, 1988, pp. 95–96 passim.

370 Mircea Eliade, 1978, pp. 130–131.

371 J. E. Cirlot 1976, pp. 173–175 passim; Ad de Vries, 1974, p. 288; Tom Chetwynd, 1988, pp.

2. 123–124. passim.

372 Miriam and José Arguelles, 1977, pp. 44–45 passim.

373 Ad de Vries, 1974, p. 288.

374 Miriam and José Arguelles, 1977, p. 41.

375 Homer, 1961, pp. 177–194 passim.

376 Dante, Divine Comedy, Canto I, as recorded in Miriam and José Arguelles, 1977, p. 41.

377 Mark P. O. Morford, Robert J. Lenardon,1977, p. 395; Edith Hamilton, 1953, p. 151; Edith Hamilton, 1953, p. 151.

378 Goethe, 1973. pp. 39–42 passim, 70–99 passim.

379 Edith Hamilton, 1953, pp. 151–152 passim.

380 Ad de Vries, 1974, p. 463.

381 Edith Hamilton, 1953, p. 152.

382 Brian Bates, 1983, pp. 172–176 passim.

383 Edward F. Edinger, 1991, pp. 142–144 passim.

384 Ibid., 143–144 passim.

385 Nor Hall, 1980, p. 187.

386 Ibid., p. 187.

387 Frances Thompson, 1980, p. 41.

388 Ibid., p. 46.

389 Ibid. p. 47.

390 Ibid., p. 48.

391 S. G. J. Ousley, 1976, pp. 67, 73.

392 M. P. Pandit, compiler, 1966, p. 31.

393 Ibid., p. 31.

394 S.G.J. Ousley, 1976, p. 64–65 passim; Edward F. Edinger, 199, p. 147.

395 M. P. Pandit, compiler, 1966, p. 31.

396 Alex Jones,1983, pp. 6–18 passim.

397 C. G. Jung, 1977, p. 116.

398 Sri Aurobindo, as recorded in Editor, 1969, p. 45.

399 C. G. Jung, 1975, p. 185.

400 Ad de Vries, 1974, p. 219–220 passim.

401 C. G. Jung, 1975, p. 185.

402 Tom Chetwynd,1987, p. 182.

403 Ibid, p. 70.

404 Jung, as recorded in Barbara Hannah, 1981, p. 22.

405 R. A. Schwaller de Lubicz, 1985, pp. 96, 102.

406 C. G. Jung, 1977, p. 293.

407 Edward F. Edinger, 1991, p. 147.

408 Marie-Louise von Franz, 1980, p. 265.

409 Ibid., p. 265.

410 C. G. Jung, 1971, p. 513.

411 Patrizia Norelli-Bachelet,1974, p. 66–67 passim; Patrizia Norelli-Bachelet, 1975, pp. 14, 69.

412 Edward F. Edinger, 1991, p. 147.

413 MarijaGimbutus, 1982, p. 108; Barbara G. Walker,1988, p. 374.

414 Ibid., p. 374.

415 Ibid., p. 374; J. C. Cooper, 1985, p. 74; C. G. Jung, 1975, p. 73.

416 Ibid, p. 89.

417 Ibid., p. 73; Barbara Walker, 1988, p. 374; J. C. Cooper, 1985, pp. 73–74 passim.

418 Patrizia Norelli-Bachelet, 1975, p. 67.

419 Edward F. Edinger, 1987, p. 137.

420 Ibid., p. 137.

421 Tom Chetwynd,1987, pp. 68–71, passim.

422 Marie-Louise von Franz, 1984, pp. 163, 211, 215, n. 7.

423 Timothy Ware, 1982, p. 230.

424 Ibid., p. 232.

425 Edward F. Edinger, 1991, p. 83.

426 Ibid., p. 83.

427 J. C. Cooper, 1985, pp. 73–74 passim.

428 C. G. Jung, 1974, pp. 51, 53, 64.

429 Ibid. p. 255.

430 C. G. Jung, 1977, pp. 92–93 passim.

431 Fritjof Capra, 1982, pp. 78–79 passim.

432 Edward F. Edinger, 1991, p. 47–48 passim.

433 Hans Jonas, 1963, pp. 62–65 passim, 15–16 passim, 165–169 passim.

434 J. C. Cooper, 1985, pp. 48–50 passim.

435 Joseph Campbell, 1974, p. 20.

436 Genesis 3:5. The Jerusalem Bible. The Old Testament. p. 17.

437 Stephan A. Hoeller, 1982, pp. 157–158 passim.

438 Friedrich Rest, 1959, pp. 10, 31; J. E. Cirlot, 1976, p. 289; C. G. Jung, 1977, p. 333; Joseph

3. Campbell, 1974, pp. 296–298 passim.

439 C. A. Meir, 1967, pp. 5–11, passim, 26–27 passim.

440 C. G. Jung, 1974, p. 382; C. G. Jung, 1976, p. 513.

441 J. E. Cirlot, 1976, p. 287.

442 Edward F. Edinger, 1981, pp. 58, 66; Joseph Campbell, 1974, pp. 296–298 passim.

443 Malcolm E. Duncan, 1976, pp. 70, 150–153 passim, 158–160 passim; Ad de Vries, 1974, p. 438.

444 E. A. Wallis Budge, 1969, pp. 473, 506–507 passim, 517, 521.

445 Robert Lawlor, 1982, pp. 72–73 passim.

446 E. A. Wallis Budge, 1969, p. 501.

447 Ibid., p. 510.

448 Ibid., p. 502.

449 Ibid., p. 511.

450 Malcolm E. Duncan, p. 70, 150, 158.

451 Cornelia Brunner, 1963, pp. xi–xv passim, 126–127 passim.

452 H. Rider Haggard, 1978, p. 141; Cornelia Brunner, 1963, p. 73.

453 José A. Argüelles, 1975, p. 145.

454 Ibid., pp. 145–149 passim.

455 Ibid., pp. 148–149 passim.

456 Erich Neumann, 1954, pp. 91–82 passim, pp. 83–99 passim.

457 Anthony Stevens, 1982, pp. 274–275 passim.

458 José A. Argüelles, 1975, p. 145–147 passim.

459 Anthony Stevens, pp. 274–275 passim.

460 C. G. Jung, 1977, p. 148.

461 Thomas Aquinas, 1966, p. 370.

462 C. G. Jung, 1974, pp. 288–289 passim.

463 Robert Graves, 1978, pp. 51–52 passim, 58.

464 C. G. Jung, 1970, pp. 287, 314.

465 Robert Graves, 1978, p. 358.

466 Corinne Heline, 1983, p. 61; Barbara Walker, 1988, p. 151.

467 Corinne Heline, 1971, pp. 39–41 passim.

468 Corinne Heline, 1983, pp. 60–61 passim; Djwal Kul,1976, pp. 79–78 passim, plate 6, plate 7.

469 C. G. Jung, 1975, pp. 211–212 passim.

470 Tom Chetwynd, 1987, pp. 69–71 passim.

471 Patrizia Norelli-Bachelet,1975, pp. 14, 68.

472 Djwal Kul, 1976, p. 78–79 passim, plate 8.

473 M. P. Pandit, 1966, p. 32.

474 James Hillman, 1979, p. 55.

475 Ibid., p. 55, 145.

476 Ibid., p. 54.

477 Ibid., p. 56.

478 Marie-Louise von Franz, 1986, pp. 153–154 passim.

479 Ibid., pp. 153–154 passim.

480 Patrizia Norelli-Bachelet, 1975, pp. 14, 69.

481 Ibid., p. 2; Sri Aurobindo, as reported in Patrizia Norelli-Bachelet, 1975, pp. 1–2, 12–13.

482 Barbara Walker, 1988, pp. 525–526 passim; Ad de Vries, 1974, p. 477.

483 Bear, Sun, Wabun, 1980, Upper Saddle River, NJ: Prentice Hall. pp. 32–33 passim; Barbara Walker, 1988, pp. 525–526 passim.

484 Sun Bear, Wabun, 1980. p. 33.

485 C. G. Jung, 1977, pp. 98–99 passim.

486 Tom Chetwynd, 1982, p. 303.

487 Sun Bear, Wabun, 1980, pp. 32–33 passim.

488 Erich Neumann, 1974, pp. 48–49 passim, pp. 240–243 passim.

489 Mircea Eliade, 1974, pp. 18–19 passim; Erich Neumann, 1974, pp. 49, 242–243 passim.

490 Ibid, p. 245–246 passim.

491 Ibid., p. 248.

492 C. G. Jung,1970, pp. 251–349 passim.

493 C. G. Jung, 1974, p. 395.

494 Ad de Vries, 1974, p. 366.

495 Erich Neumann, 1974, pp. 242–243 passim.

496 C. G. Jung, 1975, p. 211.

497 Ibid., p. 211–213 passim.

498 Patrizia Norelli-Bachelet 1974, p. 66.

499 C. G. Jung,1974, pp. 434–436 passim.

500 Jean Shinoda Bolen, 1984, p. 76.

501 Ibid., pp. 75, 78–81 passim.

502 Mark P. O. Norford, Robert J. Lenardon, 1977, pp. 101–103 passim.

503 Edward F. Edinger, 1991, p. 58.

504 Alex Jones, 1982, p. 119.

505 Ibid., p. 119, 112–114 passim.

506 Ibid. p. 114.

507 Ibid. pp. 114–115 passim; M.P. Pandit, 1966, p. 31.

508 Erich Neumann,1974, pp. 98–100 passim.

509 Ibid., pp. 98–99 passim.

510 Edward F. Edinger, 1991, p. 38.

511 C. G. Jung, 1977, pp. 134, 152–153 passim.

512 Ad de Vries, 1974, pp. 386–397 passim.

513 C.G. Jung, 1977, pp. 236–237 passim.

514 C. G. Jung,1977, p. 196; Sri Aurobindo, 1971, pp. 337, 346–347 passim; Sri Aurobindo, 1971,

4. pp. 337, 346–347 passim.

515 Brian Branston, 1980, pp. 286–294 passim.

516 Sri Aurobindo, 1971, pp. 338, 339, 346.

517 The Revelation of John 8:9, The Holy Bible. The Revised Standard Version. The New Testament. pp. 972–973 passim.

518 The Revelation of John 21:22, The Holy Bible. The Revised Standard Version. The New Testament. pp. 979–981 passim.

519 Ad de Vries, 1974, pp. 187, 188, 247.

520 Ibid., p. 188.

521 Heinrich Zimmer, 1972, pp. 154–155 passim.

522 C. G. Jung,1977, p. 120.

523 C. G. Jung,1977, p. 210.

524 Helen Luke, 1975, p. 71–76 passim.

525 C. G. Jung,1976, pp. 406–407 passim.

526 Erich Neumann, 1974, p. 158, 219.

527 C. G. Jung, 1976, pp. 406–407 passim.

528 Ibid., p. 406.

529 Edward F. Edinger, 1981, p. 83.

530 C. G. Jung, 1977, p. 47.

531 Alex Jones, 1982, pp. 20–22 passim.

532 Ibid., pp. 112–114 passim; S. G. J Ousley, 1976, pp. 74–75 passim.

533 Tom Chetwynd, 1987, pp. 67–68 passim.

534 Patrizia Norelli-Bachelet, 1974, pp. 66–67 passim.

535 Corinne Heline, 1977, pp. 58–59 passim.

536 Edward F. Edinger, 1991, p. 72.

537 Ibid., pp. 43, 72, 74.

538 C. G. Jung, 1976, p. 94.

539 Ibid., p. 90.

540 Ibid., p. 93.

541 Ibid., p. 94.

542 Ibid., p. 96.

543 Ibid., pp. 95–96 passim.

544 Maria Gimbutas, 1982, p. 108.

545 J. C. Cooper, 1985, p. 72.

546 Ibid., p. 74.

547 Ibid., p. 74.

548 Ibid., p. 74.

549 C. G. Jung, 1975, p. 115.

550 Emma Jung, Marie-Louise von Franz, 1972, p. 180; Charles Squire, 1975, p. 416.

551 C. G. Jung, 1975, p. 89.

552 Ad de Vries, 1974, p. 188.

553 Barbara G. Walker, 1988, p. 374.

554 C. G. Jung, 1975, p. 183.

555 Liz Greene, 1984, p. 260.

556 Mark 1:16. The Holy Bible, The New Testament, p, 786.

557 Nor Hall, 1980, p. 188; Max Zeller, 1975, p. 170.

558 Ibid., pp. 170–171 passim.

559 Nor Hall, 1980, p. 224.

560 J. C. Cooper, 1985, p. 72.

561 C. G. Jung, 1975, pp. 118–119 passim.

562 C. G. Jung, 1976, pp. 204–205 passim.

563 Nancy Qualls Corbett, 1988, p. 138.

564 C. G. Jung, 1974, pp. 48–52 passim.

565 C. G. Jung, 1974, p. 51.

566 C. G. Jung, 1977, p. 160.

567 Nor Hall, 1980, p. 118–124 passim.

568 Marina Warner, 1976, p. 257.

569 Karl Kerenyi, 1979, pp. 41–60 passim.

570 C. G. Jung, 1975, pp. 240–241 passim.

571 C. G. Jung, 1977, p. 453.

572 Barbara Walker, 1988, p. 483.

573 John Layard, 1988, pp. 178–179 passim.

574 Barbara G. Walker, 1988, p. 483.

575 Ibid, pp. 482–483 passim.

576 C. G. Jung, 1976, p. 341.

577 Ibid. p. 341.

578 Barbara G. Walker, 1988, p. 4.

579 C. G. Jung, 1970, p. 174; C. Jung, as reported in James Hillman, 2007, p. 20.

580 Patrizia Norelli-Bachelet, 1981, p. 69.

581 Edward F. Edinger, 1991, pp. 83–84 passim.

582 Barbara G. Walker, 1988, p. 49.

583 Edward F. Edinger, 1991, p. 147.

584 Tom Chetwynd, 1987, pp. 166–167 passim; Aniela Jaffé, 1979, p. 77.

585 Ibid., pp. 78–79 passim.

586 Ajit Mookerjee, 1971/1972, pp. 77–79 passim.

587 Ibid., p. 132.

588 Ibid., p. 18–25 passim.

589 Corinne Heline, 1977, p. 86.

590 Ibid., p. 83, 90.

591 C. G. Jung, 1977, p. 22.

592 C. G. Jung, 1977, pp. 95–101 passim; Ajit Mookerjee, 1971/1972, pp. 77–79 passim, 119.

593 C. G. Jung, 1977, p. 99.

594 Eugene Monick,1980, pp. 30–31 passim.

595 Ibid., pp. 30–31 passim.

596 Ad. de Vries, 1974, p. 240.

597 C. G. Jung, 1975, p. 211.

598 S. G. J. Ousley, 1976, p. 98.

599 Corinne Heline, 1977, p. 2.

600 Marie-Louise von Franz, 1974, pp. 9–10 passim, 73–74 passim.

601 Corinne Heline, 1977, p. 90.

602 Theodor Abt, 2005, pp. 152–165 passim.

603 Ad de Vries, 1974, p. 477.

604 Christine Downing, 1981, pp. 38, 79, 135, 149–150, 193, 233.

605 Ibid. pp. 38, 79, 135, 149, 150, 193, 233.

606 Ad de Vries, 1974, p. 477.

607 C. G. Jung, 1977, pp. 98–99 passim.

608 Ibid. p. 98.

609 Sun Bear, Wabun,1980, p. 32.

610 Sri Aurobindo, 1972, p. 11.

611 As reported in Robert J. Sardello, Randolph Severson, 1983, p. 2.

612 James Hillman, 1982, pp. 35–36 passim.

613 Sri Aurobindo, 1972, pp. 11–14 passim.

614 Russel A. Lockhart, 1982, p. 14–18 passim.

615 Ibid. pp. 18–19 passim.

616 Ibid. pp. 18–19 passim.

617 Ibid. p. 19.

618 James Hillman, 1982, p. 39.

619 Russell A. Lockhart, 1982, p. 19–20 passim.

620 Robert J. Sardello, 1983, p. 9; Tom Chetwynd, 1982, p. 130.

621 Robert J. Sardello, 1983, pp. 6–7 passim.

622 Ibid., pp. 6–7 passim.

623 Sri Aurobindo, 1972, p. 12.

624 James Hillman,1982, p. 87.

625 Robert J. Sardello, 1983, pp. 13–14 passim.

626 Randolph Severnson, 1983, p. 31.

627 Edward F. Edinger, 1991, pp. 58–59 passim.

628 S. G. J. Ouseley, 1949, pp. 22–24 passim.

629 Ibid., p. 25.

630 DjwalKul, 1976, plates 2, 9, pp. 28–29 passim.

631 Carlos Castenada, 1968, p. 11.

632 C. G. Jung, 1976, pp. 214–215 passim.

633 Marie-Louise von Franz, 2008, pp. 9–20.

634 Sri Aurobindo, as reported in M. P. Pandit, compiler, 1966, pp. 196–197 passim.

635 Edith Hamilton, 1953, pp. 29, 144.

636 Ibid., pp. 29, 144; Mark P. D. Norford, Robert J. Lenardon, 1977, pp. 101–102 passim.

637 Jean Shinoda Bolen, 1984, p. 78.

638 Ibid. pp. 79–81 passim. 91–92 passim.

639 Ibid., p. 81; Mark P. D. Norford, Robert J. Lenardon, 1977, p. 101.

640 Alex Jones, 1982, pp. 106–109 passim, 49–50 passim, 37–38 passim.

641 Corinne Heline, 1971, p. 40.

642 As reported in Patrizia Norelli-Bachelet, 1974, pp. 66–67 passim; M. P. Pandit, compiler, 1966,

5.   pp. 257, 273.

643 C. G. Jung, 1977, p. 16.

644 C. G. Jung, 1977, p. 25.

645 Ibid., p. 21.

646 Ibid., p. 21.

647 Ibid. p. 25.

648 C. G. Jung, 1977, pp. 278–283 passim; Patrizia Norelli-Bachelet, 1974, pp. 66–67 passim.

649 Ibid., pp. 66–67 passim.

650 M. P. Pandit, compiler, 1966, p. 31.

651 Adolph Portman et al., 1977, p. 142.

652 Ibid., p. 142.

653 M. P. Pandit, 1966, p. 31.

654 Marina Warner, 1976, p. 266.

655 M. P. Pandit, 1966, p. 31.

656 S. G. J. Ouseley, 1976, pp. 75–76 passim.

657 Karl Kerenyi, 1978, p. 22.

658 Edith Hamilton,1953, pp. 29–30 passim.

659 Ibid., p. 30.

660 Karl Kerenyi, 1978, pp. 22–23 passim; Edith Hamilton, 1953, pp. 29–30 passim. 188–192 passim.

661 E. A. Wallis Budge, 1969, p. 104; Leonel Casson, editors,1983, pp. 90–91 passim.

662 Marie-Louise von Franz, 1975, pp. 50–51 passim.

663 David Werther, et al. 1985, pp. 14–16 passim.

664 Hazel Henderson, 1981, pp. 190–194 passim.

665 Ibid., pp. 221–222 passim.

666 Erich Fromm, 1982, pp. 132–139 passim.

667 Ibid., pp. 132–139 passim.

668 Ibid., pp. 129–132 passim.

669 J. E. Cirlot, 1976, pp. 331–332 passim.

670 Sun Bear, Wabun, 1980, pp. 134–135 passim.

671 J. E. Cirlot, 1976, p. 82; Ad de Vries, 1974, p. 335.

672 Franz Cumont, 1956, p. 39; Henri Frankfort, 1961, p. 10.

673 E. A. Wallis, 1969, pp. 196–197 passim.

674 J. E. Cirlot, 1976, pp. 144–145 passim.

675 Franz Cumont, 1956, pp. 152–155 passim.

676 J. Marvin Spiegelman, PhD, Mikusen Miyuki, PhD,2018, pp. 29–113 passim, 103–113 passim.

677 J. E. Cirlot, pp. 65–66 passim.

678 C. G. Jung,1976, pp. 168–170 passim.

679 Ibid., p. 170.

680 Barbara G. Walker, 1988, p. 295.

681 Ibid., pp. 368–369 passim.

682 Ibid., pp. 368–369 passim.

683 Paul Friedrich,1978, p. 26.

684 Ibid., p. 26.

685 Ibid., p. 26.

686 Ginette Paris, 1987, pp. 27–28 passim.

687 James Hillman, 1981, pp. 21–26 passim.

688 C.G. Jung, 1975, pp. 8–9 passim.

689 R. A. Schwallerde Lubicz, 1985, pp. 96, 102, 216.

690 Robert Lawlor, 1982, p. 12.

691 Tom Chetwynd, 1987, pp. 68–69 passim.

692 Ibid. p. 70.

693 Edward F. Edinger, 1991, pp. 83–84 passim.

694 Stephan A. Hoeller,1982, pp. 31.

695 Ibid. p. 32.

696 M. P. Pandit, Compiler, 1966, pp. 31–32 passim.

697 J. E. Cirlot,1976, p. 221.

698 Ibid. p. 221.

699 Ibid. p. 221.

700 Corinne Heline, 1977, pp. 53, 60, 64.

701 M. P. Pandit, Compiler, 1966, p. 274.

702 J. E. Cirlot,1976, p. 332.

703 C. G. Jung, 1976, p. 244.

704 Ibid., pp. 244–246 passim.

705 J. E. Cirlot, 1976, p. 332.

706 C. G. Jung, 1959, p. 767.

707 Sri Aurobindo, 1970, pp. 325–326 passim, 346–347 passim.

708 Liz Greene, 1984, pp. 28, 29 passim.

709 Patrizia Norelli-Bachelet, 1974, pp. 66–67 passim.

710 Alex Jones, 1983, pp. 20–22 passim, 42–43 passim.

711 Ginette Paris, 1986, pp. 16–19 passim.

712 C. G. Jung, 1970, pp. 300–301 passim.

713 Alex Jones, 1983, pp. 106–107 passim.

714 M. P. Pandit, compiler, 1966, p. 32; James Hillman, 1981, pp. 21–22 passim.

715 C. G. Jung,1970, pp. 247–248 passim.

716 E. Wallis Budge, 1969, pp. 53–54 passim, 437–444 passim.

717 Sonu Shamdasani, editor, 1996, pp. 75.

718 C. G. Jung, 1970, pp. 284, 299.

719 Friedrich Nietzsche, 1974, p. 46.

720 J. E. Cirlot, 1976, pp. 309, 310 passim.

721 Marie-Louise von Franz, 1986, p. 40.

722 C.G. Jung, 1965, p. 389.

723 Marie-Louise von Franz, 1986, p. 123.

724 Ibid. p. 123.

725 C.G. Jung, 1974, pp. 48, 304n., 491.

726 Ibid. p. 491.

727 Marie-Louise von Franz, 1986, p.p. 110, 111.

728 Ibid. p. 110.

729 Corinne Heline, 1977, pp. 38, 41.

730 Nor Hall, 1980, p. 8.

731 Corine Heline, pp. 46, 48.

732 Ibid. pp. 46–47.

733 Marie-Louise von Franz, 1986, pp. 120–123 passim.

734 Ibid. pp. 124–125 passim.

735 Marie-Louise von Franz, 1986, pp. 120–123 passim.111–116 passim.

736 Ibid. pp. 138–139.

737 Ibid. pp. 139–141 passim.

738 Edward f. Edinger, 1991, p. 83.

739 Tom Chetwynd, 1986, pp. 121–122.

740 Tom Chetwynd, 1982, pp. 318–319.

741 Patrizia Norelli-Bachelet, 1975, pp. 109–110.

742 Ibid. p. 69.

743 Corinne Heline, 1974, pp. 103–104.

744 Ibid. 195–197 passim.

745 Sally Nichols,1980, pp. 227–247 passim.

746 Ibid. pp. 214, 215–225 passim.

747 Editor, 1969, pp. 27–28, 45–46, 48–49.

748 Patrizia Norelli-Bachelet, 1974, pp. 66–67 passim.

749 C. G. Jung, 1975, p. 211.

750 Ad. de Vries, 1974, pp. 382–384 passim.

751 The *I Ching* or *Book of Changes*, 1967, pp. 3–9 passim.

752 Robert Wm. Krajenke, 1976, pp. 40–44 passim.

753 Patrizia Norelli-Bachelet, 1974, pp. 69, 109, 110.

754 The *I Ching* or Book of Changes, 1967, pp. 10–15 passim.

755 R. A. Schwaller de Lubiz, 1985, pp. 96, 102.

756 Henri Frankfort, 1961.

757 Robert Lawlor, 1982, pp. 26–27.

758 Ibid. p. 27.

759 David L. Miller, 1984, pp. 152–153.

760 Ibid. p. 152.

761 Pierre Grimal, editor, 1973, p. 237; Ibid. p. 237.

762 David L. Miller, 1984, pp. 152.

763 Tom Chetwynd, 1986, p. 9.

764 Ibid. p. 9.

765 Ibid. p. 9.

766 Ibid. p. 9.

767 Edward F. Edinger, 1991, pp. 161, 215.

768 C. G. Jung, 1976, pp. 96–98 passim.

769 Ad. de Vries, 1974, p. 477; Marie-Louise von Franz, 1980, pp. 71–72.

770 Barbara G. Walker, 1988, p. 507; Editor, 1967, p. 415.

771 C. G. Jung, 1977, p. 98.

772 Ibid. p.p. 98–99.

773 Ginette Paris, 1986, p. 12.

774 James Hillman, 1980, p. 26.

775 Ibid. p. 27.

776 Ibid. pp. 24–25.

777 Ibid. p. 29.

778 Ibid. pp. 29–30.

779 Ibid. pp. 27–29 passim; James Hillman, 1981, pp. 60–61 passim.

780 C.G. Jung, 1876, pp. 100–101, 172.

781 C. G. Jung. 1976, p. 259.

782 Ibid. pp. 259–260.

783 J. E. Cirlot, 1976, pp. 346–350 passim.

784 Ibid. pp. 349–350 passim.

785 Djwal Kul, 1976, plate 2.

786 C. G. Jung, 1987, p. 81.

787 R. A. Schwaller de Lubicz, 1977, p. 49.

788 C. G. Jung, 1977, p. 72.

789 Tom Chetwynd, 1982, pp. 185, 186.

790 C. G. Jung, 1965, p. 183.

791 C. G. Jung, 1975, pp. 228–229; J. E. Cirlot, 1976, p. 135.

792 C. G. Jung, 1975, pp. 184n, 185.

793 Sri Aurobindo, 1972, pp. 17, 19.

794 C. G. Jung, 1975, pp. 33–37passim.

795 Maria Gimbutas, pp. 186–190 passim.

796 Ibid. p. 187.

797 Barbara G. Walker, 1988, p. 415.

798 Ibid. p. 415.

799 Ibid. pp. 306–307; C. G. Jung, 1976, pp. 14–16 passim.

800 Ibid. p.p. 15–16.

801 Maurice and Robert Burton, 1976, pp. 330–331passim.

802 Ad de Vries, 1974, p. 343.

803 J. E. Cirlot, 1976, pp. 56–60 passim.

804 Ibid. pp. 56–57

805 Ibid. p. 119.

806 Editor, 1967, pp. 536, 536a, 536b, 537.

807 Edward F. Edinger, 1991, p. 40.

808 Ibid. p. 209.

809 Ibid. p. 209.

810 Ibid. p. 209.

811 Marie-Louise von Franz, 1986, p. 72.

812 Tom Chetwynd, 1986, p. 100–103 passim.

813 Marie-Louise von Franz, 1986, p. 83.

814 Ibid. p. 144.

815 Ibid. p. 144.

816 L. Alcopley, 1968, pp. 3–15 passim.

817 Ibid. p. 114.

818 F. M. Cornford, 1957, p. 14.

819 Ibid. pp. 7–11 passim.

820 Ibid. pp. 155–158 passim.

821 David Bohm (as reported in Marie Louise von Franz, 1986, p. 153.)

822 Fritjof Capra, 1982, p. 53–54 passim.

823 Marie- Louise von Franz, 1986, pp. 147, 148.

824 Ibid. p. 151, 152.

825 Ibid. p. 154.

826 Edward F. Edinger, 1991, pp. 147–151 passim.

827 Patrizia Norelli-Bachelet, 1974, pp. 67–68 passim.

828 Edward F. Edinger, 1991, pp. 86, 93–95 passim.

829 Ibid. p. 86.

830 Ibid. p. 93; Dayne Rudhyar, 1971, p. 123.

831 C. G. Jung, 1977, pp. 226, 227; Edward F. Edinger, 1991, pp. 12–13.

832 Ibid. p. 12.

833 E. Wallace Budge, 1971, p. 44.

834 Ibid. p. 44.

835 Ibid. pp. 44, 47

836 Marie-Louise von Franz, 1974, pp. 108, 131.

837 James Hillman, 1981, pp. 22–23.

838 Marie-Louise von Franz, 1974, p. 108.

839 Edward F. Edinger, 1991, p. 72.

840 M. P. Pandit, compiler, 1966, pp. 32; Tom Chetwynd, 1987, pp. 69–71 passim.

841 M. P. Pandit, compiler, 1966, pp. 31; Tom Chetwynd, 1987, pp. 69–71 passim.

842 M. P. Pandit, 1966, p. 31.

843 Tom Chetwynd, 1987, pp. 69–70.

844 Ibid. pp. 125–127 passim.

845 Ibid. p. 70.

846 Edward F. Edinger, 1991, p. 83.

847 The I Ching or Book of Changes (1967), the Richard Willhelm Translation, Book 1, p. 10.

848 Ibid., passim.

849 Corinne Heline, 1977, p. 38.

850 Ibid. p. 40.

851 Barbara G. Walker, 1988, pp. 482–483.

852 Thomas Merton, 1976, p. 82.

853 John 6:33, p. 158.

854 1 Corinthians 10:17.

855 Barbara G. Walker, 1988, p. 92.

856 Thomas Merton, 1966, p. 13.

857 Ibid. p. 29.

858 Ibid. p. 35.

859 C. G. Jung, as reported in Barbara Hannah, 2018, p. 243.

860 Thomas Aquinas,1966, pp. 155–156.

861 Editor, 1969, pp. 39, 45, 56–57.

862 Barbara G. Walker, 1988, p. 99.

863 James Hillman, 2007, pp. 20, 28.